D0349764

THE SECRET HISTORY

OF KINDNESS

THE
SECRET HISTORY
OF KINDNESS

LEARNING FROM HOW
DOGS LEARN

Melissa Holbrook Pierson

W. W. NORTON & COMPANY
NEW YORK · LONDON

To Amy Cherry,
dauntless editor and patient friend

Copyright © 2015 by Melissa Holbrook Pierson

For information about permission to reproduce selections from this book,
write to Permissions, W. W. Norton & Company, Inc.,
500 Fifth Avenue, New York, NY 10110

For information about special discounts for bulk purchases, please contact W. W. Norton
Special Sales at specialsales@wwnorton.com or 800-233-4830

Manufacturing by RR Donnelley
Book design by Dana Sloan
Production manager: Louise Mattarelliano

Library of Congress Cataloging-in-Publication Data

Pierson, Melissa Holbrook.
The secret history of kindness : learning from how dogs learn / Melissa Holbrook
Pierson. — First edition.
pages cm
Includes bibliographical references.
ISBN 978-0-393-06619-7 (hardcover)
1. Dogs—Training—Philosophy. 2. Dogs—Psychology. 3. Dog trainers—Psychology.
I. Title.
SF431.P54 2015
636.7'0835—dc23

2014045932

W. W. Norton & Company, Inc.
500 Fifth Avenue, New York, N.Y. 10110
www.wwnorton.com

W. W. Norton & Company Ltd.
Castle House, 75/76 Wells Street, London W1T 3QT

1 2 3 4 5 6 7 8 9 0

5656 9816 5/15

If there is anyone that holds that the study of
the animal is an unworthy pursuit, he ought to
go further and hold the same opinion about the
study of himself.

—ARISTOTLE

He began to train Piggy-Beast to do all kinds
of tricks that no one would have believed an
ordinary Småland pig could possibly do. It was
all very secret and Piggy-Beast enjoyed himself
and learned very quickly, especially because every
time he did something well he got a tidbit from
Emil.

—ASTRID LINDGREN, *EMIL AND PIGGY BEAST*, 1973

THE SECRET HISTORY

OF KINDNESS

INTRODUCTION

⋎

It is wrong, always, everywhere, and for anyone,
to believe anything upon insufficient evidence.
—W. K. CLIFFORD, *THE ETHICS OF BELIEF*, 1877

Facts do not cease to exist because they are ignored.
—ALDOUS HUXLEY, "PROPER STUDIES," 1927

One rarely thinks of rats as heroes. Maybe it takes a young Belgian Buddhist monk to think they are, and moreover to make them so.

In 1995, Bart Weetjens was pondering a great worldwide problem. Landmines have been deployed in every major conflict since 1938. The earth is littered with them. The World Health Organization says that "since the 1960s as many as 110 million mines have been spread throughout the world into an estimated 70 countries." Unexploded ordnance and mines have been responsible for death or injury to estimated hundreds of thousands of people, many of them children. Weetjens desperately wanted to help. Demining was both expensive and dangerous—people often tripped mines before locating them for disposal.

This is when Weetjens coincidentally learned that researchers had successfully trained gerbils for scent detection work. An idea was born: He happened to own pet rats. What better animal for this task

1

than one light enough to avoid activating the explosive devices—as well as preeminently suited to scent detection because it has more genetic material devoted to olfaction than any other mammal?

The African giant pouched was determined to be the type of rat best suited for the work to be undertaken in Africa. The Belgian government provided a grant for the feasibility study, but since pouched rats initially proved a little hard to breed—it would ultimately take a year before they got the recipe right—the lead biologist of Weetjens's nonprofit, named APOPO, ran experiments to see if Norwegian hooded lab rats could be trained to detect and dispose of TNT-scented objects. They could. Easily.

In 2000 the operation was moved to a large training minefield in Tanzania, where now the pouched rats (the size of chihuahuas and leashed to harnesses that might be a perfect fit for the diminutive dogs) were enrolled in the training. In a startlingly simple procedure, they were first classically conditioned to associate the sound of a click with an imminent reward: *click,* here's some food; *click,* food; *click,* food. The click itself, which would normally be meh to a rat, became exciting after being paired with the truly exciting primary reinforcer that is food: in a bit of transferred magic, the click soon functioned as a reward itself despite having no rewarding qualities of its own. Next the animal was trained to "point" on the target scent (or rather, to hold his nose in the designated hole for five seconds, an unnaturally long time for a rat). He received a double reward for that: a click, and then the food. Very quickly, his pointing behavior was thereby strengthened, that is, more likely to be repeated. In fact, guaranteed, inasmuch as anything in this world is guaranteed. As if he were complying with some sort of law.

In truth, he was. A universal natural law like that of thermodynamics, or Kepler's laws of planetary motion.

In the first live field test, held in Mozambique in 2003, the rats performed flawlessly, locating every buried mine. The next year, the first group of mine detection rats passed the International Mine Action Standards licensing test and the program was granted operational accreditation. More than a year before its deadline of March 2014, APOPO exploded the last three landmines in the Gaza Province of Mozambique. It had cleared more than 6 million square meters by uncovering 2,406 landmines, 13,025 small arms and ammunition, and 922 UXOs. The organization next began work in Thailand, upon that country's request.

Weetjens and his rats were not satisfied to stop at demining. Exploiting the same native abilities of the rat for scent search—easily channeled to human use by way of that natural teaching technology known as positive reinforcement—his organization put another third-world scourge between the crosshairs.

Tuberculosis is a massive problem in Africa. Conventional diagnosis is done with microscopes, with a reliability rate of 40 to 60 percent. But once they had been trained to detect the peculiar odor given off by Mycobacterium tuberculosis, rats were able to increase the rate to 89 percent, and at a speed far beyond the abilities of the human eye: it takes them two-hundredths of a second to identify the presence of the bacterium. Rats can accomplish in seven minutes what takes an entire day for a human technician with a microscope. In two years, by mid-2009, APOPO's TB detection rats had evaluated more than 50,000 sputum samples, identifying over a thousand TB infections that would have been missed by conventional microscopy.

* * *

IT IS hard for most of us to imagine a person for whom coming to sit in a chair upon request represents a triumphal entry into a world of new possibilities, of a fuller life than previously available.

"Simple" is a relative concept. Throwing a ball is simple—for an

animal with opposable thumbs. Knowing you shouldn't eat out of
the garbage can is simple—unless you are a dog. Obeying a request
to behave in a socially acceptable manner is simple—except when a
neurological defect makes it impossible to comprehend the notion of
social acceptability.

Operant conditioning, the manner in which learned behavior is
acquired, is a form of semantics: a way to make the incomprehensible understandable for the individual, by transferring the universal
motivation of self-interest to anything that does not already contain
it. It gives to any act the reason why. Which is not otherwise simple.

*And then one cold morning, it happened, entirely out of the blue.
"Come sit,"* I said, standing by the chair. The child looked at me
calmly, walked quietly to the chair and sat (actually looking quite
pleased). Ah! I cannot express the joy of this moment. Balloons!
Bubbles! Aeroplanes! We twirled through the air together, and the
parents, who were watching, were thrilled. "We thought our child
would never do that," one of them said. But they did do it, and it
was the carefully built scaffolding of operant conditioning that made
it possible.*

*It seems such a simple thing—"come and sit in this chair"—but
it is not. It is terribly important that one does learn to do it, because
being able to sit in a chair (when asked) is a gateway to a host of different experiences in our culture, with mainstream schooling being
only one of them. In the days following this event, the parents told
me that many things were changed by it—the child's toilet times and*

* In technical terms (and to me the technical holds a kind of magnetic fascination; I
think being in the presence of precision must be an elemental joy), the words "come
sit here" represent a discriminative stimulus, or SD, which had been given meaning
during a series of Discrete Trial Training sessions in which an instruction is given and
the response followed by consequences either positive or negative.

dinner times, car rides, and so on. And then of course the program itself—with the ability to sit at the table for longer and longer periods (and therefore also concentrate *for longer periods), the child made the most extraordinary progress. It was amazing to witness.*

Being able to sit is a way in *to a richer world. And behavioral therapy can point the way there.*

This account of a memorable moment in the education of an autistic child, from a piece called "Learning How to Sit and Operant Conditioning," appears in a blog titled Psych and Sensibility written by an anonymous (but clearly authentic) Australian student in psychology. The author is also a student of literature, which is why he or she is able to see in a single use of applied behavior analysis the grander meanings of its timeless theme: transformation.

Indeed, in the next post, which is titled "John Donne, autism, and ABA therapy," the writer discusses the realignment of worldview that a parent of an autistic child can be forced to undergo in permitting the momentary yet awful distress caused by "redirection": it is necessary to break down the old order for a new one to rise in its place. Before the child can understand that compliance yields positive results *for her*, she has to be sometimes forcibly placed in the position where she is able to experience it firsthand.

The brutal, beautiful poetry of Donne's "Holy Sonnet 14" is invoked to describe what on the part of the parent is an act of true faith: "Batter my heart, three-person'd God, for you / As yet but knock, breathe, shine, and seek to mend; / That I may rise and stand, o'erthrow me, and bend / Your force to break, blow, burn, and make me new." The cumulative effect of this thoughtful student's explorations of the ways in which applied behavior analysis can open worlds to the mentally impaired is poetry itself, or the thing that poetry is meant to address—the big stuff that cannot be gotten at any other way. Like something that starts as an ideological change and mysteriously becomes a geographical one. You are first in one place. And then you have traveled to another.

Understanding how behavior works is like going somewhere new, while staying inside the same brain. It comports precisely with the wisdom of Saint Augustine: "The world is a book and those who do not travel read only one page."

*   *   *

THE SUN-BLEACHED boy in the video is named Hrafnkell; he is a nine-year-old Icelander. Reportedly exceptionally intelligent, he has yet to learn one elementary life skill many children far younger already have attained, and for its lack he has been mercilessly teased. Even the younger boy sitting across the table—brother?—snickers at his perplexed fumbling. Soon his parents will no longer be able to find Velcro-tabbed shoes to fit him, and anyway, it is having a bad effect on his self-esteem. Yet nothing so far has enabled him to master tying his shoelaces.

The teacher speaks no Icelandic, and Hrafnkell no English. But as we are about to see, they will communicate in a substantive, and finally eloquent, language: the one in which the brain learns. For this, they will need no words.

The teacher has broken into constituent parts the act that to most of us quickly became so fluid it now seems a single motion—if we are even aware we are doing it at all. The boy concentrates as he tries to think about where to begin, which the instructor has demonstrated by making an X with her arms: *Cross the two ends.*

Click.

He looks a little surprised at the sound made by the toy clicker in her hand, but it quickly vanishes under a smile; he looks to her to make certain the sound means the reward is justified. He reaches into the small plastic bag on the table—"Yep, just one," she says, nodding, in reply to his look of uncertainty—and drops something small and hard into a bowl. He is obviously pleased, smiling broadly now, ready for the next step. Now he loops one end of the lace around and under the other. *Click.** Another reward goes into the bowl.

The first day's lesson runs for twenty minutes. The next morning (Hrafnkell is yawning) they put in fifteen. And then it is done: he can tie laces now. What he could not accomplish for years is taken care of in a little over half an hour.

The reward must have been something potent for a little boy, something to push him over a barrier made of equal parts humiliation and resistance. But it doesn't look like anything we imagine it must be, say, Legos or candy. You have to still the video to look closely at the bag. Navy beans? He is working for navy beans. And enjoying it.

With this method known as TAGteach ("teaching with acoustical guidance," essentially clicker training for humans), skills are taught painlessly and efficiently, sometimes to those who have found it difficult to learn in any other way. Something about our brains—an evolutionary development that rooted so deep and long ago it is functional even in abnormal or simpler mammalian brains—responds most naturally to learning by feedback, most successfully when action results in instantaneous reward. Being taught in the

---

* In another example of luscious technical distinction, the sound of the click, because it has been paired with, or conditioned to, the receipt of something desirable, is called a conditioned, or secondary, reinforcer. APOPO's rats began to work for, and enjoy, the secondary reinforcer of a click because they knew it signified something good was on the way. And "something good" in operant conditioning is defined as anything that is basic to the survival of all organisms, including food, water, sex. These are thus known as primary reinforcers. For a child, attention, play, rest, and food are all primary reinforcers; they have survival value.

way we were built to acquire knowledge feels "right" to us, and unsurprisingly gets the job done best. In the artificially constructed learning environment, a "token economy" mimics the way things already work: the perfectly thrown spear gets dinner. We are made to learn quickly how best to stalk, to aim, to take into account wind and weight and a hundred variables. Our survival depends on it: Assess, decide, do, see what works. Do again, *because* it works.

The stickers, lollipops, or play breaks that are most valuable to a child are too unwieldy to offer immediately upon achieving what have been decreed target behaviors, especially when these are intended to be part of a chain of steps that will eventually merge into a single compound behavior: as soon as he gets the toy, the kid is going to shut down the lesson, no matter if it isn't finished yet. So, tokens (which can be anything, including dried beans) are used. These can be collected and later exchanged for rewards the subject finds particularly worthwhile, whether treats, fun activities, or desired items like toys. This mode of operant conditioning has been found especially successful with autistic and developmentally disabled children, many of whom were unreachable by other means. "One of the most important technologies of behaviour modifiers and applied behaviour analysts over the last 40 years has been the token economy," experts in autism have noted.[1] Token economies have proved powerful motivators toward unprecedented achievement not just for the impaired but also for athletes, musicians, dancers, business managers, and average children. If the concept of a token economy sounds somewhat familiar, it should: much of our behavior is shaped by the receipt of tokens we call money.

It seems peculiarly human in its symbolic nature, this learned valuation of inherently valueless objects. Only humans could develop a system so complex and so cunning.

Hold the self-congratulation. Ten years ago, researchers in the relatively new field of behavioral economics began running a series of experiments on a group of capuchin monkeys, and in no time had turned them into . . . us. One report on the results, which found that monkeys not only quickly grasped the concept of currency but knew exactly what it was good for, ran under the headline "Gambling, Prostitution, and Theft Rampant Among Yale Monkeys." Indeed, the capuchins were observed horse trading, bargain hunting, practicing "utility maximization," responding to shifts in the value of their coin, occasionally lifting an unwatched token, assessing risk in potential exchanges, and finally, in what was called the first observed example of paid sex among primates other than us, achieving parity with human society.*

Reward is a powerful shaper of behavior. B. F. Skinner, the psychologist who codified how operant conditioning works, knew this by 1938, and thousands of experiments since—studies so fascinatingly designed they constitute one of the great joys of being alive in the early twenty-first century—are still mere elaborations on his findings. Then again, anyone with a dog is already familiar with the workings of the comparative cognition lab. Only to them it's called the kitchen.

· · ·

MY DOG led me on down the path. There was something imperative in her chase. There started to be something imperative in mine, too. What we were being pulled toward was related somehow, that I knew. But we each had our own interests in the matter. This, too, revealed itself as related to the subject and the solution both.

---

* After seven years of study, the architects of these experiments, psychologist Laurie Santos and economist Keith Chen, both of Yale, told *Mental_Floss* magazine, "Whatever mechanism in the brain that's driving these biases is one and the same in capuchin monkeys and in us. That means these strategies are 35 million years old."

In attempting to teach her, I would receive the more important lessons. She taught me about learning, and hence about us: the ways in which all beings are similar, and the costs of not acknowledging it. She did it by first leading me to a science containing discoveries about the way we learn that had potential beyond the scope of me and her, which was big enough. But it was as if Mercy knew what this end would be: confidently, she went straight toward a great revelation. My dog was so smart it was scary.

● ● ●

LIFE IS enriched immeasurably by acquiring books at yard sales. No matter how little money or shelf space you have, books at yard sales are always free and end up fitting perfectly into your bookshelves. Or that's what I tell myself.

Somewhere in some year, I'm pawing through a cardboard box; my species in its natural habitat. Near the bottom there is a small book with a torn dust jacket, exactly the kind I would normally shove aside in hope there was something better underneath, something I'd actually want to read. The type and the design of the cover announced it that most disposable genre: dated self-help. Wait, that's redundant. For every year brings its new trend in the last word of what you ought to do and how. With all that mutual cancellation the possibility of improvement is always null. I'd already given up. I read novels instead.

Anyone Can Have a Happy Child looked pure seventies by its design—font choice as telling as perms and Sperry Top Siders—and therefore its advice must be long contradicted. It probably prescribed frequent spankings.

Only thing is, I then had a young child and wanted him to be happy; I had no idea where this Holy Grail was hidden. I read the back

of the jacket and stopped cold. But here was the germ of the new training technology that was working miracles with my disorderly border
collie. I had no idea anyone had ever prescribed it for people, too. "The
teachable moment, which is the key to teaching values and behavior,
happens right after you praise a child for something he has done that
pleases you, that represents a valued behavior you would like to see
repeated and, more than repeated, become a part of his personality."

Yet this was, in a sentence, the sum of *The Behavior of Organisms,* in which B. F. Skinner described the means by which behavior
is acquired or modified. *Behaviors that are reinforced by their consequences increase in frequency; behaviors that are not reinforced decrease
or extinguish.* His theory was adapted for practical use by some specialized animal trainers years later, and later still was streamlined
and came to be popularly known as clicker training. Now here was
Jacob Azerrad, Ph.D., clinical psychologist and professor of behavior
therapy, telling us it would work as well on kids as on border collies.
It's not a big book, but it's a terribly profound one. Great truths—the
kind that smack you upside the head and leave the world spinning
for a while afterward—are often dumbfounding in their simplicity.
The book's ideas had fallen out of fashion, if they were ever in it, but
I couldn't see how it could fail. (One parent gave it a five-star review
on a bookseller's page with the headline "This Book Saved My
Life.") There's not a whole lot to do to ensure your children are well
behaved and contented; it requires only watching them and catching them doing the right thing. Ignore the wrong thing. Reward the
right one. It works like magic.

Of course, the notions of "right" and "wrong" are subjective,
grown-up ones; all a child knows is "this worked for me" (got me
something I liked) or "that didn't work for me" (I got nothing).
Azerrad's description of how this functions is adaptable: substitute

"dog," "dolphin," or "nations" for "children" and its observations are every bit as world-changing.

> *Children's behavior, good or bad, is directly related to the conse-*
> *quences of that behavior. In almost every instance, it is worthwhile*
> *for them to behave as they do. As a consequence of their behavior*
> *they are rewarded, with time and attention and a heavy degree of*
> *parental involvement. It doesn't matter to children whether they're*
> *being rewarded for behavior adults think is "bad" or "good." In*
> *either case, the rewarded behavior is likely to continue. . . . Behavior,*
> *whether positive or negative, is simply the result of the consequences*
> *that attend a particular way of acting.*

He goes on to remind the reader that in Salem, Massachusetts, in 1692, the reportedly bizarre behavior of certain people, including many children, was deemed the result of their possession by the devil. We know what happened then. Today, Azerrad maintains, the belief in possession by demons is alive and well, although known by different names: "emotional disturbance," "problems." While we no longer torture, stone, or burn to death the afflicted, we now simi-larly "put our reliance on equally ineffective and destructive (at best, nonproductive) ways of removing" the purported witches from our midst.* We believe there are unseen devils in the mind, and the way

---

* As a follower of Skinner (professor of psychology Carl D. Cheney, in "The Source and Control of Behavior") puts it in more precise terms: the mythical constructs of "human nature" and "the mind" represent "an appeal to impalpable entities in the face of ignorance of actual controlling factors." Therefore, if they are made the "objects of education, therapy, or conditioning programs, failure is certain." Failure of this sort can exist along a spectrum ranging from execution as a witch (or other, more current, evildoer) to a bundle of money thrown away on therapy. And I say this as someone who has gladly spent more than half a lifetime in therapy, which has been extraordinarily illuminating, if not as helpful as I'd hoped.

to "exorcise" them is by talking. If in the therapist's office we identify and "understand" our problems, they will go away. He thinks
this is balderdash. "This procedure is almost as doubtful as burning
witches." Treating behavior is the way to change behavior.

In many ways behaviorism is world-changing—for parent, dog
trainer, or statesman alike—and one of its most startling calls is to
remove the notion of values from our understanding of what causes
behavior. We have a deep-seated belief that actions originate in values. We try to do good, and we hope the same of others. There is
no denying that to most of us our sense of values is important. Yet
behavioral scientists have proof that individuals act in accordance
only with their own desires and serve their own ends (although,
often, serving others is deeply rewarding to us as social creatures).
It is the theory's first rule, in fact, that the actor is the only one who
determines what is reinforcing to him or her. The values of anyone
else are beside the point. To insist that others act in accordance with
values that represent no inherent reward to them in a subtle but very
real way denies them full self-determination. *I* decide what is good
for you; *I* think you ought to do what *I* think best. Otherwise known
as coercion.

We may hope and wish all we want, but our children, our dogs,
and our fellow citizens are all looking out for number one, as the
saying goes, and number one decides what number one wants. Not
me, not you. An individual may offer the behavior of a big smile and
hearty thank-you, and possibly a sizable tip, if the chocolate cake
you give her is her favorite thing in the world, and she's hungry; the
person who gags at the sight of cake and moreover has just eaten a
five-course meal will find it unpleasant, to say the least. A desire to
be generous and kind by offering chocolate cake can be quite different from actually being generous and kind.

And so relating to others by means of the way behavior has been proved to work—as opposed to how we believe or hope it does—can paradoxically cause us to treat others in a genuinely ethical way. Instead of *wanting* to be considerate or just, we embody those principles in the way we relate, by taking into account only *the other*'s desires. Our intentions do not come into play, except when they are rewarding to us; consequences are all that matters to an organism.

Strangely, this forgotten little book from thirty-five distant years ago, found by chance during a backyard archaeological dig, fits into the puzzle that was dumped out of the box in a heap when I first got a dog. It took me twenty years to fit enough pieces together to see the intricately colored painting of nature it had been made of: love and science.

Looking back now, after long travels at the end of the leashes behind two dogs who both knew the way when I did not, I wonder why I didn't realize long ago how utterly fantastic, mind-blowing, and richly consuming biology, evolution, and behavior were? To me when I was young, it was a lot of . . . science. Science had charts, and numbers, and lines on graphs. Real, pulsing blood: that was in novels, stories, poems. Science was dry. (Though I confess at least to getting the appeal of Bunsen burners.) Science had none of the electric charge of Shakespeare, of Faulkner.

I persisted in this gross misapprehension for a significant piece of my life. But then came the revelations of science, and suddenly it bloomed open for me, sang operas, wove tapestries from threads in colors that made my eyes vibrate. The truth of what we are made of. Before, I had tried for the big picture by jumping dot to dot in the words of poems' lines, listening to the meaning of silence in the caesuras. I thought this was big stuff, Eliot and Stevens making my head hurt in a pleasant way.

But what I mistook for the big picture was merely brushstrokes in it, and evolution, ethology, and biology revealed themselves as All

Ye Need to Know. Every motet, cathedral, sculpture, ballet, is captive to the all-encompassing work called Survival of the Fittest. It is so complete, so magisterial, so intricate that I cannot imagine a god more staggering to contemplate than one single aspect of this wonderment that is us (and the rest of animal creation): pheromones, or the muscles in the face that telegraph our emotions, or the brokenwing display of the piping plover. Put it all together, all the billions of tiny gears and bolts, and you are standing under one overarching organizational principle of the whole—the symphonic theme—and that is *what works*. What works for our cells will cause those cells and not these to survive; what works for organisms will survive in them (thanks, Darwin); what works to the aims of language will survive as words; what works in behavior, gets us the cookies, will survive in our actions (thanks, Skinner). Art-making is a subset of language—that which can be expressed no other way than this— and is subject to the laws of its own evolution. But laws nonetheless: that which science seeks.

Survival of the Fittest. Not a musical title, certainly, but the single reason why. The reason we are here (which is, um, to be here), the reason at the bottom of everything we do. Art written by science.

Perhaps I may be excused my teenage excursions in the other direction. My dorsal lateral prefrontal cortex, the seat of wise decisions, was as yet not completely developed. But, being inside the experience, how was I to know?

CHAPTER ONE

∀

This part of the story, mine, begins in Brooklyn's Prospect Park, in the cultivated wildness that seems impossible, a gift, in the middle of a dense and great city. There, in the expanses of lawn and woods that cover 585 acres of former farmland and forest carved into careful serenity by Frederick Law Olmsted and Calvert Vaux in 1867, every morning before nine a microcosm of humanity convenes to show its essential nature. First, though, all you see is dogs. Hundreds of them, in all shapes and sizes and proclivities, running and playing. Some go missing for a time in the bushes, searching for some part of their animal past as hunters, which they find (and chase) in the form of squirrels or, more distressingly to their human companions, by way of excrement. This, whether the product of the horses improbably present in the middle of a modern city or of the homeless for whom the park is less a playground than a hygiene station, also provides a view of another stage of canid evolution, since wolves may have first been drawn to human settlements by their outlying latrines.

The dogs' owners also display a wide variety of their own elemental behaviors. In fact, it would be a challenge to view the scene for more than a few minutes and not be struck by the idea that the most interesting thing about dogs is the people they are attached to. Other forces, atmospheric winds, convected my thoughts. In the dog park, I would watch as the veil of the present suddenly ripped down the center seam. Behind it was playing, on continuous loop, a batch of grainy color 8mm home movies. On top of the adults moving through the park were now superimposed their younger selves. The guys throwing Frisbees endlessly for their equally relentless charges, because that is what makes the beloved dog happy (the predatory instinct again, this time redirected to a flying plastic disk), were once again eight-year-old boys. A mother, indistinct in a doorway, smiled and waved, turned and shut the door. Then there was a tear-stained face, only six years old but already looking ancient, that flashed over the visage of the guy whose bulldog strained against a choke chain in an effort to simply greet the free dogs who bounded up to meet him. The dog was summarily jerked away; no fun for you. (Why? No reason except for what was contained in a thirty-second clip that was somehow also a five-act tragedy.)

Beliefs start early, and they start in the wet clay of the young self. What I chose to see, too, was formed in my own age of innocence. That I even stood there too long, mesmerized by the dance of others' relationships, and held these images in my mind for years, is a function of my own story, my own desire to comprehend and perhaps fix my own history by proxy. Dogs are ideal for the purpose: in the absence of regaining our own pasts, gone for good, we either rework or repeat them in the present. First, I had to get my own little proxy. It makes sense: she was black and white.

. . .

IT IS rarely a good idea to own a dog much smarter than you are. With Mercy, we simply didn't know what we were getting into. She was born of that moment in a young marriage when you are doing everything possible to forestall the discussion about children. A dog is the perfect avoidance behavior.

We avoided our way into pet ownership on the weekend of our first anniversary, after spending three days talking about it while receiving visitations from the ghosts of possibility: the resident golden at the bed-and-breakfast, the beagle appearing and disappearing behind the unreadable gravestones of a two-hundred-year-old cemetery, the blenderized spill of herding-dog puppies at the riding stable. On the way out of town, the animal shelter was placed directly in our path.

And she was there. It took a few moments, but there she was: the future. In a cage with two brothers throwing themselves, black-and-white dice intent on the fortuitous winning roll, against the wires. Years later, when it grew obvious that her personage deserved a full-scale biography, and not by just one but two writers, we attempted to trace the whereabouts of her brothers. Letters, calls, investigations, yielded nothing. What is a biography without the first two chapters of family history? The frustration of not knowing anything about her was enormous, never more so than after she died, and the silence of an intolerable nothing pressed heavy from all sides.

The black puppy with four white paws hung back, regarding us, calm in the knowledge of her own brilliance. That was what did it: the smoldering lights of her eyes. "That one." We pointed. She was brought forth, into our arms, the puppy from the cage that bore a hand-printed tag: "Husky/Labrador retriever." Whatever. It might as well have read, "Vixen/devil," or "Watershed/challenge." We had no idea about dogs. Although we were soon to get one. For the record, she was almost pure border collie. The dogs that "do not make good pets," warned a book by a herding-dog authority we later read in our headlong quest to figure out what we had done. For now, she squirmed in our arms as we filled out the paperwork.

I looked down at the top of her black head and thought, "Wow. Insects." I could see the fleas crawling through the fur but did not know what they were, that's how advanced was my animal husbandry. At the first rest stop on the highway, spinning like a top at the end of the rope that acted as temporary leash, she finally squatted and relieved herself of a mass of brown liquid the density of stew.

There were probably still some worms left inside her, but I couldn't be entirely sure.

With the entry to the Brooklyn Bridge in sight at last, an unearthly sound erupted from deep in her throat, followed immediately by a warm sensation in my lap. Welcome to New York. We had decided on the way to name her Mercedes. But she was forever Mercy to us.

*   *   *

SHE WAS up all night long, chewing on the furniture, crawling underneath the platform bed where her teeth had access to electrical cords but we had no access to her. All night long. And this was after the endless night during which we had taken turns cradling her as she moaned and cried piteously, gut roiled into agony by the worming pills. By day she stole our socks and chewed our bills and our books, then took us on Nantucket sleigh rides as she careered at top speed up the sidewalk in unbroken haste to get to the dogs or children she had spied at the head of the block. When she got there, she threw herself upon her objectives with vigor. She didn't even know what she intended to do with them; she was in the grip of some possession, whether by neurochemistry or malevolent spirit of the dead none of us could figure. It was on the fifth night of uninterrupted sleeplessness that we knew something had to be done: we would not survive, or she would not, or all three of us would go down, separate but equally aflame.

The next day, we got on the phone with the only other dog owners we knew in New York. These friends, careful, perfectionist, overeducated, bookish sorts, were sure to have done their homework when they acquired their long-haired dachshund children. And so they had: within a day we were in possession of a borrowed video-tape called *Sirius Puppy Training* by Dr. Ian Dunbar and a typed list of ten trainers, with phone numbers.

Who to choose? No perfectionist but rather a randomist from the heart, I allowed my inner know-nothingness to guide me. It pulled me straight to number three. Polly Hanson, of Brooklyn. Why not two, or seven? I dialed. She answered. After listening to a haphazard pour of woe and complaint, she asked if tomorrow morning was good for a visit. Tomorrow morning was soon, but not soon enough.

When the bell rang, Mercy raced from one end of the long hall to the other while Polly climbed four flights of stairs. The door opened on a pixieish woman my own age with a radiant smile. Seraphim on a house call. She seemed not to notice the young wolf launching herself to waist height by means of strong springs, bouncing down the hall as we proceeded to the kitchen. I took a chair, but Polly lowered herself to the floor. "Tell me about Mercy!" she said in the manner of one asking about Christmas morning. I blathered on as if this were the world's first, and most peculiar, dog (she was, wasn't she?). All thirty pounds of Mercy had crawled into Polly's lap, and she proceeded to work little shark teeth up and down sleeves and the fingers stroking her fur; Mercy was an amateur contortionist. The next thing I knew, she uttered a yelp and scrambled out of Polly's lap, then stood quietly staring at her newly surprising chew toy.

It brought me to a stop, too. "What'd you do?" I asked in mild shock.

The cocktail-party smile was undiminished. "I did exactly what her mother would have done. She bit too hard, and I let her know."

"But how?"

"I bit her."

I had not seen a thing. Just as I would no doubt have missed her mother's rebuke, swift and neither more nor less than required by the transgression.

In a few minutes, Polly stood up and gathered her canvas bag. "I know what is the matter with your dog."

What? Oh, what? My marriage, and the growing, insensible love I felt for this impossible creature, hung on her pronouncement. Gravely she intoned: "Your dog needs the Park Cure."

Obviously, I did not know what the Park Cure was or what it entailed, only that if this doctor with healing hands prescribed it, I would do anything to provide it.

"Be downstairs with Mercy at seven-thirty tomorrow morning. I'll pick you up." I nodded yes. I could not have known it then, but I was agreeing to an education. I was agreeing to a world changed by one dog, and by luck.

CHAPTER TWO

⅄

Obedience to law is liberty.

—BOETHIUS (ATTRIB.)

To be driven by appetite alone is slavery, and
obedience to the law one has prescribed for
oneself is liberty.

—JEAN-JACQUES ROUSSEAU, 1762

Burrhus Frederic Skinner was born in 1904 in Susquehanna, Pennsylvania, near the border with New York. The town, of about 3,500 residents, occupied itself with building railroad cars and quarrying bluestone. Coal dust rose into and then fell continuously from the air.

He and his younger brother grew up in what he later described as a "warm and stable" home, with a lawyer father and housewife mother. The boy who became an adult with an impossibly high forehead—there looks to be an extra two inches in his cranium compared to the norm—was one of those inveterate inventors, the sort of child who was impatient with the slow or inefficient and sought to improve the works of any machine he pondered. There was endless opportunity, in that young and uncontained American world: "Our yard was a mess, the town was a mess, the surrounding countryside was largely primeval or on its way back to that condition"—in other words, heaven. The disorder offered itself sacrificially to the mind that could order it. He and a chum built a cabin out in the woods. In considering how to improve his door-to-door business selling elderberries, he devised a flotation system to separate out the unripe fruit. He attempted, but did not succeed, to build a perpetual motion machine.

The teenager moved ninety-three miles northwest to attend the male-only Hamilton College in central New York. He received an A.B. in English, and upon graduation returned home to embark on life as a writer. It succeeded about as well as his perpetual motion machine, notwithstanding his receipt of an encouraging letter from no less a personage than Robert Frost. Bookish, curious, unsatisfied: like any ambitious young person without a plan, Skinner headed to New York City. There he found employment as a clerk in a bookstore. One can imagine him in thrall to the shelves, sampling the wares as much as selling them. He had previously pledged himself to the ideas of Francis Bacon; if Skinner had a religion, which he no longer did, having abandoned Presbyterianism, it would have been empiricism. "Nature, to be commanded, must be obeyed," Bacon had said, a priori encapsulating what was to inform the life's work of his disciple 350 years later. Near the end of his life, Skinner would write:

> *Science, not religion, has taught me my most useful values, among them intellectual honesty. It is better to go without answers than to accept those that merely resolve puzzlement. I like Bertrand Russell's reply to Pascal's wager. Pascal argued that the consequences of believing in God were so immense that only a fool would not believe; but, said Russell, suppose God values intellectual honesty above all else and that he has given us shoddy evidence of His existence and is planning to damn to hell all those who believe in Him only for the sake of the glittering prizes.*

He could in this way be seen as a sort of pantheist, who finds God— another name for truth—in the works of nature, which inform men on the ways in which they operate, instead of the other way around.

This is where, by the sort of accident that later appears perfectly designed, he encountered the works of Pavlov and the psychologist John Broadus Watson, the founder of behaviorism. The can of worms in which Skinner would later find himself, unable to escape, was opened here.

Watson was a champion of the purely objective observation of behavior in which recourse to introspection had no place; he was a proponent of the new scientism that was being overlaid on all sorts of natural processes at the turn of the twentieth century, from eating to sex to childrearing. He held the chair in the psychology department of Johns Hopkins University, until he was divested of the post when it was discovered he was having an affair with his graduate student assistant. Whatever he believed about the propriety of his personal decisions, he held that the human is primarily shaped by his environment, and famously stated that the world needed "not more babies but better brought up babies." In 1910, *Harper's* published his manifesto "The New Science of Animal Behavior," replete with diagrams of the mazes and contraptions he had used to closely attend to what animals did in them in response to various stimuli. In it he pronounced:

> *Reasoning . . . is a very much over-rated psychological process, even in adults. The amount of actual reasoning going on in the minds of most of us, after the pattern of the old conventional type—*
> All men are mortal.
> Socrates was a man;
> *Therefore, Socrates was mortal—is just about* nil. *What we do is to* think.

*Past connections and associations will appear in the mind when
we are in a situation which demands some action.*

The last assertion contains the fundamental notion that Skinner
modified in founding a new field, the experimental analysis of
behavior, or behaviorism. Life already marks it well. In essence, Watson maintains that our past experiences inform our future actions
through associations with antecedent stimuli, as in the famous Pavlovian *sound* followed by *salivation* effect. If in one situation we have
experienced something good—pleasurable, beneficial—we *associate*
that happy sensation with the recurrence of the same situation. And,
naturally, we are then apt to try to make the situation recur.

Naturally. We knew that.

Watson's is a radically simple idea of the sort that presents itself
as already understood, when in fact no one had said anything quite
like it. What Skinner discovered is likewise anything but simple,
instantly flipping received wisdom on its head. *It is past consequences,
and not free consideration of future acts, that selects behavior.* Now we
grow alarmed, having been asked to assume a whole new worldview.
But we had built so much upon the old one!

As we know well, all new ideas, even ones that come with easily observable proofs, are met with initial resistance, but none are
so resisted as those that tamper with our self-conceptions, especially
those on which religions are based. This is what the Skinnerites
were up against. Pushing at the stone fortresses of God-and-man
using only their big foreheads.

More heresy was in store.* Watson came close to severing the

---

* Watson ended up leaving the academy for greener pastures (and possibly ones less
censorious of inappropriate exploitation): he pioneered psychologically based advertising as vice president of the J. Walter Thompson agency on Madison Avenue.

artery running from the heart of who we believed we were: fundamentally separate from the rest of the animate world. "We can reason about playing the piano all we care to, but we cannot play the *Spring Song* until we have learned to control each separate movement by the slow and very same process that the animal employs."

The young man reading these words—who would later come to elaborate Watson's partial slice of a functioning model for behavior—was one who had since childhood approached the world as a series of problems needing solutions largely in the form of a new contraption. Devise one, then, he would.

But he would not be the first to do so; more than an inventor, perhaps, Skinner was an improver. He would refine the devices of Watson's contemporary, Edward Lee Thorndike,* known as the father of comparative psychology, and *then* all hell would break loose.

Thorndike's doctoral dissertation, successfully defended in 1898 at Columbia University, was the first in psychology to be based on studies of animals. He made "puzzle boxes" of levers, strings, and doors, from which his subject, cats, would find their reward—freedom (and, gilt on the lily, food too)—if they learned how to release themselves. They surely did: whether by observing another cat finding the lever or by happening on it by accident, their responses quickened until leveling off; when graphed, the rate described the shape of an S. Upon testing, other species showed the same response. If

---

* Thorndike left a lasting impression on the psychology of learning, in one example by devising the tests on which are based those used to this day to determine enlistment qualifications for the U.S. armed forces. He spent the bulk of his career at Teachers College of Columbia University.

Julie Vargas, president of the B. F. Skinner Foundation, maintains that a thorough search of Skinner's written record during the years 1928 to 1931, the period in which he discovered operant conditioning, turns up no mention of Thorndike. She is convinced that Thorndike's work did not inform Skinner's in any way.

animals learned through insight, as previously believed, the graph would have shown an abrupt drop instead of the gradual curves it did. That getting out of a box was the reward for which they would work so tirelessly could be the thesis of an experiment for which Thorndike himself was subject: Test the idea that man is enough like other animals that in designing an experiment he will instinctively choose the most universally desired reward that can be conceived. *Freedom from restriction.*

He codified his findings into the "law of effect," which became the foundation on which Skinner's own experiments, also using puzzle boxes of a sort, were built: if an act is followed by a "satisfying state of affairs," its repetition will be strengthened, and if it is followed by an "annoying state of affairs," it will be weakened. This learning occurs automatically, and all animals learn the same way, Thorndike stated. Further refined, his "law of exercise" consists of two parts: the law of use—the more often an association is used, the stronger it becomes—and the law of disuse—the longer an association is unused, the weaker it becomes. Finally, there is the "law of recency," which states that the most recent response is the one most likely to reoccur, all other things being equal.

Much later, Skinner would observe, "The rat is always right," but since scientists are men and not infallible rats, they have a tendency to wander off the solidity of their well-built bridges and right into the sucking mud at river's edge. For his part, Thorndike went knee-deep into the muck of eugenics, brightly offering his belief that "there is no more certain and economical a way to improve man's environment as to improve his nature." There is also no more certain or economical a way to discredit the legacy of your work, too.

Leaving shore in a writer's small boat placed Skinner adrift on a wide sea. He decided to put in at the harbor of school again. He entered Harvard at age twenty-four as a graduate student in psychology, but he found his most like-minded mentor in William Crozier, who headed the new department of physiology. Crozier, like Watson, aimed to study "the animal as a whole" without the wayward preconceptions of interiority. Data became his student's firmly held faith, too. He started building devices. Then, when his lab rats pressed levers inside the special boxes he had made, the cumulative recorder he also invented, an ingenious computational device prefiguring today's computer—rate of response showing as an uptick along a horizontally advancing line—sanctified his confidence in evidence. He was about to go Pavlov one better.

Skinner discovered that the rate of the rat's bar-pressing response was dependent not on what happened *before*, as with Pavlov's bell and the salivation reflex it triggered, but rather on what happened *after* the bar was pressed. The appearance of a pellet of feed caused the rat's future act—pressing on the bar again, say, or not doing so, or doing it faster and faster, or for a longer or shorter duration between rewards. The rat's behavior thus *operated* on the environment, and his future acts were always controlled by its effects.

Skinner named this effect operant behavior. And he called the process of setting the contingencies of reinforcement responsible for producing the behaviors operant conditioning. There are four quadrants, he discovered, into which the modifiers of all behavior can be organized (apart from those that are the result of instinct and thus a part of the repertoire of inherited behavior). Both punishment (that which suppresses behavior) and reinforcement (that which strengthens behavior) come in two flavors each: "positive" and "negative." Despite the popular connotations of those words, here they refer only to addition and subtraction.

Positive punishment is the addition of an aversive stimulus, or whatever will reduce the frequency of a behavior (making an unpleasant noise, hitting, cutting off breath by pulling against the windpipe with a choke chain).

Negative punishment occurs when you remove something desirable (turning your back to remove attention; closing your hand over the biscuit if the dog grabs for it rudely).

Positive reinforcement is the introduction of anything that will make a behavior reoccur. (Receiving your paycheck every other Friday makes it much more likely you show up on Monday; the dog sits in front of a door and then he gets to go outside, so he learns to sit before a door.)

Negative reinforcement represents the removal of an unpleasant stimulus in order to increase the frequency of a behavior. (The mosquitoes at dusk are so hateful you are sure to carry a bottle of insect repellent in your bag wherever you go in summer; a pinch collar administers a painful pressure on the neck until the dog walks politely, at which point it releases.)

Many behaviors can be taught two or more ways, say with negative reinforcement or with positive reinforcement, but one tends to be more effective, that is, its effects are longer-lasting and— important from the standpoint of the emotional state of both teacher and student—without the roster of problematic side effects that frequently accompany certain methods. Or that, in the case of positive punishment, always accompany it: among them fear and anxiety, which impede learning and lead to a reluctance to engage in any but whatever is the least action that can be performed to avoid the discomfort. Given this, it is interesting to note how often punishment is held up as the *morally* right choice of behavior modification technique, albeit rarely the more effective one. Its popularity "at one time" (meaning still, though less and less) grew out of the puritanical strain of pedagogy that held to spare the rod was to spoil the child.

Even to the time of my grandmother, who so proudly wielded a butter paddle on the behinds of her misbehaving children and grandchildren that she inscribed that maxim on it before bestowing it as a gift (she was retiring it upon going into an old-age home). My sister, alone among forty cousins, won this prize of prizes in a lottery.

Lest this appear a long-ago remnant of outmoded technique, about eighteen hours ago I was sitting at a cocktail party talking with a friend as we watched her eight-year-old and a pal play catch in the hotel garden. "My stepfather believes the old-fashioned methods of childrearing are the best," she related, adding that he advised her to spank her son. " 'It works on my dog,' " he repeated often, with an edge of aggressive come-on. He wouldn't let it go. "I get the feeling he's trying to challenge me," she mused. No doubt.

"Works on" is a telling phrase in this context. Why would anyone *want* someone to hit a child? It begs so many other questions they start chasing each other in the mind, a little like rats. Some of these will be answered later in a technical discussion of how punishment affects behavior. For now I will just mention that all four approaches to modifying behavior pull behind them a trainload of specific physical and emotional consequences. These are what B. F. Skinner studied exhaustively—and dispassionately, assigning no moral weight to any of them but merely noting their effects. He was a scientist who had no compunction about applying electric shock to intelligent animals that had no hope of escaping, but who went on to publicly conclude that punishment was an ineffective means of shaping behavior. In that I find something especially trustworthy, if strange.

. . .

THE SCHEDULES on which reinforcement is delivered, Skinner's experiments led him to realize, are a critical part of the *quality* of the resulting behaviors, which is to say their strength—how deeply entrenched, how easily forgotten or replaced. Schedules of reinforcement are the gearbox in the engine of behavior: they transmit power, at varying speeds, so the wheels move. Without them, you won't go far. The gear needs to be selected properly, too, to match engine speed, or it cannot run optimally. Skinner had found the production of behavior to grow stronger, weaker, or liable/resistant to "extinction" (disappearance) depending on the rate of reinforcement. There are two categories of reinforcement schedule—a continuous schedule and an intermittent schedule—while within the latter are four subtypes: the fixed-ratio, the fixed-interval, the variable-ratio, and the variable-interval.

(This is no doubt the point at which the whole lecture hall has come either to be napping or checking their Tumblr. But then the students miss the explanation of their own behavior, including and especially the appeal of incessantly pecking on devices with little screens, which deliver various levels of reinforcers—some awesome, some so-so—at various times, thus making our predominant communicative technology most compelling from a behavior-modification standpoint. The intent adoration with which one stares at one's smartphone can only be compared to the gaze lavished on a deeply beloved—who likewise delivers a variety of pleasures on an unpredictable schedule. Romance's dark mystery—why we often fall hardest for those who blow hot and cold—is fully clarified under the scientific light of the intermittent schedule.)

The rats used by APOPO had been trained to detect mines and TB using operant conditioning, with its carefully employed schedules of reinforcement. The autistic child who for the first time complied with a request to sit in a chair did so because of the schedule of reinforcement that helped teach him what the request meant. So, too, the boy in Iceland who experienced the freedom and confidence that comes of mastering a common skill. And to not understand the power the schedule of reinforcement wields over our every moment is to not see the danger as it heads right at us.

The variable-ratio schedule is the most potent of all: if you wish to maintain a behavior at utmost strength, you will be advised to put it on this schedule of reinforcement after establishing it by first using continuous reinforcement.* Very little, in fact, is going to get in the way of the will to repeat a behavior that has been rewarded unpredictably. It generates a thrill of anticipation; we find they're the things we can't stop ourselves from doing, even when we know we should. Like texting. Which behavior we will maintain even if we are risking death to do so.

In 2013, texting while driving surpassed drinking and driving as the greatest hazard to American teens: researchers estimate there are now more than 3,000 annual teen deaths nationwide and 300,000 injuries from using mobile devices behind the wheel. What is so alluring about the activity, to the point that we are committing vehicular homicide all over the place but blithely justifying it with the belief that it can be done safely (as those who do it claim, against all evidence)? Its schedule of reinforcement.

The ping that says a text has arrived—which, significant to the matter of the schedule, *may* or *may not* reveal a reward: a date, a profession of love or lust, a yes of any kind—is irregular, and for that, irresistible. We'd check spam messages all day with the same immediate attention because the ping has been conditioned to be

---

* On the other hand, dropping reinforcement entirely is the sure way to extinguish a behavior entirely, unless it continues getting reinforcement from some other source: You trained your dog to come by giving her a treat every time she did, but once the recall seemed reliable you stopped giving her treats. Slowly, she stopped responding reliably, and soon, at all. Now, staying over by the fence line sniffing grass, while not as much fun as getting a cookie, is more rewarding than nothing. Dogs, like everyone else, know which side their bread is buttered on.

reinforcing (having previously signaled welcome messages on occasion). The sound of an incoming message is a conditioned reinforcer, and it shapes our behavior just as the click does the trainee of any species. We are helpless not to respond, because it is the *reward center in the brain* that is doing the responding. You can't just say no to the mesolimbic dopamine system.* You, or rather your prefrontal cortex, which is the part of you that feels like "you," is left out of the loop.

The reason this particular schedule of reinforcement is the most compelling, to man or rat, is once more probably located in our evolutionary past: food is obtained only occasionally, not on every hunting expedition. Ironically, or obviously, the variable-ratio schedule of reinforcement also happens to be the same on which the gambling addict is made.

Up to this point, in declaring that B. F. Skinner had in fact discovered the magic key to behavior—the reinforcer and its effect on the future—I have been guilty of an oversimplification. Or maybe just a partial truth. At the time he was in the laboratory developing his theory of operant conditioning, the science of neurochemistry was barely in its infancy. It is now known that it is the neurotransmitter dopamine that is specifically responsible for identifying rewards. In fact, every conceivable reward yet studied has been found to trigger the release of dopamine. (Although it had been chemically synthesized much earlier, its role as a neurotransmitter was not discovered

---

* "This circuit (VTA-NAc) is a key detector of a rewarding stimulus. Under normal conditions, the circuit controls an individual's responses to natural rewards, such as food, sex, and social interactions, and is therefore an important determinant of motivation and incentive drive. In simplistic terms, activation of the pathway tells the individual to repeat what it just did to get that reward. *It also tells the memory centers in the brain to pay particular attention to all features of that rewarding experience, so it can be repeated in the future.* Not surprisingly, it is a very old pathway from an evolutionary point of view." (Emphasis mine; Icahn School of Medicine at Mount Sinai, Neuroscience Department Laboratories website.)

until 1957.) So it is not, precisely speaking, the reward that changes behavior; rather, it is the release of the pleasure chemical in the brain caused by the reward. Anything that stimulates the flow of dopamine is desired by us, and therefore we do whatever it takes to get it, again and again. "Anything" includes nicotine and heroin, as we know; also sex, power, receiving money or compliments, practicing religion, and waging war. It might be argued, and has (a 2011 article in *ChemViews* magazine is titled "Could Dopamine Be the Most Evil Chemical in the World?"), that free will is a billboard advertising nothing more than the action of this chemical in the brain. It is the opposite of free: it alone forges the shackles of profound addiction.

It gets more interesting.

Researchers initially assumed it was the *receipt* of the reward—the lovely feel of milk chocolate growing soft on the tongue; the moment the coins start clattering from the mouth of the one-armed bandit—that opened the dopamine faucet. Nope. As biologist Robert Sapolsky explained in a 2011 lecture to the California Academy of Sciences,[2] monkeys in Skinner boxes who were trained to depress levers a set number of times in order to get a food reward did not experience the dopamine rush after they accomplished the task and received the food. Rather, it spiked when they saw the signal light that meant the session was going to begin. Before they received anything at all.

When they were moved from a fixed-ratio to a variable-ratio schedule of reinforcement, the dopamine released in advance of the working session *almost doubled*; here is the real reason behaviors that are rewarded unpredictably become stronger. And they are strongest of all—i.e., the dopamine spikes are higher still—when those unpredictable rewards are unpredictably sized, as in gambling: most of the time you win nothing, sometimes you win a little, and infrequently you hit the jackpot. Indeed, "jackpotting" has become a standard tool in the positive-reinforcement dog trainer's kit. Every once in a while, the desired behavior yields not one but a whole handful of treats and among them some particularly delicious ones. Accompany this with a lot of happy excitement and the appearance of a favorite tug toy, too, and you're "throwing a party"—the dog has suddenly won big, and you've vastly increased the chances he'll repeat the behavior that preceded this surprise. He wants more dopamine, too, just as we all do.

As Sapolsky puts it, "Dopamine is not about pleasure, it's about the *anticipation* of pleasure." If you block the flow of the chemical, the behavior that previously excited it simply won't reoccur. We act in order to get the rush. Period.

* * *

ALTHOUGH B. F. SKINNER also had no way to know that sixty years hence we would all become willing subjects of our own behavioral experiments in the form of personal computing devices, he did predict the exact outcome of the responses they elicit. In *The Behavior of Organisms,* published in 1938, he set forth the terms of this new law, as universal and generally unyielding as that of gravity.* What was revolutionary about what he called operant conditioning was that it sought to explain all behavior, whether the explanation (in the form of an originating stimulus) could be seen or not. In fact, that was its difference from classical, or Pavlovian, conditioning.

He wrote: "The kind of behavior that is correlated with specific eliciting stimuli may be called *respondent* behavior"—bell rings, dog salivates—while "such behavior as is not under this kind of control I

---

* Or rather, an abundance of laws: *The Behavior of Organisms* is chockablock with them. The Law of Prepotency; the Law of Chaining; the Law of Algebraic Summation; the Laws of Conditioning of Type R, and of Extinction of Type R; the Law of Inhibition. And so on, and on.

shall call *operant*," when the response is "a posterior event," meaning that "no correlated stimulus can be detected upon occasions when it is observed to occur." Translation? It is a behavior freely given in anticipation of a *future* stimulus (while the salivation is more or less compelled, being a reflexive reaction to something that has already happened). The act—whether pecking on a bar to make a pellet of feed appear, or an infant's cry that is made in anticipation of the offer of the nipple—precedes the stimulus that has been conditioned by it.

It sounds dry and unthreatening, but the implications of what Skinner was saying were neither. It is solely the presence of a behavior (along with its qualities, such as strength and duration) that points to the fact of its having been caused by a reinforcing stimulus, and on what schedule. The behavior describes the type of reinforcement or lack thereof. No prize, no act. No punishment, no nothing. We never act in a vacuum, and Skinner considered thoughts a vacuum—or at least a red herring. There was always something concrete, something feelable or eatable, that encouraged or dissuaded everything we did, no matter whether "we" were white rat or varicolored human. God, intention, and will were as vapor: they were thoughts, and they didn't make us act. (Emotions such as fear, anxiety, desire, and sadness are byproducts of the rate and type of stimulus—real, natural, but not causative.)

This is greatly simplified from the original statement—a book that runs, after all, some 470 pages replete with charts and graphs—but it *can* be simplified. And that is another of Skinner's perceived transgressions: the unfathomable complexities of being human could not possibly be so easily distilled. It is counterintuitive. We live inside the mind that creates the intuition that we are richly intuitive; how could this same mind permit the notion that we are not?

Yet Skinner stringently tested his law in the laboratory and in his own life—*and it never failed*. Not with rats or pigeons or even when he later looked back on his own years through the lens of behavior analysis at the millions of minutes, each one a decision, that comprise a life. His autobiography runs to three volumes.

He describes teaching his daughter, when an infant in his lap, to raise her arm by turning the table lamp on and off. He describes visiting his horse-crazy girl's riding stable and seeing that traditional horse training was organized to depend, unnecessarily and inefficiently, on applying aversives; in a few moments he shaped some new behaviors using positive reinforcement. No one was impressed. But why *wouldn't* people wish all animals, including themselves, to live happier, less restricted, less painful lives? Everywhere he looked he could see how things could be rearranged in fairly short order. That no one seemed much inclined was a source of never-ending frustration to him.

So he repeated his experiments, in different genres (fiction, science, philosophy) and venues (his daughter's grade-school classroom, demonstrations for the popular press, work for the government), but the results never changed. All behavior is shaped by what happens after it: a pleasant outcome—pleasure defined only by the individual at a specific point in time and due to internal factors that may be in part determined by biology or history—and the behavior will repeat. No outcome and the behavior will be extinguished. He was forced to reiterate his finding that this is how all organisms learn, whether mollusk or graduate student. The rat does not lie and neither did the data recorder; its black marks on white offered irrefutable data about what causes us to do things. If a behavior occurs, it is being rewarded, even if the reward is masked by the complexities of our environment or our history. It is there, for the existence of the behavior tells us so.

In the Skinner box, life was simplified; there was something to do and a food pellet that resulted, or there was not. There was no couch, TV, or comely female rat; there was no church or book to write or society of others.* In the wider world, rewards can cleverly hide, but they nonetheless teach us what it takes to get them. He would write more about this, with increasing fervor and frustration, using illustrations from politics, society, history, and daily life. It was as if he thought that, surely, the list could be made long enough for people to finally get it. Then they would see the lawness of his law.

Radical though his discovery was, if Skinner had merely published *The Behavior of Organisms* in 1938, he would be remembered in science courses as someone who once figured out what made some animals we don't care much for anyways tick. His discovery, elaborated for practical application and disseminated by students of his, still would have had the substantial impact it later did on the fields of animal training and husbandry, on the development of TAGteach, and on effective treatments for the autistic and mentally disabled, and he would be fondly regarded for these. And marginalized, because they would stay in their Skinner boxes, ones with doors that quietly close on the gymnasium, the zoo, the psychiatric hospital.† He would be considered, if he was thought about much at

---

* Actually, at some point there was: a psychiatrist at Boston Psychopathic Hospital named Clare Marshall spent a year in Skinner's lab at Harvard in the fifties, when Skinner was a professor there, studying the reinforcing effects of sexual contact. "When a male rat pressed a lever, a receptive female dropped into the experimental space. The event could be scheduled in various ways and proved to be, to no one's surprise, highly effective," Skinner reported in the third volume of his autobiography.

† Nothing is more marginal (if popular) than the fellow animals we have, through intellectual sleight of hand, set apart from us. Books on animals—let us not forget that Blake wrote "animal books"—are in the back of the store, next to the shelves devoted to building your own compost bin and near the titles on car maintenance. Their sales figures betray an interesting fact, though: as individuals we are endlessly fascinated by animals; as a culture, not so much.

all, as a slightly eccentric tinkerer who at the behest of his wife on the birth of their second daughter designed a safer crib—dubbed the baby-tender, or the air-crib—that did away with hazardous bars that could catch and injure limbs and that permitted a baby to sleep in a climate-controlled environment unfettered by clothes or bound in blankets. Even the provocative and misleading title given the *Ladies' Home Journal* article on the crib, "Baby in a Box," might have gone the way of all such periodical silliness, long biodegraded ("On Choosing a Hat," "How to Live Cheaply"). If he had just stopped with describing how lab rats formed lever-pressing behaviors at differing strengths and did not extrapolate his findings to the shaping of human behavior by our social systems, his image would be far different than it is today: a man who himself is widely misunderstood, even if his theories have now permeated much current teaching and therapeutic methodology.

Cognitive behavioral therapy, widely used to treat a variety of phobias, addictions, and repetitive troubles, is a direct descendent of operant conditioning. So are hundreds of motivational apps that help us lose weight, stop smoking, exercise more: textbook operant conditioning. In a multitude of other fields, what Skinner learned about the way we learn has become so mainstream today—in therapy, business (where it is known as organizational behavior management), targeted marketing, and education—we can no longer identify the source. Here is a brief summary (by Wallace Hannum, retired professor of educational psychology at the University of North Carolina at Chapel Hill) of the reception of Skinner's theory, from applied behavior analysis to nameless "common knowledge":

Skinner has traveled from being the most influential theorist in education in the 1950s and 60s to perhaps being among the least influen-

tial today. At least this is true as far as reputation. It is very difficult to find educators today who claim to be Skinnerians whereas 40 years ago almost all teachers embraced his ideas. Although his star has faded and his theory is very much out of favor, today you still find many teaching practices that have theory origins in Skinner. Today we don't claim to be Skinnerians but our teaching practices would often indicate otherwise.

Skinner gave us behavioral objectives, the use of reinforcers (rewards), individualized instruction, the simple-to-complex sequencing of content, the use of active practice by students, the use of frequent feedback to students, criterion-referenced testing, self-pacing, mastery learning and many more concepts in wide use in education today. Skinner remains very influential in schools although we no longer consider his theory to be important or even correct. We don't write about using Skinner's ideas and we don't talk about this, but when you look into classrooms you see a lot of Skinner today.[3]

You do *see* a lot of Skinner in many fields but you do not *hear* about Skinner "in a good way," as they say. His discovery is alive and well while he himself is perceived to have been a loose cannon from a period of psychology that has been fortunately superseded.*

* * *

---

* An award-winning, widely read book by Lauren Slater, *Opening Skinner's Box,* as recently as 2004 repeated the claim that the scientist raised his daughter Deborah in a "Skinner box." Deborah, who was elsewhere rumored to have had a psychotic break, sued her father, and committed suicide, wrote a strong rebuttal in the *Guardian.* (Deborah Skinner Buzan, "I Was Not a Lab Rat," March 12, 2004). Buzan is an artist, and her older sister Julie is the president of the B. F. Skinner Foundation in Cambridge, Massachusetts. Its slogan: "Better Behavioral Science for a More Humane World."

A FULL fifty years after his most controversial work was published, his name retains a will of its own in pop culture. There is no more lively a corner of it than *The Simpsons,* which was conceived to deflate every hypocrisy great and small on the American scene. Having a character named after you on the epochal show is a dubious yet certain sign of arrival. Principal Skinner is described as "a stereotypical educational bureaucrat." A humorless automaton, meant to exemplify the polar opposite of a kid like Bart, with whom we all identify in his joyful lack of impulse control and happy disregard of anything as dumb as careful consideration. Come to think of it, the Simpsonian caricature of Skinner perfectly captures the prevailing image of a Skinner subject: living in a box, content to repetitively press on a bar.

The reason for the schism between the utility of his theories and the malignancy of his reputation is located in the fact that after 1938 he refused to keep his ideas in the realm of rats (or, soon, almost exclusively those animals famously labeled in 1966 "rats with wings" by New York City's parks commissioner). He was about to expand his repertoire considerably, with a performance that was designed to show the world he was not "just" a scientist; he was a philosopher whose ideas—of a far more solid type than the airy products of that fictional "homunculus" we erroneously believe guides the self—were made in the scrupulous precincts of the experimental lab. He was a *scientist-philosopher.* So, in a characteristically perverse act, Skinner chose fiction to express his plan for an improved society based on behavioral science. *Walden Two*, his utopian novel, was published in 1948.

The choice of a fictional voice can be seen as the spoonful of sugar that would make his socially prescriptive medicine go down easier—to the dismay of uncounted high-school students since—but it is possibly overdetermined. It was certainly a bit of a literary error. In a 2003 paper ("The Double Life of B. F. Skinner") in the *Journal of Consciousness Studies*, Bernard J. Baars makes a plausible case for an unacknowledged personal motive in Skinner's lifelong, sometimes strangely bitter, disavowal of the merit of "consciousness" as a material aspect of life: his postgraduate failure to become a writer of fiction, particularly of the Joycean stream-of-consciousness type that was all the rage when he was a young student. Baars maintains that this conflict remained very much alive, and irritating to the scientist, as his autobiography attests. The latter is indeed riven with doubts, as well as what appears to be a very private anguish that Skinner the man attributed to being misunderstood as Skinner the scientist. Instead, some of his professional decisions may have been guided in part by a more personal sense of failure and unattained goals.*

"I let Frazier say things that I myself was not yet ready to say to anyone," Skinner would write about the main character who dia-

---

* Although from a glancing knowledge of his work it would seem incompatible with Skinner's views on psychology that he should permit the validity of Freudian theory, in fact he did—he acknowledged the workings of defense mechanisms in himself, for example, and was generally fascinated with key ideas of psychoanalysis such as the function of repression. The abstract of an illuminating paper by Geir Overskeid of the University of Oslo, titled "Looking for Skinner and Finding Freud":

Sigmund Freud and B. F. Skinner are often seen as psychology's polar opposites. It seems this view is fallacious. Indeed, Freud and Skinner had many things in common, including basic assumptions shaped by positivism and determinism. More important, Skinner took a clear interest in psychoanalysis and wanted to be analyzed but was turned down. His views were influenced by Freud in many areas, such as dream symbolism, metaphor use, and defense mechanisms. Skinner drew direct parallels to Freud in his analyses of conscious versus unconscious control of behavior and of selection by consequences. He agreed with Freud regarding aspects of methodology and analyses of civilization. In his writings on human behavior, Skinner cited Freud more than any other author, and there is much clear evidence of Freud's impact on Skinner's thinking. [American Psychologist 62, no. 6 (September 2007): 590–595.]

grams the theoretical foundation of *Walden Two*. The novel indeed marks a great leap of sorts, from the multiple tables and graphs of *The Behavior of Organisms* labeled "Differential Reinforcement of Responses Alternately Above and Below Critical Values" (figure 111) and "Original Extinction at Different Drives" (figure 137) to a hopeful—many said far worse—fictional utopia where people wander happy, with not a combative bone in their bodies. World War II had ended, more or less, just a couple of years before Skinner was gripped by the need to set forth his vision of a cooperative and peaceful society. " 'Why don't we just start all over again the right way?' " breathlessly asks a character who is a young veteran of the recent horrific war; he was also a former student of another character the author thought to name "Professor Burris." This is representative of the novel's coded attempts at cleverness; stiff and expository, it wears the clothing of literature but with a bad fit.

Walden Two's thesis echoes Skinner's seminal discovery of operant conditioning with the answer to a question no one was asking. If all behavior is the result of contingencies, then something in our environment supplies them. We were controlled anyway, usually with aversives rather than reinforcers; why not reengineer our social institutions to reward good behavior rather than punish bad behavior?* Our laws were built largely upon threats—*Do this, or else*—and many of our religions promised eternal damnation. Wars were punishments doled out by nations to other nations; fear of negative consequences was the prime mover in schools and the

---

* Why punishment is a bad thing—apart from the fact that it is a *bad* thing and no one but masochists generally choose it over positive reinforcement—is a large subject and will receive its own attention in due course. For now it is enough to observe, again, that on a functional level it retards learning in general, stifling creativity and novel behavior.

workplace.* More prisons were built all the time (if they acted as deterrent or rehabilitation, as claimed, the evidence was not compelling). These were simple facts met, Skinner believed, with wholesale denial. Let's have done with it and then see how much happier and productive we could become, went the implicit argument. He wrote the book in seven weeks.

It was, according to *Life* magazine, an insult to the genuine innocence of Thoreau's natural utopia, Walden, and a "slur upon [its] name, a corruption of an impulse . . ." The *New York Times* found it "alluring in a sinister way, and appalling, too." The notion of "behavioral engineering" on its face seemed fascist to the public. To *Walden Two*'s relatively few proponents—enough, though, to start a raft of utopian communes, at least one of which, Los Horcones in Hermosillo, Mexico, is going strong forty-five years later and includes a therapeutic Center for Children with Behavioral Deficits—it was clear we operate from so deep inside the well of society's already established systems of behavior modification (religion, government, school, and the family) we are unable to see how they in fact control

---

* From B. F. Skinner, *Science and Human Behavior* (1953):

Narrowly defined, government is the use of the power to punish. Although this definition is sometimes offered as exhaustive, governmental agencies often resort to other kinds of control. The source of the power to punish determines the composition of the agency in the stricter sense. The strong or clever man is a sort of personal government whose power derives from his strength or skill. He may acquire henchmen who exercise the actual control over the group but who are in turn controlled by him through personal strength or skill. The underworld gang often shows a governmental structure of this sort. In the organized government of a modern state, the specific task of punishment is assigned to special groups—the police and military. Their power is usually sheer force, amplified by special equipment, but the power of the ultimate governmental agency may be of a different nature. For example, the police and military may be recruited after appropriate education, they may be controlled through economic measures, or they may act under religious pressure.

our "freedoms" completely. Although the common outrage directed at Skinner's proposal for a newly engineered society was based on a belief that it would rob us of our essential liberties, if the basic tenets of Skinner's law of the acquisition of behavior are true, so is this: we cannot give up something we do not have.

Words that mean one thing in a scientific context often have other meanings in the vernacular; so with "positive" and "negative," as already described. More loaded still is the word "control." This is where *Walden Two* seemed to slam the door in the face of the reader for whom it meant only one thing: loss of self-determination and the introduction of totalitarianism. In fact, Skinner was sickened by tyranny, and the book was his answer to protecting society against its incursion. Yet, like the picture of the girl in a bikini meant to illustrate the dangers of inappropriate dress, some things are so hot they quickly burn to ash anything else in their proximity. Such is the case with rationality, where a proposal to introduce behavioral "controls" represents a struck match.

Skinner later acknowledged he brought the problem on himself, but he was unapologetic about not attempting to avoid it: "I knew the word was troublesome. Why not soften it to 'affect' or 'influence'? But I was a determinist and control meant control, and no other word would do."

If one can be identified, this is the point at which Skinner's legacy began to curdle—in advance. To many it remains difficult if not impossible to understand clearly what Skinner was proposing. It seemed anodyne to him, built as it was upon his unshakable belief that humans were governed by the same laws of behavior as other organisms. After all, he had spent so much time graphing the proofs of what worked, and how, in modifying behavior, in every possible permutation of experiment that occurred to a scientist devoted heart and soul to empiricism, that it would bore the socks off even the most ardent rat lover. It could hardly have been sinister. It was fact.*

The sensitive, music-loving, poetry-writing Burrhus Frederic Skinner, who believed at least on one level that he was merely telling us we *needn't live in fear of reprisal*, that we could refashion our social institutions in consonance with the way he had discovered we learn most effectively, was taken aback by the vehement reaction to *Walden Two* (even if its sales, which initially crawled, were eagerly graphed by the author in exactly the same way he quantified his lab animals' responses, not to mention his own writing behavior).[4] It all seemed bizarre to him—even though he had also courted exactly this response, as his autobiography hints. Ever afterward the angry remonstrances his works called forth seemed to catch him by surprise.

---

* Even a brief critique of the novel that attempted to be as fair-minded as the author intended his planned society to be would so retard our progress toward the further reaches of operant conditioning's application with man's best friend that we might not get farther than Sit. Suffice it to say that among critics there was horror and antagonism aplenty, along with misunderstanding. On the book's side, there was overreaching and patent simplification, as well as elision in certain crucial aspects of the working plan. Feminist scholars have taken it to task for its obvious sexism, although Skinner professed complete egalitarianism. This view, from fifty years later, comes as close as it is possible to get to an evenhanded approach to the book and its legacy; for some reason, its humor is the most reassuring aspect of its probable hit in the critical bull's-eye.

Genetic differences make different people react differently to the same reinforcements; genetic differences also make people seek out different experiences, which alter their learning histories. In other words, some kid at a real Walden Two is going to throw a cat off a building to see how it lands; another is going to spend hours alone at a computer console; another is going to invite his cousin under the lilac bushes to play doctor. They are not all going to turn out delightful—or even happy, self-controlled, and productive, all of which are now suspected to have strong genetic components (anxiety, thrill-seeking, and happiness level all appear genetically driven). Though Skinner always included genetics in his formula for predicting behavior, today's science has proven that he never gave it as much weight as it merits. [Susan X. Day, "Walden Two at Fifty," Michigan Quarterly Review, XXXVIII, no. 2 (Spring 1999)]

He would sometimes write rejoinders to his critics, but they were pale and defensive, and rarely read anyway. For now, he would only reiterate that no one person, not even Frazier, "controlled" the society in the vernacular sense: "*Walden Two* is a designed culture in which the designer has arranged his own demise as leader. There is no hero, no philosopher-king, no Führer, Duce, or Caudillo. That is the answer to the inevitable question—who is to control? No one." A statement like this, even supported by the substance of the book's lengthy disquisitions on political organization clad in the style of conversation, could not dissipate the fog of fear that rose from a general misunderstanding of the science that underlay his prescription for society, New and Improved. That is because Skinner himself had misunderstood how well practiced (hence resistant to extinction, another proof he apparently forgot) a behavior was the traditional self-conception. One can now see grandiosity on top of naïveté in his apparent belief that a single offer to show how his discovery might better human lives could smoothly eclipse two thousand years of entrenched belief about why we did the things we did. He hoped with one novel he could change nothing less than who we believed we were.

• • •

IF *WALDEN TWO* did not exactly establish B. F. Skinner as a literary talent but rather as a divisive social commentator, then what he did next, after a return to strict science with his books *Science and Human Behavior* (1953), *Schedules of Reinforcement* (1957), three other texts on education and contingencies of reinforcement, and 1957's *Verbal Behavior* (in which he made the case for language as just another behavior, built like all of them), could be seen as a further reaction to disappointment. Perhaps one could go so far as to say disgruntlement.

If I can be forgiven the temptation to psychoanalyze the man who is sometimes (erroneously) viewed as psychoanalysis's chief antagonist, the publication of a book bearing the title *Beyond Freedom and Dignity* may be seen as a purposeful, if subconscious, wish to make some noise. Specifically, a loud shout at a world that appeared to have definitively rejected his literary talents.

The backlash from this offensive would hit him square in the character.

Upon the book's publication in 1971, he appeared on the cover of *Time* magazine in a cadaverous caricature under the legend "B. F. Skinner Says: We Can't Afford Freedom." What he meant by *Beyond . . .* could never be coolly considered when affixed to the sacred term *freedom,* and especially not after outraged rebuttals began to fly immediately. Their contrails soon crisscrossed the sky until the blue beyond could not be seen. B. F. Skinner was about to become even more than famous, as he may have wished; he was to become infamous, arguably one of the most maligned and misunderstood scientists since Darwin.

The comparison is apt on more than one level. Skinner's law describes how behavior is formed by a sort of evolutionary process— actions that bring benefit to the organism are repeated, intensified, or further shaped, while behaviors that are not rewarding become extinct. And both men discovered natural laws that called into question deeply cherished beliefs. Darwin survived his inquisition fairly intact, notwithstanding the fact that to this day there remain segments of society who disbelieve. But Skinner remains in limbo. Part of the reason is revealed by looking back on his written record, and especially at the earnest, somber author of it who perennially speaks, in those black-and-white interview clips preserved in the technologic purgatory of YouTube. He seems slightly naïve, or perhaps bullheaded, almost to have missed the true import of his discovery, even as he presses us to heed its importance: his findings changed the narrative trajectory of humanity, for they repositioned the origin of everything the species did. How could he have not understood the effect this might have? In one breath he was talking about pigeons, and in the next he started to talk about us.

What he said was not easy to hear. Even if, to my ear at least, it sounds like "You're finally free." In his most controversial book, he intended to deliver positive news:

> *In the traditional view, a person is free. He is autonomous in the sense that his behavior is uncaused. He can therefore be held responsible for what he does and justly punished if he offends. That view, together with its associated practices, must be re-examined when a scientific analysis reveals unsuspected controlling relations between behavior and environment. . . . Science does not dehumanize man, it de-homunculizes him.*

• • •

The project of *Beyond Freedom and Dignity* was to bring the science of operant conditioning into the realm of practical social application, perhaps to defictionalize it and make it less easy to dismiss than *Walden Two*. This was why, after all, Skinner had so closely attended to the rates of response of pigeons pecking at colored disks in his boxes—not because he found the birds fascinating, but because he felt more than certain that what he was able to get them to do implied something usefully important about a universal mechanics of behavior. In the space of a half hour, he could teach a pigeon to perform a figure eight; by gradually stretching the ratio of reinforcement, he was able to induce a pigeon to peck more than 10,000 times for a single piece of grain.

There is nothing more central to the scientist, or to the storyteller, than implications. These are what drove Skinner, during all those years in his basement lab, after all those miles of numbers on the paper streaming from his cumulative recorder. "I have long been concerned with [operant conditioning's] implications," he began a paper titled "Answers for My Critics." He had worked so tirelessly in order to glimpse those implications, while the implications his critics drew from his implications—wholly separate—got written into their own stories.

* * *

FREEDOM IS perhaps the most difficult of all concepts for humans to consider dispassionately. We have come to an age, if we were ever not in it, where to say "We are fighting for freedom" seems sufficient to justify nearly any act of aggression or defense. It is the one rationalization that goes unquestioned, because freedom—notionally and in many cases actually—is the same as life itself. Even if we can't always define what we mean by the word, much less how we gain it by launching offensives in its name on people half a world away.*

The collective despair over all sorts of deadly hypocrisies hit a defining crisis during the sixties, when the Vietnam War raged seemingly without end.† This was when Skinner began writing his

---

* In his classic study of the way obfuscations can be employed to throw truth off the boat, "Politics and the English Language," 1946, George Orwell observed: "It is almost universally felt that when we call a country democratic we are praising it: consequently the defenders of every kind of regime claim that it is a democracy, and fear that they might have to stop using that word if it were tied down to any one meaning."

† At the same time, almost as if they came from the same impulse (and some believe the same source), protest against war and environmental degradation went hand in hand. It's striking, reading literature of the sixties—even so-called entertainment, such as the Travis McGee crime novels of John D. MacDonald—how concerned, and despondent, thinking people were about the ruination of the natural world. Fifty years on, the concern has all but disappeared from popular culture, except if the current fascination with postapocalypse and zombies can be seen as a sublimated resignation to a self-delivered fate.

manifesto on social change, the one that would change the way his work would be considered for decades to come.

• • •

YET IT may be that Skinner's greatest mistake, more than in 1971 assigning himself lead sledgehammer in the demolition team set to dismantling "the traditional view," was made fourteen years earlier when he tackled verbal behavior. This was considered the province of linguists, not behaviorists. In a time of increasingly concentrated scientific specialization, as Skinner's era was soon to become, crossing disciplinary borders can be the equivalent of declaring war. It is easy now to see what was about to go wrong when Skinner posited a behaviorist approach to language—not only does it assume, as with all other behavior, that it is no product of projected will but rather of the environment working on speech; it again implies we are not fundamentally different from other organisms. In *Verbal Behavior*, Skinner was primarily aware of offering a theoretical (not experimental) framework for understanding how language is constructed. It did not necessarily contradict other schools of linguistic thought—for instance, generative linguistics' innate tendency to grammar could well have been evolutionarily structured in such a way as to require operant conditioning for full implementation—but in many cases can be easily enfolded into them. There was at any rate no neurobiological proof to the contrary available at the time Skinner floated his theory of verbal behavior.

His most vocal critic, however, saw Skinner's assertion that language is primarily acquired behavior as antithetical to his belief that it was the product of some separate and special human endowment—in fact, linguist Noam Chomsky believed there was a mechanism in the brain devoted to language in humans alone. Again, though, given the state of neurology then (and now) the Language Acquisition Device was never precisely located. (This may be why Chomsky later absorbed this notion into a more general theory of grammar as nativist.) To the layman, too, Skinner's idea seemed to contradict a deeply held belief: that within us is a free intellect that is the author of our words. These express our highest humanity, since they are the conduit of our yearnings and our pain, our joy and our dismay; they are the raw material of art. The drive to express ourselves in words feels practically essential to being human. Our words emanate from the heart of experience. Even from the very soul.*

In *Verbal Behavior,* on which Skinner worked for twenty-three years, he put forth his thesis on speech as behavior, albeit an especially complex one. (He never disavowed, here or elsewhere, operant conditioning's interplay with such inherent forces as instinct or biological drives, although two of his brightest students would later explicitly outline the shortcomings of his work in this regard, in an influential paper based on their practical experience training a far greater diversity of animals than Skinner had.)† As he wrote in his autobiography, "The human species had taken a giant step forward when, through evolutionary changes in its nervous system, vocal behavior came under operant control. Mating calls and cries of alarm had evolved because of their survival value, but vocal behavior was

---

* Both of these notions—the existence of a "soul," and the idea that because we *feel* we made a decision to do something it was our thoughts that were the cause of our doing it—are rejected by Skinner as the chimeras of a "mentalist" attitude. That is, one in which we interpret data incorrectly, if understandably, from a sort of dark prison within "the mysterious world of the mind," which is in fact "an unwarranted and dangerous metaphor."

† "The Misbehavior of Organisms" by Keller Breland and Marian Breland (*American Psychologist* 16 [November 1961] 681–684) will be discussed later, along with their groundbreaking work in practical applied behavior analysis in the course of running their company Animal Behavior Enterprises.

acquired because of its consequences during the lifetime of the individual. Verbal behavior as we know it then followed, and in turn the rapid evolution of cultural practices, including 'rational thought.'"*

It was a review of this book (beloved largely and predominantly by its author) that had a more lasting effect than the work itself ever would. In 1959 the journal *Language* published a thirty-three-page review by Chomsky that appeared to demolish the central thesis of Skinner's *Verbal Behavior*.

Skinner had received a prepublication copy of a review of his new book by "a linguist I had never heard of" and put it aside despondently after reading only a little bit. "I could not see how a review beginning that way [citing four immediate errors] could be of any value, and I stopped reading," he recalled. Nonetheless, it "soon began to receive far more attention than my book," he admitted,

---

* The belief that we engage in an act we have come to consider "rational thought" is, to Skinner, wholly separate from the question of whether or not behavior originates from such a thing. His answer is no, and in his view clinging to this mistaken assumption holds us back from creating a society in which creativity—the province and ability of all higher animals, humans having it only in more degree than other species—could be truly unfettered. To Skinner, creativity is simply another behavior, built in the same manner as every other. The persistent but demonstrably false belief that only humans exhibit creativity is the primary reason we delayed its investigation in other animals; only relatively recently have both observational and experimental evidence been upending received wisdom. Novel behavior has now been recorded in a variety of other species, including primates of several sorts, birds, dolphins, and dogs. This makes sense since the ability to be creative lends a clear evolutionary advantage. It is neither plausible nor possible that only one species, the human, could go through the same milling process as the rest of creation and come out with something so major that no other animal has. Where would that genetic material come from—and what could have kept it solely within our bodies?

Although there is yet no absolute proof because the question is inherently subjective, there is one way in which we may be truly different from other animals, and it concerns this very (complex) behavior: The *feeling* that our thoughts are causal agents of the things we do would not have arisen if speech had not.

noting that it inspired a former student to begin a speech by half-humorously announcing, "Behaviorism is dead and it was a linguist who killed it." The allure of the cognitive paradigm, "mentalism" as Skinner had it, was powerfully at work. The first in a long series of dominoes had been tipped.*

(At least one persuasive *a posteriori* proof of Skinner's belief that language is operantly acquired remains, and we have met it before: the ongoing success of behavioral conditioning in teaching autistics

---

* The effect of Noam Chomsky on the reputation of B. F. Skinner and the way his "radical behaviorism" is thought of today cannot be overemphasized. A paper titled "The Case Against B. F. Skinner 45 Years Later: An Encounter with N. Chomsky" by Javier Virués-Ortega in *Behavior Analysis* 29, no. 2 (Fall 2006) collates evidence:

The review of Skinner's Verbal Behavior *(1957) by the linguist Noam Chomsky (1959) has seemingly had a deep impact on research trends in psychology and attitudes toward behaviorism among several generations of psychologists. Leahey (1987) [T. Leahey,* A History of Psychology *(Englewood, NJ: Prentice Hall)] stated that "Chomsky's review is perhaps the single most influential paper published since Watson's Behaviorist manifesto" (p. 347). According to Arthur W. Staats, psychologists who study language from different behavioral standpoints were affected: "There was a group called Group for the Study of Verbal Behavior. O. H. Mowrer, C. E. Osgood, J. Deese, L. Postman, and myself, among others, all people studying verbal learning were there. They were nominally behavioral, but they weren't radical behaviorists. There were none at that time. They were behavioral but without a specific behavior-analytic background. Chomsky's article really affected them. It had a big impact" (A. W. Staats, personal communication, January 18, 2004). Knapp (1992) [T. J. Knapp, "Verbal Behavior: The Other Reviews,"* Analysis of Verbal Behavior *10:87–95] reported that from 1972 to 1990 Chomsky's review "was cited once for each two citations of Verbal Behavior itself . . . perhaps a unique relationship [between a book and its review] in the history of social sciences" (p. 87).*

Outside the field of behaviorism, Chomsky's paper is considered to be a classic, and is cited as final evidence of the inadequacy of behaviorism as a general framework for animal behavior and human affairs. . . . Smith (1999) [N. Smith, Chomsky: Ideas and Ideals *(Cambridge University Press)] stated that, "[Chomsky's] review of Skinner's major book . . . [is] perhaps the most devastating review ever written. . . . [It] sounded the death-knell for behaviorism" (p. 97).*

to speak; early, intensive behavior shaping à la Skinner has permitted countless children who might otherwise have been unable to enter regular classes at appropriate age level. "The behavioral approach in general has been much more effective than those based on psychoanalysis, holding therapy, auditory training, sensory integration, swimming with dolphins, weighted jackets, facilitated communication, vitamin therapy, and others," declare the authors of one paper on the subject, leaving out only "application of snake oil" in their list.[5] Skinner would have been gratified by the findings. In 1999 a report from the U.S. surgeon general concluded, "Thirty years of research demonstrated the efficacy of applied behavioral methods in reducing inappropriate behavior and in increasing communication, learning, and appropriate social behavior."[6] And, after summarizing various studies on the success of behavioral treatment, a textbook on treatment states, "[I]ntensive behavioral intervention produces substantially better outcomes than other treatments for young children with autism."[7] Otherwise, Skinner's magnum opus on language can be found at the bottom of the dustbin, soaking in the rancid spoilage of decades.)

It was, perhaps, Skinner's simple misfortune to have finally published his work on language when the impact of Orwell's *1984* was at a height, and in the same field as the antagonist who as a young student had been profoundly impressed by the British author and his potent warnings on the abuse of power. Just as the linguistic theories of Chomsky and Skinner are not mutually exclusive, their beliefs on politics and society align more closely than either of them admitted. What followed between the two of them has an aspect of tragedy: it was all for nothing, really.

. . .

IN THE matter of Chomsky v. Skinner, the wrong hot buttons were pressed not by a pigeon but by the behaviorist—and again, the word "control" was one of the hottest. As a critic later pointed out, echoing Skinner's own admission in his personal writing that he knew the word was a "problem" but that he couldn't (or wouldn't) stop himself from using it because it was *scientifically precise,* "The notion of control, anathema to the politically oversensitive, means only 'causation' in its purely functional sense, and need not alarm." But alarm it did.

It almost seemed that Chomsky misunderstood everything Skinner said. He was straight-on angry, and he dug deep into the lexicon of attack: "illusion," "notion," and "hypothesis"; finally he accused Skinner of entertaining "a serious delusion."

Skinner never responded publicly to the review; a measured, point-by-point rebuttal to the "ungenerous to a fault; condescending, unforgiving, obtuse, and ill-humored" review ten years later, by the University of Minnesota's Kenneth MacCorquodale, came too late and moreover preached only to the choir in a journal of behavioral analysis. Yet it is doubtful that even had it appeared in *Language,* the review's original venue, it would have made much difference; by then, Chomsky's piece had been reprinted three times. Primed by this battle with Skinner over linguistic theory, when *Beyond Freedom and Dignity* appeared over a decade later, Chomsky was more than ready to engage his foe again.

Notwithstanding the troubles Skinner had perhaps brought upon himself, Chomsky clearly took relish in redoubling them. He once more dismantled Skinner, if not Skinner's arguments, this time in a publication for general readers. *The New York Review of Books,* its circulation only slightly north of 100,000 but wielding a disproportionate influence (Tom Wolfe, during its heyday in 1970, called the magazine "the chief theoretical organ of Radical Chic"), published "The Case Against B. F. Skinner" at the end of 1971. It was in truth less a "case" than a completion of the list of fire-breathing descriptors begun in Chomsky's earlier review: *vacuous, empty, dogmatic, fraudulent, fascist, impoverished, unscientific.*

The vehemence of the response to this wholly new scientific theory made it Darwin all over again. And in fact, as research biophysicist John R. Platt explains, appalled reception by some quarters of the public is not the only similarity between the two scientists.[8] Both "started from a small set of problems and forced a radical rethinking of everything else in the field"; too, "Darwin, like Skinner, was accused of . . . treating man as a mere animal." The crime of *Beyond Freedom and Dignity* was its depiction of operant conditioning as behavior's own natural selection—Skinner had pointed out that "the environment does not push or pull, it *selects*"—but more damagingly, it generalized from pigeons to human beings. Using the same type of reasoning had enabled Darwin to feel confident he should include man in evolution's scheme. Platt says that "learning by reinforcement may go back 500 million years or more, so it is primitive, even though not quite so primitive as the survival mechanism," and he wonders only why the codification of the law of behavior "has taken so long and has been so resisted."[9] It is a question with no good answer. Or then again, maybe more than we can count.

• • •

SKINNER MAKES us twitch. Still, and maybe always. In his book *Listening to Prozac,* psychiatrist Peter Kramer wrote of the deflating realization that followed on the ostensibly good news that pharmacology had found a way to rid people of the Black Dog that had skulked in humanity's shadow for much of known history. "When one pill at breakfast makes you a new person, it is difficult to resist the suggestion, the visceral certainty, that who people are is biologically determined." It is even more difficult to accept the supposition that pretty much everything else people do is determined by contingencies of reinforcement. Yet the success of the SSRI continues what Darwin and then Skinner unwittingly began: the disassembly of the grand foundation on which we built so much that matters to us, the notions of free will and personal striving.*

---

* Again, "We need attribute nothing to inner states," Skinner held, insisting that contingencies of reinforcement explained everything. Research in the field of neuroscience has to date largely borne out his theory. In a fascinating paper titled "Free Will and Free Won't," published in *American Scientist* (vol. 92 [July–August 2004]: 358–365), cognitive neuroscientists Sukhvinder Obhi and Patrick Haggard reported on experiments intended to determine how movement is related to the perception of control. They cite a previous study at the University of California, San Francisco, in 1983 in which Benjamin Libet and colleagues found that subjects' "neural preparation to move" actually *preceded* conscious awareness of the intention to move by 300 to 500 milliseconds, suggesting that "a person's feeling of intention may be an effect of motor preparatory activity in the brain rather than a cause"; their findings "ran directly contrary to the classical conception of free will." An experiment in 2003, by Daniel Wegner of Harvard, appeared to present proof that "the human brain constructs feelings of causal agency after an action has taken place." In summation of this exploration into the nature of intention, the authors suggest an intriguing possibility: that an illusory sense of control over our actions is a primary element of consciousness itself. To open this perception to doubt is to threaten our very sense of self.

This habit of our brains to place a retroactive narrative gloss on voluntary muscle action may well also operate with an involuntary one that most people are familiar with; perhaps our signal center makes no distinction between the two. When, during sleep, a leg muscle twitches (in scientific terms, myoclonus, thought to originate in the spinal cord and used by the body to map neurologic pathways), the dreamer commonly instantaneously constructs a meaningful story that *feels* as though it preceded the movement: you're standing on a hillside and a rock slips underfoot, and bingo! your foot actually moves.

In turn, this might be related to the story-making impulse that elides facts and incorrectly recovered memories to come up with a story the individual is convinced to be true—but is not. It is known as confabulation, and in the past couple of decades has become a favorite subject of neuropsychology. Future research may well be able to identify an involuntary compulsion to form explanations for phenomena the brain can't instantly explain, complete with beginning, middle, and end: the storytelling impulse.

Though it might not seem to fit, the act of self-control—seen as parallel to free will—is accounted for in the world according to operant conditioning. In a chapter by that name in his 1953 work *Science and Human Behavior*, Skinner argued that an individual "controls himself precisely as he would control the behavior of anyone else— through the manipulation of variables of which behavior is a function." If you think about it long enough, most objections to Skinner's apparent denial of human individuality can be easily subsumed into the theory: the person who is able to turn down that second (or third) glass of wine even though she'd love to have another is not necessarily above its allure, nor is she employing self-control that emanates from decisiveness in a vacuum. She simply may find the memory of waking clearheaded the day after one glass more rewarding than the pleasure of feeling tipsy. We have willpower, but it is the product of the same law of behavior that affects all creatures' actions: we do something, it produces pleasure or it produces pain or it produces nothing, and the result determines whether we continue doing it, stop doing it, or do it differently, and *these are the only options*. The bedrock rules of behavior function to our preconceptions much like the swallowing of that yellow and red capsule.

. . .

KAREN PRYOR, a biologist and animal trainer who beginning in the mid-seventies helped resuscitate operant conditioning as a functional tool not only for training but for interpersonal relations, is fond of quoting Arthur Schopenhauer when she relates the history of behaviorism's reception: "All truth passes through three stages. First, it is ridiculed. Second, it is violently opposed. Third, it is accepted as being self-evident."

Of course, the law of operant conditioning, like gravity before

Newton and the heliocentric nature of the solar system before Copernicus, predated the arrival of the man who observed and named it. As political scientist Harvey Wheeler, author of *Fail-Safe,* wrote in 1973 for a symposium on the implications of Skinner's discovery for a nonpunitive society, "[T]he world has always been an operant-conditioning world[; i]f it had not been, operant conditioning could not have been discovered in the first place." You don't need to "believe" in Skinner, in the same way you don't need to believe in Newton to get smashed on the head by a falling beam.

And you don't need to profess radical behaviorism to admire its functionality. All you need to do is watch a few sessions of clicker training.

Skinner experimented on animals to arrive at his principles of behavior, but his object was never animal training. Nonetheless, for the past sixty years his ideas have found elegant use in the field. It may or may not be merely coincidental that he was a consummate trainer himself. In the early fifties, he published a paper titled "How to Teach Animals" in *Scientific American* and claimed that using his methods it would be an easy matter to teach a dog tricks like touching a cabinet handle with his nose or performing "a little dance." Only thing was, up to that point he had never done such a thing.

A writer from *Look* magazine—along with a Dalmatian—decided to call his bluff.

At Skinner's workshop, the Harvard Psychological Laboratory in Cambridge, the feeling is that a man can have a dog doing anything reasonable he could want a dog to do within twenty minutes of their first encounter. We doubted that, and visited Skinner with a camera on our hip and Agnes on our leash. Dog and psychologist were introduced to each other. Skinner asked us what we would have the dog do, and we said, "Run up the wall." Twenty minutes later, we were convinced.[10]

It is one of the first depictions in the popular media of a technique of positive-reinforcement behavior modification known as shaping.

The pictures accompanying the piece show Agnes fairly throwing herself at a high spot on the wall. And just because he could, Skinner also shaped the behavior of the dog, again within twenty minutes, to open the lid of a trash can by stepping on the pedal.

The readers of one of America's biggest-selling magazines probably looked at the Muybridge-esque photo sequences of Agnes and thought, Pure magic! at the very same moment they wished they could teach their dogs something, anything, although not necessarily how to open the kind of garbage can they had bought precisely in order to keep the family pet *out*.

· · ·

SKINNER LIVES, though he died in 1990. His obituary on the front page of the *New York Times* stands as one of the most measured explications of his work as it was, uncolored by bias. It ends by noting that his final request was that there be no funeral.

I sit for an afternoon in front of my TV tuned to YouTube. Here he is, a professor at Harvard, demonstrating the shaping of behavior: holding a remote control that operates a grain dispenser, he will have a pigeon turning 360 degrees, counterclockwise, in about a minute. Another clip shows a classroom of children, in fifties black-and-white, bent assiduously over their teaching machines. It's a startling sight: every one of them is as focused, eager, as a trader on Wall Street. Even the little boys wearing buzz cuts who in large numbers in a later age would be diagnosed with a condition requiring medication. Dr. Skinner explains that with his machines in their classroom, these children are now able to learn at their own pace; the faster students are no longer in effect punished by having to wait to learn whether or not their answers were correct, and the slower students do not become discouraged. They were more directly connected to the teacher, the author of their lessons, and the results of their work were quickly rewarded with what became a genuine treat—more work. These apparatuses never found general use, until, that is, their descendants took over the world: the home computer may be the preeminent teaching device, for better or worse, in the universe today. It functions by shaping our digit-poking behavior with immediate reinforcement. It is a Skinner box with a microprocessor.

Now he addresses an unseen audience of fellow psychologists: the quintessential nerd, with his delivery largely bloodless, though occasionally a drop of wit seeps out before vanishing into the dry air. For a man accused of a secret desire for social domination, he is rhetorically bland. No glint of the madman in his eye behind the Buddy Holly glasses, no red-faced exhortation. He explains quietly, patiently, over and over again, as if the presentation of what he knows to be fact will finally be heard, so we can get on with changing our fate, progressing toward a society rebuilt according to scientific truth. As if what he has to say can deliver us from evil.

CHAPTER THREE

҉

"Patience, patience, Davie!" father would say. "A
dog must understand what he is doing. You don't
want the blind obedience of a slave."

— CLARE BICE, *A DOG FOR DAVIE'S HILL*, 1936

Things were easier then. This is not just good-old-days syndrome:
driving a car along the filaments of the city street web *was* much easier
back in the day, but more to the point, so was parking. For the first
year of Mercy's life, it was a cinch even in the lot for Prospect Park
employees. A year later—every undeserved gift of privilege quickly
becomes taken absolutely for granted, hence irks like hell when lost—
the suspicious eye of Parks Department authority was slowly pivoting
toward us. A new technology briefly threw them off the scent. A fellow dog owner who was a graphic artist took a photo of the official
parks windshield permit, then scanned and reproduced it for distribution to the inner circle. The price of admission was utter dedica-
tion: you loved your dog enough to drive him to the park from the
far reaches of the borough for a morning constitutional seven days a
week. We treated each other better than blood family. Even to the free
distribution of that inestimable gift, a prebarcode scam.

Polly opened the car door and her own black shepherd mix jumped out and began investigating the perimeter of the parking lot to make certain no one had trespassed since his last visit. I started to clip a leash to Mercy's collar. "No, just let her out." But, but. How would she know to follow me? "Teach her that she needs to follow you," Polly added simply. The religion in Prospect Park was fundamentalist off-leash, and I was to become a zealot among extremists. (This was the core of the Park Cure: its magic was exercise. Dogs were free to race, chase, play, investigate. Then, exhausted, they went home and exemplified the Good Dog, the one who did nothing but sleep.) This instruction to eschew a leash—that relatively recent commonplace, symbol of the latter twentieth century's general fear of wildness and its fetish for containment both—also provided introduction to a foundation principle of positive-reinforcement training: he who controls the resources controls the mechanism that changes behavior. I was a resource cornucopia to my dog, out of which spilled most of what mattered most to her: food, fun, kinship. I could not be a squirrel, though I could provide a squirrel surrogate by throwing a ball. When she was thirsty and there was no dirty puddle or toilet bowl, I was her only source for water. The line was drawn at dead fish or fecal matter with which to anoint her pulse points; she would have to obtain her own canine Chanel No. 5.

I would like to report that I walked forth boldly into the Long Meadow and an eager embrace of the new, but I did not. I was without faith then, and the faithless have only their own fear for company. *My dear puppy! Would I ever see her again?*

It was apparent, and borne into reality from that moment on, that the learning curve in the park rose higher, more swiftly, than any I'd yet experienced. Mercy would turn out to be a specialist in teaching the hard lesson. Polly, and here is where stupid luck played its card, was an autodidact of the science that was just beginning to reemerge from under the snowmelt of a long dark season. Two trajectories of knowledge, launched from different countries—the University of Minnesota's experimental psych lab and the field of modern ethology founded by Konrad Lorenz, the author of *On Aggression* and *Man Meets Dog**—took decades to finally intersect in the airspace over applied behavioral analysis. A teaching technology that had passed like the freemasons' secret handshake from academic scientist (B. F. Skinner) to the first commercial animal trainers in the U.S. (Marian and Keller Breland and Bob Bailey), then to their student, a dolphin trainer and later canny caesar of a clicker-training empire (Karen Pryor), was finally making itself seen. The dog people were waking up.

* * *

FOR ME, it was like being parachuted into Harvard soon after naptime cookies and milk. The then-small company of dog owners met every morning between seven and nine to walk the circuit of trails through the woods and into the meadows of Prospect Park. It was our park alone; we knew to avoid the Vale of Cashmere, which belonged to men wishing to meet other men with whom to vanish behind the shrubs, and we stayed away from the abandoned gazebo near the decrepit Boat House, sleeping quarters for the homeless. Our dogs unfortunately discovered their latrines in

---

* The Austrian Lorenz, who shared the 1973 Nobel Prize "for discoveries in individual and social behavior patterns" with two other ethologists, Nikolaas Tinbergen and Karl von Frisch, had his own experience with regressive reception of his work, which was based in straightforward observation of instinctive behavior in species like the greylag goose. It "is necessary to describe various patterns of movement, record them, and above all, render them unmistakably recognizable," he maintained, yet descriptive science was belittled by a pervasive "denial that has been elevated to the status of religion."

the nearby bushes. These were the days before Brooklyn became Brooklyn, neat and well tended and densely populated by expensively shod bohemians. In this era the morning park was empty but for those with no other place to go and ten or twenty dog people who wished to bestow on their dogs a hefty dose of exercise and socializing before the 9 A.M. bell rang. That was the hour leashes had to be attached again and civilization was expected to reappear. (To the contrary, we believed our half-wild selves the true civilizing impulse, for we were not only not shady in any obvious way, we also picked up litter. But mythmaking is a primitive and pervasive habit through every strata of society all the way to the heights of park bureaucracy. When we left, the park was in fact given back to the demimondaines who crept through its dark voids until we came back again the next morning.) We were oddities who refused to use the morning hour the proper way: preparing to take the subway to the job in Manhattan. We were, in polite employment terms, freelance, or perhaps gently used. One was a Vietnam vet on disability, another was a dog trainer, the rest writers or musicians or actors with too little on our plates and too much unseemly affection for our dogs. In other words, we were thorough misfits, and so we bonded as steel to magnet. We ran to the assistance of each other whenever one of our charges required emergency bathing in a stream (see above, at *latrines*) or chasing down when they had found, like the prize in a box of Cracker Jacks, a rat carcass they were determined to consume in private and in full. One of our group, a nightshift registered nurse who was also a Goth of gentle demeanor and vegan proclivity, would sit on a log in the woods to quickly administer the vaccines that we had ordered in bulk, so that we saved both money and stress on our dogs. All together we formed a sort of hippie commune, sharing just about everything, including our countercultural tendencies; having gone to college in

Vermont headed the typological list of characteristics marking the Brooklyn homesteader twenty years ago.

Instead of better pot farming, our collective's aim was improved companion animal husbandry. So we read up on the canid's natural diet, merging that knowledge with an established distrust of corporate America. Thus, over a short period, group feeding habits progressed from premium, small-batch commercial kibble to home-cooked meals. (Revisiting M. F. K. Fisher's *How to Cook a Wolf*, the great writer's 1942 manual on facing down wartime shortages, provided the recipe for a pet food slurry made from oats, vegetables, offal, and bits and ends—who else ate it? I didn't want to know—that we bought cheap from the United Meat Market on Prospect Park West.) After two hours of recreation in the park, we put all the dogs together in their den, also known as Polly's battered Mazda. They either napped or talked revolution while we breakfasted at a Greek diner called Katina's. Afterward, Polly paused at all the recently occupied tables along our path to the door, quietly scraping remains of omelets and bitten toast into a napkin. She aimed a disarming smile in the direction of the stunned busboy and left with dinner in her pocket for her therapy dog, Smedley (named for Major General Smedley Butler, author of *War Is a Racket*). During our perambulations she had already explained that "dog food" was a relatively recent commercial invention from the thirties meant to capitalize on the surplus meat from horses and mules that had been supplanted by the coming of tractors and automobiles. When that source was gone, the cans were filled with former mustangs rounded up from their natural range. And when that was outlawed, an ever-resourceful industry discovered that anything could be sold to pet owners if it had a colorful label, inventive name, and advertising campaign: who could think ill of a product evoking beef fresh from the cowboy's lasso? No matter that what was more likely in the package was anything swept up from the kill floor, including feathers, beaks, brains, and animals felled by sickness instead of the stun bolt; the extruded "food" also contained grain hulls and processing by-products. Polly did not have to work hard to convince us that coffee-shop leftovers represented a great leap in nutritional quality. Then, within the year, most of us left all bagged dog food behind to follow her lead once more in advocating what would soon become a newly fashionable diet, at least among the capitalistically suspicious: Biologically Appropriate Raw Food—BARF. (Our dogs rarely did, except after accessing the park's abundance of feces and the precursors of garbage. Prospect Park was not short on either, and only now do I realize how much of my subsequent life's course was determined by both. What became home, the people I now call friends, the loves won and lost; all traced back to what was left behind by a population of homeless and West Indian revelers whose barbecues proved too lavish for any available trash receptacle.)

In addition to teaching me how to feed my dog, how to teach her to live at least partly successfully in the human world, and so many other things of lasting value I cannot count, Polly gave me even more useful lessons.

The phenomenon known as leash aggression was rife on city streets. It had two causes: the first that the dog's inability to flee from a source of fear left him with only one other option, and the second that on a leash, a dog does not have full use of body language. Hence he is prevented from approaching a potentially dangerous animal on an arc, and to meet with his body on the oblique. An otherwise passive dog would soon get in the habit of imitating Cujo, mouthing off and posturing wildly, at the mere sight of another dog a block away. If both of them had been off-leash, free to handle the matter the way dogs will, all this would be different. But for now, the dog's thinking was, "Whoa, here's a scary thought: what if that dog is going to attack me as soon as I get near, and I can't get away? For some reason I can't read what he's saying about his intentions. . . ." The only thing for it, then, was a preemptive threat display. The humans would soon get into the act, too, yelling, "Keep your goddamn dog away from mine!" with the result that all that noise and anxiety ratcheted up the dogs, and the next thing you knew, a perfectly lovely day was blown apart. And it would happen every block. (The dog, meanwhile, would be thinking: It worked! It worked! No attack. Let me be even more fearsome the next time!)

I cannot honestly say whether Polly was a keener student of human or of dog behavior. Her method of defusing the situation on the street never failed, for it depended on human vanity, and that never failed, either.

She saw a canine terror up the block, straining against the leash until he was on hind legs, writhing and snarling, white teeth flashing. This was Polly's signal to affix a wide smile on her face and make direct eye contact with the human now being trundled down the sidewalk to an appointment with destiny. Before the other got there, she would call out in flutey tones, "Oh, my goodness! What a *gorgeous* dog."

The person's demeanor changed in a flash. *A compliment, for me!* The frown of anticipatory anger would invariably disappear, replaced with the eagerness of "Tell me more." The dog would keep snarling and straining, of course, but it was no longer of any account. This gave Polly time to give her own charge an alternative behavior to perform—she had also taught me an obvious truth that was still startling the first time I heard it: a dog who's performing a spin or a Go Find! can't simultaneously be making ugly faces at another dog—or at the very least offer a counterconditioning treat from the bag at her belt. That way her dog was learning that "approach of angry dog" equaled "yummy treat coming," with the result that the dogs under her care always looked to her with happiness when they heard another dog growl.

Her routine never varied, no matter how pathetically ugly the other creature, but the owners did not know this. All they heard was that someone liked their dog, their shadow. In the next moment, they were floating away in a bubble of satisfaction. Noise? What noise? What opportunity for the blessed release of human aggression?

*   *   *

THERE WAS nothing I would not do for Mercy. It turned out that she would do almost anything for me, and that she did so without being aware did not diminish the vastness of her acts. My desire to make her happy by providing for her biological, social, and intellectual imperatives—how I became aware of their depths was a joint project of Polly's peripatetic lectures and Mercy's eyes looking into mine—meant that I first had to learn what these were.

*   *   *

I FOLLOWED Polly the first day not only into a park. I followed her into an unavoidable examination of systems, because Mercy had begun her lifework of changing everything that appeared to me. She has continued to do so even though ten years after she entered my life she left it. Untimely gone.

That is another story, the private yet universal story of grief. It is a tale of one fifty-pound dog, her God-given drive to eat, coupled with a transcendent ability to fulfill it; she led me to construct a theory I have yet to abandon, one correlating larceny with high intelligence in dogs. The narrative would continue with half of a flourless butter-chocolate birthday cake meant to serve thirty, two blocks of suet hung too low on a neighbor's branch, and a large tin of shea butter, one with a presumably locked lid. This would then bring us to a plot

point concerning blood lipids and stroke. But we are not writing that
story, which ends too predictably anyway, with death and the way it
encloses people and makes them utterly uninteresting. One of them,
for instance, will stay up late at night, floating motionless in a sea of
snapshots spreading to the shores of the walls. The other will get an
electric shock from even a glimpse of her image, but will nonetheless
look out the window and watch a black form trotting up the road,
pausing at the end of the drive, and will hear her voice (how? she
never spoke) clearly say: *See? I'm back.*

This is not that small and usual story. This is one about systems,
even though the subject was a gift from this very particular dog we
are not really writing about, even as we are.

The only remnant of this sidelined tale that will appear is just
an anecdote, but still it rings and rings in the mind, over and over.
Prescience is an odd thing: Is it just a good guess paired to inscrutable luck? Is it foreknowledge? Can it ever cause one to change the
future? If so, I wish I could be back at the park one morning, standing next to Polly as we watched Mercy race back toward the garbage
cans that were overflowing after a weekend of wanton barbecuing.
(As with all dogs, Polly taught, management is the first weapon in
the arsenal of "discipline": it is no more fair to ask a dog to self-
control hardwired biological drives than it is to demand a hungry
toddler forgo the ice-cream cone in his hand. Polly was asked frequently by despairing clients, "How oh how do I keep my dog out of
the garbage?" and her silent answer was the gift of an impenetrable
bullet waste can. Case closed. But anyone who has ever lived with
a border collie knows that management needs to be practiced with
strategic superiority, and it's hard for a mere human to be superior
to a border collie. For those with this experience, then, my statement
that Mercy exploited higher mathematics—and humor—will not
sound far-fetched. She first measured my speed at a run, multiplied

it by ground distance, then divided it by her known velocity to arrive at the precise moment when she could stop pretending she had forgotten about the font of all goodness, away from which she had been led on leash. That's because her hapless owner had determined they were finally far enough to let her off again. Consummate actress, she would play along, heeling obediently, until she knew by her calculations that it was time to turn and run. I followed, shouting curses— at my repeated idiocy as much as at her invincible cunning—while she sorted through the napkins and ketchup packets to enjoy every last rib bone, cupcake liner, hamburger bun, and mayonnaise smear on the dirt.)

"If Mercy dies before her time, it will be because of something she ate."

She managed to get through ten years of garbage eating before Polly's prophecy finally came true, but not for lack of trying to get the job done sooner: we became midnight habitués of the emergency phone line to the all-night vet, and one night I drove, panicked, toward the hospital down the 2 A.M. avenues of Brooklyn, weaving at high speed, while Mercy lay across my lap and retched between faint pantings. I know I have forgotten many more incidents of frenzied alarm, of trips to vets in many states. Somewhere I still have a file folder filled with the bills, and the final X-ray, silent gray ghost, of her bones and the soul they gave up.

Polly's husband, a laconic type who delivered his yarns with dry wit, one-upped Mercy's exasperating dietary habits with the memory of a former dog. This was a real champ who once, in obvious gastric distress after a foraging expedition, squatted for the eighth time that night and as he did so caught the whiff of something enticing nearby. While still straining to expel the watery dregs of his earlier excess, he reached out and eagerly lapped up something yet more toxic.

Polly's viewpoint was that of the dog rather than the human, and once she started my world to tilting, it continued until it was fully upside down. Everything looked different from there. People still on the other side saw a dog who "stole" and was "bad." She encouraged the understanding that a dog who managed to fulfill his imperative to obtain food, even against the high odds that prevailed against him in the human sphere, was not bad. He was *quite* good indeed. These were our values, not the dog's; what in their evolution could possibly have informed them that an armchair cost two weeks' wages and therefore should not be peed upon like the tree it resembles? (It even takes a while for a child to get the concept of income, and that's only after we start giving them an allowance.) How were they supposed to arrive at the knowledge that the steak on the dinner table, which smells both tastier and very much like what their wolf genes tell them they should eat, is not for them but the weird dry nuggets in the bowl on the floor are? The imposition of such capricious Puritanism on another species started to seem bizarre, not to mention ineffectual, like abstinence pledges for hormone-crazed teens. (Good luck overcoming a genetic urge 150,000 years in the making.) In light of biological fact, our recent moral constructs look like hysterical nonsense at best, dangerous ultimatums at worst. And nowhere more dangerous than when they are applied to another species. Dogs, in their presuffrage state, are serfs without a vote. No, they're prisoners. They can't even take a pee when they want.

Happenstance: that was why received wisdom was now detonating all around me in a rain of shards. It was happenstance that I met this particular woman and not some other, happenstance that caused what seemed to demand infinite reconsideration of nearly everything. What began with dogs then progressed. It would have been easier on my exploding brain had it not radiated out and out to finally take in every system, but the world has no real seams. The Scotch Tape we placed at the fictive junctures of animal and human, the places we seemed to want behavior to originate, what belongs to the province of heaven and what of earth, externality and interiority, all started peeling up.

A stentorian voice of tradition had spoken for centuries of what dogs were like and what we had to do to manage them; it emanated from the How to Train Your Puppy book that came with the small ball of white fluff who arrived in my childhood home heartbreakingly innocent (it said to smack the dog with a rolled newspaper and push her nose into the urine stain, so we did). Now a different voice was speaking, demanding full reconstruction of one firmly held set of beliefs, all others immediately called into question thereby. The shock was Copernican: the universe suddenly had to be reenvisioned. The shock was also retroactively deeply painful, because I now knew we had, under the guidance of tradition, abused the dog I knew was the very soul of sweetness. She had no way to know what was expected of her, because she did not instinctively partake of a twentieth-century middle-class system of property value and because we never taught her what we wanted her to do. We only punished her for infractions her nature made it impossible for her to comprehend.

Polly's program was absolutely devoid of coercion, that which had been a central feature of animal training, not to mention social institutions, for much of recorded history. She achieved every end that was said to be attainable only with physical restraint, leash pops, a knee to the chest, or shouts, without any of them. The proof was before us. She walked her dogs leashless on the sidewalks of Brooklyn, even though that was perhaps inadvisable. Her supporting statements were backed with the force of science—she had studied at

Wolf Park in Indiana with Dr. Erich Klinghammer; she attended seminars presenting the latest in canine research and was a voracious reader of training manuals, which she tested against both professional experience and book learning using an exquisitely tuned bullshit meter—as well as logic and, always, the perspective of the dog itself. It appeared to be a wholly novel approach, but she was merely on top of a wave that was cresting on a large sector of the animal-training profession, where learning theory was beginning to be applied decades after a furor had erupted over its appearance in the field of behavior analysis. The reason such trainers embraced the dog, and not what we had long believed the dog was—two different things, with enormous implications for happiness and welfare— must remain hidden in the inseparable tangles of personal history. Certain people manifest a peculiar impulse to identify with the Other, the foundation of compassion. In the years to come, I would notice how often the dog's greatest champions were those who themselves had experienced powerlessness. That, too, is another story, here now abandoned after this glancing mention, but no less centrally planted in the heart of all that follows.

Dogs scratch themselves. Each time Smedley's hind leg vibrated to dispatch an itch on his elbow, Polly simply repeated some words. Through association, or classical conditioning to be more precise, and because he was a very smart black dog, he would soon "Play your guitar" on cue. I did this too with Mercy, another smart black dog, naming everything, and soon she had a number of cute routines, none of them alas "Come" when she was in full flight after prey, which in the urban environment largely consisted of squirrels and chicken bones. Classical conditioning practiced this way was haphazard at best, imprecise and rarely becoming fully entrenched unless it was, alas, something negative; that sticks readily to us all—

analysand, lab rat, or common man alike. The nasty stuff takes up permanent residence in the ganglia while we can barely recall some pleasantness from the day before. These incidents belonged to the class of so-called superstitious behavior: a car happened to backfire or a child did some scary thing (and everything a child did including standing there soon became scary to my border collie) at the exact moment she passed a certain doorway. Then the doorway became the cause of fear.

A year after I began following Polly—in the way a novitiate follows the liturgy of the hours—she informed me she had been learning something new. At a toy store in Park Slope I bought a little metal clicker the shape of an alligator. She told me how to "load" the clicker, like a debit card: *click*, give treat; *click*, treat; *click*, treat. Then I could use it to mark the exact second Mercy was doing something I liked, and the sound was a bridge between her act and the payoff she earned. The next thing I knew, my dog had 40 words in her lexicon and it didn't quickly become 140 due only to my lack of imagination. (Some years later, two border collies named Rico and Chaser came to the attention of scientists, who studied the way they acquired language; the former was found to know the names of 200 objects and the latter 1,022. They could learn a new noun in a single trial, and it was theorized they did so by "fast mapping," the way some scientists believe children acquire language—and children alone, until the border collies showed up.) It was from this time that I started to feel I could speak whole paragraphs to her which she comprehended; lovely, the sense that this was the result of some woodland magic—the longed-for childish dream of cross-species communication—or one of those paranormal signs love threw onto the trail for one to happen upon, but it was of course something more mechanical. (The mechanical is quite magic enough for me now.) Mercy had learned that separating out the frequencies in the white noise emanating from these tailless and perplexing creatures on two legs had meaningful consequences, that's all. There was nothing more meaningful for my dog than food; for other dogs it's a Frisbee or ball, and all one had to do was listen to them for a minute when they were saying so. Then one was in possession of the key that would unlock the bottomless treasure box of communication. In its true state, it is a loop, actor and acted-upon changing roles back and forth until they are simultaneously both. When information passes between two beings, neither is fully master or mastered. The click is information, like a sentence: *That's exactly it—good.* The proof of the dog's comprehension is that he does it again, interestingly not only for the treat the sound presages, but *also for the sound itself*, for another bit of rewarding information. In turn, this information, transformed by its reception, is offered back to the interlocutor.

Trial and error is nature's teaching methodology, so animal systems are constructed to capitalize on it. Clicker training is the purest distillation of this mode of learning—*Aha! doing this works; doing that doesn't*—and it injects choice and desire into an equation that in the traditional configuration relied on coercion and the domination of one by the other. The type of learning that opens possibilities to the organism, as opposed to that which only drives toward avoiding negative consequences, excites feelings of pleasure in the brain. The learner wants more. The moment this is twigged is likely to become etched deeply in memory. It is that startling. It can be interpreted as nothing else. *I get it!* The instant that Mercy did, I would swear that a transparent window into her brain had appeared, and now I saw gears spinning, engaging. *So this is how it's done! I have the key!* She went joyfully looking for more locks. There was little she could not learn, now that she discovered the myriad advantages of learning. Her body radiated happiness. Because I loved her, her happiness was mine.

.   .   .

Maybe all this was not by happenstance, though. Maybe Mercy was wiser than fate: a fifty-pound god, omniscient. My dog, the author of all this.

CHAPTER FOUR

꒦

Man is a complex chicken.

—B. F. SKINNER, 1938

In 2008 in Sequim, Washington, a small town of fewer than 7,000 to the north of Olympic National Park and on the shore of Juan de Fuca Strait, through which runs the U.S.–Canadian border, a strange but quiet revolution was gaining strength, one week and a roomful of participants at a time. Its leader was a white-haired man named Bob Bailey. His followers were armed not with placards and raised fists, but with toy clickers and cups of pellet feed. In the second ranks behind them, completely unaware of their conscription in this march toward what in fact has been the lofty goal of every revolution in history—the eradication of suffering—were some small white chickens.

These were set, one at a time, on 2½-by-5-foot folding tables. Watching each bird with an intensity never before evoked by these creatures with rather limited behavioral repertoires (they walk, they peck) were animal-trainers-in-training who had come here, often from far away, to spend five days and a not inconsiderable sum of money sharpening their skills.

It was for many the challenge of a lifetime to study with one of the world's most knowledgeable behaviorists. A participant recalled being "exhausted as my brains liquefied and dripped out my nose from all I was attempting and learning and struggling with"—because the simple animals demanded deep focus from their handlers and then it turned out that "simple" has so many gradations it can make a person cry. (Bailey has acknowledged on camera, "The process of operant conditioning is really simple, but it's not easy.") On a whiteboard by the doorway, someone had markered a target with arrows pointing to it; "Bang your head here," read the caption. Since their intellectual faculties are relatively shallow, chickens demand a precision that, say, dogs or other social animals who are adepts with interpretation do not. On top of this, the handler has to figure out the physics of what she is doing, minute subtleties in timing of the food reward and its placement, which will dramatically alter the behavior of the animal. "Training is a mechanical skill," Bailey reminds his students. Chickens may be birdbrains, but they're engineered, again like all of us, to respond to meaningful stimuli. Here the chicken was always right. If it did something that was different from what the human had thought it should do, it was the nonfeathered animal who had made the mistake. Every time.

Who was teaching whom? The answer is not as it seems; not much in chicken camp is. Step by step over several days, the trainers succeeded in staging what resembled a chicken circus: a hen climbs a ladder to a 1-foot-wide platform, executes a 180-degree turn, walks across a tightrope to peck a Ping-Pong ball on a tether, then descends another ladder to encounter two bowling pins of different color; by prearrangement, it knocks down the yellow followed by the blue. Every section of the routine has been built painstakingly from smaller bricks of behavior, sometimes taught in reverse order in a process called backchaining. Other hens drag bread pans a distance of 2 feet by grasping a loop of string in their beaks or peck a black dot on a placard upon being cued with a laser beam—and only upon the cue. Meanwhile, the handlers are sweating. They face pop quizzes and the occasional correction: if Bailey considers a student is "putting the screws" to a chicken by withholding the cue or the reinforcing pellet (either of which is rewarding to the animal) for a beat too long, he will instruct the handler to pick up her chicken and take a time-out. He is mindful of the effects of human error on the animal. But he is not that derisively termed being, a softie. He is a former Navy man. Fairness is a collateral advantage of efficiency.

Participants, who strive to become as observant of their birds as Bailey is of them, experience the intense week under his watchful eye as something of a Zen retreat. It is an exercise in introspection, where the true lesson is not color or pattern differentiation through a bird's eye, but self-knowledge. The week's primary discovery, in the words of one dog trainer who attended, was that "if you want to change animal behavior you have to learn to see, read, and change your own behavior first." This is the kind of thing you hear again and again from people who have immersed themselves in the science of applied behaviorism, also known as operant conditioning or positive reinforcement.

These are not the same thing, precisely, but the terms are often interchanged to refer to the methodology of applying Skinner to what have you.* Bailey himself had learned from two of Skinner's star students at the University of Minnesota, who had left graduate school to open the world's first commercial animal-training business. This company, Animal Behavior Enterprises, was later hired

---

* Positive reinforcement is just one of the four quadrants of operant conditioning's technique, but generally speaking the people who have studied operant conditioning also appreciate the serious side effects (not to mention the expert skill level required) of using positive punishment. For almost all companion animal training applications, positive reinforcement gets the job done without complications. And it sounds nicer, too.

by the U.S. Navy to train the trainers of its Marine Mammal Program, for which Bailey was the first director of training. In order to school the military's dolphins, they were schooled first in the principles of operant conditioning—using chickens just as Bailey's later students would.

Fifty years on, these pupils are here at chicken camp (which Bailey would come to hold exclusively in Sweden after years in Hot Springs, Arkansas, and in Sequim)—forty hours of nothing but attempting to learn how to shape the behavior of the two chickens each person is assigned. Many of Bailey's former students have themselves become teachers, fanning out over the land to give their own seminars and workshops, so there are even more avid watchers of chicken behavior in the world at this moment than even this strange scene reveals.

What you would hear most often from all of them is not how hard it is to learn to teach another species but how wrenching it is to find out you have to soul-search first. You have to detach from your ego, your desires, your demands, your projections, and the persistent call of traditional beliefs, which may have vanished from your intellect but are still present in your blood, from the long-ago of childhood. Training well in the scientific manner is an exacting skill, in its demands on both intellect and hands most akin to the practice of medicine, but what may be even more difficult about it is withstanding the extreme paradox it exerts. Many people are led by pure romanticism—love for a dog so abiding that a large investment in education, practice, and patience is pocket change—to the hard science of operant conditioning. Once they see it in action (never a yank, pull, scare, yell), it looks to them like justice, the very manifestation of a most vaunted ideal. The desire to be kind is the emotional diamond ring we can offer to these creatures of our affection. Yet being successful as a positive-reinforcement trainer depends on leaving the lovely messiness, the hopes and expectations, the merged emotions, the story line of love, out of the matter entirely. The method Bailey teaches works solely by identifying the appropriate reinforcer for a given situation, controlling the variables, and delivering with mechanical precision the reinforcer on its appropriate schedule. If you do it right, behavior is changed, whether the operant is bivalve or beloved. If it's not, your setup or timing is wrong. It's never the dog's "fault," and it's not the chicken's either. It's yours as a junior scientist, one who has to leave his heart at the lab door.

• • •

IN 1964, Bob Bailey supervised the Navy's first open-ocean release of a dolphin. The goal was to see if dolphins—fast swimmers who did not get the bends when returning to water's surface after deep dives—could be used to retrieve weapons-testing equipment lost at sea. And come back reliably, of course. Within five years, the Navy had held some 1,600 open-ocean exercises with dolphins; they lost only one, a female who looked out to sea and never looked back. Another time a dolphin appeared to be ignoring the acoustic recall signal, no matter how many times it sounded; finally someone noticed there happened to be a school of sharks between him and the boat. This is a caution about assuming recalcitrance on the part of an animal, at least one trained by nonpunitive means.

The people who traveled to Sequim to learn under Bailey how to apply operant conditioning were likewise not looking forward to careers with chickens. They were planning on taking the same principles they learned, say, in getting a chicken to reliably peck not the red square but the yellow one, back to their professions teaching service animals, competition horses, the mentally disabled, gymnasts. They could apply them to the dog who barks at the doorbell and achieve quiet without resorting to yells or blows, and they could apply them to the teenager who resolutely refuses to come to the dinner table on time. They also found themselves hoping, but held the wish closer to the chest than Skinner ever did, that the theory could find wider application in human society. Or at least the society in their immediate vicinity: again and again trainers schooled in positive reinforcement and those called "crossover"—from traditional, coercion-based styles—report having a moment of thunderstruck epiphany that is not far from religious conversion. This is the one in which they think to ask themselves, "Wait. I've stopped yelling at my dog. Why am I still yelling at my kids?" Followed quickly by another question: "And why is my society yelling at me?" They left Bob Bailey's chicken camp believing as firmly as Skinner himself that the law of behavior is persistent through all interactions among beings, and what is good for the chicken is good for General Motors—or for their families, schools, and governments. It was pure science. But it felt like the opening into something almost spiritual. There was no way to explain it. There was no way to explain why you'd spend a lot of money to do nothing but train chickens for a week, either.

. . .

THE RISE of Animal Behavior Enterprises, the company started in Minnesota in the mid-1940s by Marian Kruse "Mouse" Breland and her husband, Keller, is one of the great tales of applied science—and because it is enfolded in the story of B. F. Skinner, it is a great tale widely unknown.

Marian had graduated summa cum laude from the University of Minnesota, where she studied under Skinner. In an interview in 2000 with veterinary behaviorist Sophia Yin and published on her website, Marian (who died in 2001) described the usual trajectory of pure accident: seen in retrospect, it appears it could have led to only this outcome and no other. "I went to college as a Latin major with a Greek minor and I had to take a science, which I did protestingly. I took psychology. I thought it was the least painful science. I got in this special class with B. F. Skinner. He was taking a few known good students and since I happened to have straight A's, I got into his psychology class. He converted everyone. I know at least six students from that class who went on to great prominence [in the field of psychology]. He was very persuasive and he had something exciting to work on because it was new. There of course he taught the whole class on the basis of his new operant system. . . . I went on to become an undergraduate [research] assistant in the psychology department and then Skinner's graduate student after I graduated. I had added to my major so I had a major in psychology and a minor in child psychology." As Skinner's lab and teaching assistant, she had the privilege of training rats and also of doing the kind of scut work the fortunate student is given: typing lecture notes, proofreading manuscripts (including the seminal *Behavior of Organisms*), and some babysitting on the side. After graduation Kruse married her sweetheart, fellow psych scholar Keller Breland. The two had been among a group of students who successfully trained a cockroach to switch off a light.

When World War II intervened in the further course of their studies, the couple was tapped to join a small coterie moved to a top-secret location to work on a wartime project. It was a place destined to remain secret from Axis spies: the half-floor at the top of the General Mills plant in downtown Minneapolis, its moat the twining lanyards of railroad tracks upon which trains crept forward and back, bringing grain to be milled into Gold Medal flour. Above the secret lab, on the roof of the huge structure, rose a sign that could not have been invented by a storyteller of any subtlety as a metaphor for all that has preceded this point, as well as all that is to come later: EVENTUALLY is all it says, in looping script.

All too obvious for fiction, except here is a photo of the man himself standing on the roof, fedora in gloved hand, the one-word encapsulation of his entire story the backdrop to his bare head and its barer forehead, even more metaphorically precise because it is now, read from behind, backward.

(The word was an abbreviation of the advertising slogan everyone knew in those days. "Eventually you will use Gold Medal Flour, so why not now?" Pillsbury, across the river, displayed its comeback: BECAUSE PILLSBURY'S BEST!)

Inside the lab, the scientist and his students trained pigeons with the ultimate goal of conscripting them as the brains inside the first guided missile—a true smart bomb. The government had given them $25,000 and a year. In that time, they proved, beyond their own doubts at least, that a pigeon could reliably and unerringly guide a missile to its target. The pigeons pecked at a projection on a ground-glass screen, correcting course continuously. (The missile had been dubbed the Pelican, and the code name for the development was Pigeon in a Pelican; however it was commonly, and by Skinner himself, referred to as Project Pigeon.) It would have been a historical passage of weird and unlikely beauty if the project had been given the go-ahead, allowing pigeons to sacrifice themselves as our side's feathered kamikazes.

Although their final achievement was demonstrated in Washington, the brass—eager to embrace whatever "crackpot" idea (Skinner himself soon adopted the use of the word) would give an edge in a desperate fight—thought this one went too far. They alone also knew they had a more promising weapon in the pipeline in the atomic bomb. Nor could they overcome the fear that an animal, or even three, in the nosecone of a bomb might not be fully trustworthy. ("None of the birds failed," reported Marian, but two more were added as insurance anyway; "now if all three of them suddenly had headaches then it wouldn't work.") The trussed birds, strapped into plastic armatures and wearing a strip of metal conductor on their beaks, must have looked like something out of science fiction. The team was forced to realize "that a pigeon was more easily controlled than a physical scientist serving on a committee." Skinner was crestfallen. He was left only "a loftful of curiously useless equipment and a few dozen pigeons with strange interest in a feature of the New Jersey coast."

More than a decade after the war, when Project Pigeon was finally declassified, the psychologist vented a little of his frustration in a speech to the American Psychological Association, which was bestowing on him its Distinguished Scientific Contribution Award. His work on behalf of the war effort amounted to something greater than a new type of weapon; it was "a declaration of confidence in a technology of behavior. Call it a crackpot idea, if you will; it is one in which I have never lost faith. I still believe that the same kind of wide-ranging speculation about human affairs, supported by studies of compensating rigor, will make a substantial contribution toward that world of the future in which, among other things, there will be no need for guided missiles."

This is all history now, strange and hopelessly antiquated. But it is not an entirely dust-covered event. As is the mysterious way of such things, retrospect highlights the indirect way a "failure" may lead directly to accomplishments of great importance. One of these was teaching pigeons to bowl.

In an article that appeared in *American Psychologist* in 1958, Skinner recounted what happens to many a scientist with a government grant: boredom while waiting "for decisions to be made in Washington." Wasn't it a strange coincidence that a psychologist and his students who were working on a top-secret project using pigeons should be doing so in a building that would naturally attract, with its grain elevators in the middle of the urban zoo, flocks of pigeons—volunteers, as it were, circling the enlistment office? "They were easily snared on the window sills and proved to be an irresistible supply of experimental subjects." Since the group was in the process of training birds to guide a mortal payload toward enemy ships, teaching one to send a wooden ball down a little alley to knock down a set of toy pins should by all rights have been an easier, and more pleasant, activity. Instead, the bird didn't know what he was supposed to do, having never experienced league night. He was slow to swipe at the ball, and so, impatient of waiting even more, they "decided to reinforce any response which had the slightest resemblance to a swipe—perhaps, at first, merely the behavior of looking at the ball—and then to select responses which more closely approximated the final form." Not too big a deal, right?

In a later recollection, though, the writer manqué could only have recourse to poetry in capturing the impact of the sudden realization that he and his colleagues had discovered a new method of building behaviors, "free-form hand-shaping." They all "gazed at one another in wild surmise," Skinner wrote, borrowing from Keats's "On First Looking into Chapman's Homer." Using the reinforcement of "successive approximations" in steps toward a final result is the way most complex behaviors are efficiently taught, including those long chains of action seen in seaquarium shows, freestyle dog "dancing" routines, and military animal training. It is also the basis of the game known as 101 Things to Do with a Cardboard Box. In it a dog, a clicker (the bridging stimulus between the desired behavior, which might occur in a split second, and the delivery of the reinforcer that gives the sound its meaning as approval), treat rewards, a lot of patience, and a watchful eye coupled with spot-on timing of reinforcement can yield an infinite number of possibilities: dog in box, on box, under box, around box, tearing box . . . and excited to do so, because it acts as a grand buffet line of choice for the dog. You end up with an ecstatic dog, one who might grow so enthusiastic about learning he is apt to go searching for the place you hid that clicker so you could have a few moments' peace. Practitioners of clicker training, especially those who do a lot of shaping, almost all have stories of the dog who goes searching for the teaching tool, eagerly dropping it in the lap of the surprised human with a look of happy expectation.

Skinner had, more than six years earlier, trained a complex behavior chain using his lab rat Pliny (named after the Roman historian who endeavored nothing less than to enclose all of what was known about the world of his time within the volumes of his *Naturalis Historia*. Skinner had his humor, as well as his hubris). The rat learned to pull a string to remove a marble from a rack, pick it up with his front paws, and drop it into the mouth of a tube. "Every step in the process had to be worked out through a process of approximations," he explained, "since the component responses were not in the original repertoire of the rat."

What made him characterize the bowling pigeon as so much more significant than the marble-carrying rat—its occurrence a day "of great illumination," Skinner remembered more than thirty-five years later—was that the training method was so efficient. The bird "got it" quite quickly. Then there was the fact that they had achieved this end not by having to rearrange the physical environment at every step to provide the reinforcers mechanically (how cumbersome that must have been, and proof that scientists have patience far exceeding that of normal humans), but simply doing so by hand. Primates' hands are more fluidly adaptable than any static mechanism inside a box operated by the test subject. These experimenters simply thought to use a switch that operated the feed chamber door, one resembling the controller on slide carousels of yore. (The same principle is currently used, with technology updated to include a wireless remote, in the Manners Minder/Treat & Train dispenser developed by behaviorist Sophia Yin, a graduate of Bob Bailey's chicken camp and until her untimely death in 2014 one of today's most knowledgeable, eloquent, and inventive positive-reinforcement trainers. You can order one of her devices, of course, online.)

This method, Skinner wrote in 1972, "is now so commonplace that it is hard to understand why we should have been amazed at the speed with which this was done." Not quite as commonplace as it might be. But among proficient trainers from amateur to professional, from those involved in dog sport to assistance-animal training to marine mammal shows, as well as in zoos throughout the Western world, shaping is the method employed as the most economical (and often the only) way to train complex behaviors. We now take for granted long sequences—for instance the assistance animal's help with the laundry, including picking up dirty underwear, dropping it in the washer, closing the lid, and pressing the button—but until the discovery in the General Mills lab that reinforcing successive approximations toward a final result by hand is both quick and efficient, it was not commonplace at all. In fact, we did not know what some animals were capable of until the discovery was disseminated through an ever-widening list of applications. The repercussions of what Skinner portrayed as an accident arising out of boredom in an inquisitive moment would spread like the expanding ripples from a stone dropped in a pool.

That dissemination, which would remain fairly contained until Karen Pryor realized its popular potential, would begin almost immediately.

In 1943, when Project Pigeon met its premature end,* a light-bulb appeared over the heads of Skinner's two young married grad students. Marian and Keller Breland bought a farm in rural Minnesota, where they set about shaping behaviors in a number of test subjects, including chickens, parakeets, pigs, and dogs. (Marian had loved animals since she was a girl.) Their results convinced them to leave their degrees unfinished, though Marian would get hers thirty-eight years and three children later, at the University of Arkansas; Keller already held a doctorate in psychology from Louisiana State. They were eager to launch a commercial enterprise they believed held every promise of success.

Not everyone felt the same way. Indeed, it seemed that no one did. A classmate bet $10 that their animal-training business would fail; in a final ironic proof of the difficulties facing all novel ideas, even Skinner thought they would go under.

What the Brelands ultimately achieved with Animal Behavior Enterprises would represent one of the least recognized great advances in practical science. On the surface, much of their work appears trivial, if remunerative: they trained hundreds of different animals that appeared in commercials for companies as varied as General Mills—they had a leg up with that commission—and a bank whose ad featured a rabbit called Buck Bunny; it ran on TV for an unequaled twenty years. They originated the first coin-

---

* From an account of the kamikaze pigeons Skinner wrote for the *American Psychologist*:

> [Arthur D. Hyde, a research director at General Mills] closed our presentation with a brief summary: we were offering a homing device, unusually resistant to jamming, capable of reacting to a wide variety of target patterns, requiring no materials in short supply, and so simple to build that production could be started in 30 days. He thanked the committee and we left. As the door closed behind us, he said to me: "Why don't you go out and get drunk!"

operated animal shows, including a machine that would become a staple of arcades for a long while to come called Bird Brain, in which a chicken played a guessing game against the operator in return for feed. A onetime operator was none other than B. F. Skinner; he lost to the chicken. But they also published papers in peer-reviewed journals, the most influential of which, in 1961, was "The Misbehavior of Organisms," a playful reference to Skinner's classic *The Behavior of Organisms*. In it they developed the concept of "instinctual drift," or the pressure of innate tendencies to affect operant behavior. Their conclusion was derived from the application of behavior analysis during the course of working with what would amount to animals from over 140 different species and, at a single notable point, more than 1,000 individuals.

In 1955 in Hot Springs they opened, as tourist attraction and training lab, a show called IQ Zoo.* Keller died ten years later. And eleven years after that, Marian married Robert E. Bailey, who had been ABE's general manager.

In a 2012 article for the dog magazine *Bark*, Sophia Yin, continuing her chronicle of the early days of operant conditioning's popularization, described one of ABE's projects for a client, the Central Intelligence Agency. (Marian, characterized by chicken camp student Jennifer Andersen as "the scientific side" with Bailey plying "the tech side" of the operation, took the lead on many of their government commissions, some of which still remain classified.) One day in 1967 a mysterious car slowed down only long enough to deposit a cat outside the terminal at the San Francisco International Airport. The creature waited until a man entered, then it slipped through

---

* It operated until 1990. In 2004, Bob Bailey donated one of the Bird Brains exhibits to the Smithsonian Institution.

the open door. Zigzagging purposefully, as if under some unseen control, it next lay down under a bench for some twenty minutes. It looked for all the world as if it were eavesdropping on the conversation of the people above. Then, just as suddenly as it arrived, it got up and retraced its steps back out the door and into the same car, which had circled back and now moved off.

The cat had been fitted with a cochlear implant. The test had been run to see if a domesticated animal could be trained to work reliably at a distance from and unseen by its handlers. It had already been proven possible with pigeons and dolphins. Only positive reinforcement was utilized in all these successful experiments.

So much for the canard that cats can't be trained.

In addition to training animals, ABE also trained trainers, publishing manuals and holding clinics on which the chicken camps would later be based. They became teachers of teachers, and what we find being practiced in literally every corner of the world by a relative handful of professionals and amateurs alike who call themselves clicker trainers can be traced back to their methodology. It was fully grounded in the lab work of Skinner, but because ABE was a commercial entity (successfully for three decades), his theories underwent a fair amount of unique adaptation in order to work for a wide variety of species and purposes. They were in it for the success of the business, which meant they took on all sorts of impossible jobs and found the most efficient means to work them out. They took nothing from prior traditions of animal training going back centuries (as different from their methodology as different can be, except for those occasional and partial discoveries of operant conditioning avant la lettre that chance always provides over extensive time). To do so would have been to them like bleeding a patient to relieve a fever: done for eons but nonsensical now. As Bailey told Yin:

Dog training has been practiced as an ancient craft. The science of training wasn't developed until the 1940s with B. F. Skinner. Crafts generally develop over thousands of years and tend to preserve what's old and has been done before. Information is passed down in secret from master to apprentice, and the apprentice must never question the master.

In this appraisal hides a caution about believing the assertion that some aspect of training is a secret or can only be practiced by someone with innate mystical skill: the reason it can't be shared or explained, it usually turns out, is that the person can't articulate what they're doing either because they lack the scientific language—here, the language of behavior acquisition first developed in *The Behavior of Organisms*—or because it would fail its proofs. For example, the use of punishment (also known as the application of "aversives") is a common feature of traditional training. That does not mean it necessarily works, only that it has been historically employed and still goes largely unquestioned. When Bailey examined its use through the lens of science alone, separated from the religious rituals of traditional training, he found it overused and misapplied. Furthermore, he believed it was rarely necessary in most circumstances, apart from the rare occasions in which people's lives would be at stake, such as training for military applications.

Perhaps the most substantial gift of Bailey and the Brelands to the incipient revolution in how animals were treated, however, came out of their work with marine mammals. In the process of training performers for such facilities as Marineland and Sea World, they came up with the notion which they termed the "bridging stimulus," of a sound (a whistle or a click) that announced the upcoming delivery of the "primary reinforcer." In the case of a dolphin, say,

this represented the all-powerful edible reward.* Its use was necessary with an animal who might be underwater or at the height of
a splash-producing jump when the fishy reinforcer should ideally
be offered: the precise moment he performed the action that was
desired. It was critical that the reward, or its sonic stand-in, be signaled at that moment. This advance, the use of a whistle as a sign
that itself took on a little of the food reward's happy burnish, quickly
informed the work of those working professionally with captive
marine mammals. (It is a small world, back then smaller still.) And
that is how a young woman, falling into the role of trainer along the
tangents of chance, came to learn how to put on a porpoise show at
her biologist husband's new oceanarium in Hawaii in 1963.

In the absence of any other candidate, Karen Pryor was tapped to
train the performers at Sea Life Park, which was both a research and
an entertainment facility. She had previously trained her Weimara-
ner, Gus, in obedience, and the family pony's colt to accept a harness.
But these were far in degree from taking wild porpoises fresh from
the sea and ending up with the kind of breathtaking spectacle that
audiences would pay for. Pryor put herself on an educational crash
course: she read a manual written by a consultant to Sea Life Park,
a psychologist named Ron Turner. And the rest she figured out by
herself. A whole lot of rest.

*[The manual] was written in thick prose and stiff scientific jargon.
I could see why the people [my husband] had hired as trainers had*

---

* Anything necessary to survival—food, water, sex—is a primary reinforcer, that is, we
do not have to be taught to desire it. A secondary reinforcer is one that has been paired
with a primary reinforcer often enough for it to take on by association the same motivational force as a primary reinforcer; it is thus also known as a *conditioned* reinforcer.

been unwilling to digest it. It was exciting, though. Here were the rules, the scientific laws, underlying training. Suddenly I knew why I'd always had trouble with Gus on the "drop-on-recall" exercises. And why the pony, Echo, jibbed his head to the left on a right turn. I began to understand how training works. I could see that, given this handful of facts, this elegant system called "operant conditioning," one could train any animal to do anything it was physically capable of doing.

In *Lads Before the Wind,* her autobiography of becoming a trainer and behaviorist, she describes at length what that understanding yielded: a new career, and a business that would begin at last to popularize what B. F. Skinner had envisioned after he codified learning theory and delivered it to the world. It just so happened that he could not enact the changes he dreamed of directly. Karen Pryor is one of the major trustees of his law of behavior, and she took the bequest and started giving it away. She did not originate a new movement in animal welfare, but she knew how to step to the fore of a parade and lead it where it will be most visible. It is to her credit that so many pet owners the world over are doing what seems to be something new and exciting and fun: clicker training.

. . .

WHAT IS the importance to us that the Brelands trained chickens to walk on tightropes, rabbits to ride miniature firetrucks and sound sirens, raccoons to play basketball, or birds to run bases? These are just cute little animals performing cute little tricks. (Even if Professor Punch, the piebald rabbit, *was* unspeakably adorable playing on the toy piano.)

They showed us two things, it turns out.[11] Two consequential matters that arose from a chance outcome—the decision to start

Animal Behavior Enterprises—tangentially yet importantly caused by a failure of imagination on the part of a wartime committee. One is that the only limits on the complexity of behaviors that can be taught using reinforcement are the innate capabilities of the organism. And the second is that—as Bob Bailey holds on pragmatic grounds only, for he was trained as a biologist, in a field where morals hold no sway, and then hired by a military that cared above all for dependable results—the use of punishment is to be used very, very sparingly, or not at all. Out of thousands of individual animals, in hundreds of different programs, Bailey estimates he employed positive punishment (or the application of painful or aversive stimuli) only a dozen times. That is because all the behaviors he needed to teach were more reliably obtained using positive reinforcement; this decision was based not on ethics but on results. That is powerful stuff coming from the man who is possibly the world's most experienced trainer of animals, having taught over 120 different species, 1,000 human trainers, and some 10,000 individual animals. It gives him a unique podium from which to stress an interesting corollary: positive reinforcement badly applied does little harm. The same cannot be said of punishment. It can hurt, in multiple senses.

The other weighty consequence was Karen Pryor herself.

CHAPTER FIVE

The ideal society can be described, quite simply,
as that in which no man has the power of means
to coerce others.

—EDWARD ABBEY

Sometimes the book you write is not the book you thought you wrote.

The revolutionary message you so eagerly delivered to the expectant world (sitting back to await its effect, then waiting some more) goes unheard, although it was phrased so clearly, so emphatically. It's as if you'd invented a revolutionary new method of transportation, then found people were using the modules not to improve public life in a single leap, but to store outdoor furniture in the off season.

It's a dumbfounding moment, one that will propel you to go searching for a reason; you're not fond of doing colossal amounts of work to no purpose. You also desired to effect some positive change in the world, so the disappointment is not solely personal. Though perhaps there's a touch of the ego in it. Yes, though we hate to admit it, self-importance is the match that lights the authorial fire.

Karen Pryor met the moment in 1975, when her memoir of becoming a marine-mammal trainer, *Lads Before the Wind,* was published. Since most of its length was devoted to representing in different garb multiple aspects of a single discovery—how supremely successful operant conditioning proved in the training of dolphins— she naturally assumed the implicit message would be clear. That the methodology was applicable to any animal you could think of, including the human, seemed so obvious, and obviously exciting, she had only to wait a minute or two for the hurrah to sound from legions of equally enthusiastic converts. It was clear, to her at least, that the training system had worked the magic, not the peculiar intelligence of dolphins. The structure of the book—a heap of anecdotes pointing to the same moral every time—could only be intended to reveal a single thing. The science is god: right all the time.

To any reader who was truly awake, the book's long series of aha moments beside the dolphin tanks could not possibly be about something as simple as "dolphins are smart." Pryor obviously meant for some further meaning to be extrapolated from the narrative. It was her hope that these ideas would enrich every animal trainer's work.*

---

* One illustration, out of hundreds (at least one hard-won insight per page): She had to translate from clean theory to messy practice, from the pages of an academic manual by psychologist Ron Turner to the utterly individual captive wild animals in her charge. It is a little like putting together all the furnishings for a twenty-story apartment building from Ikea instructions. The precuts on each bed are slightly different, though the picture has them all the same. And this is not even to mention the cabinetry. Near the beginning of her book she describes learning to apply the "limited hold," a technique for producing "instant rather than dilatory response." (This, a page after relating another huge insight on the necessity of teaching animals that a learned behavior is to be offered only on cue; otherwise, the trainer is in the position of the army sergeant whose "platoon will advance under fire when he tells them to" but who will be "in a bad way if they may sometimes advance when he didn't tell them to." Pryor is herself always very good at extrapolating. This ability to analogize is one of the primary reasons she has become the preeminent trainer's trainer.) "A stopwatch helped the trainer stay honest; it was always tempting to leave the cue on just a little longer when you saw that your dilatory animal was about to jump. [We, too, respond to cues

One critical fact was to emerge early on in her career as the pioneering trainer at Tap Pryor's research and entertainment facility, Hawaii's
Sea Life Park. But first she would have to bolt together a new style of
training from that otherwise impenetrable psychology manual (given
her as the only tool with which to build the entire ark in which the
human-animal relationship might sail to another continent) and her
own trial-and-error work with a bunch of individuals—basically a
first-grade class with a teacher fresh from college. This is when she
fully appreciated operant conditioning as a *technology,* neither more
nor less, and amazing to both parties. It was not her artistic creation.
And so she could not possess it (though later she would certainly affix
a trademark here and there). She discovered, as Bob Bailey became
fond of repeating, that "training in the scientific manner," as it would
be called by its ever-so-slightly defensive proponents, is a mechanical
skill like any other. It required dispassionate tutelage. Her memoir was
a narrative of scientific exploration, with elements of spiritual awakening. All mysteries were explained by proof alone. (Then again, the
reading contains some literary unpredictability in the form of some
amusingly difficult personalities, finned and footed both.) This was

---

unconsciously.] If you succumbed to that temptation, however, you could end up with
the animals training *you* to leave the cue on longer and longer. . . . [Soon,] we shortened
the cue-on time to twelve seconds. Again, the laggards were out of luck. . . . We found
that we could tighten up this 'limited hold' to the smallest length of time in which the
animals could physically accomplish the behavior." In the end, the cue for the animals
to spin, a natural behavior for dolphins, was reduced to a three-second limited hold.
"The trainer punched the button, and bingo! six animals dove out of sight and then
flew into the air all over the place. It was dramatic." The audience had no idea how this
was accomplished, so it seemed mysterious and amazing. Now you know. (You also
know, if you have seen the 2013 documentary *Blackfish*, by Gabriela Cowperthwaite,
about captive orcas in marine parks, that what you see on show is a fraction of the
disturbing, and tragic, reality of forcing complex creatures to live and perform in
artificial, severely straitened environments.)

the first indication we were in the presence of something vitally new in animal stories.*

Certainly, it would be for most the first introduction to the concept of teacher training—or actually training teachers, using exactly the same methods they would then use on animals. On her new recruits to Sea Life Park (many of them young students or amateur trainers or scientists; the park's budget was extremely limited) Pryor used the "Training Game," a psychologist's invention that sounds like a riotous party game and a potential glue trap of humiliation at once. One person would leave the room, and the others would conspire on behaviors the elected trainer would try to elicit from the human guinea pig when he or she returned from the hall.

> *Putting a novice behind the whistle was a quick and cheap way of drumming training laws into the novice's head without making some poor porpoise put up with an inconsistent trainer. . . . When the subject was a human being, there was no way for a trainer to say to himself [the kind of things you hear frustrated people say of animals all the time]: "The animal can't do this," or "The animal is mad at me," or "The animal is deliberately defying me," or "The animal is stupid."*

If you couldn't get your human subject to, say, touch the wall then close his eyes, the blame would fall only on you. Figure out what you're doing wrong and then repair it: this is the meaning of mechanics. There is really only one way to fix an idle air control valve; when

---

* According to "A Brief History of Dog Training—70 years of Clicker Training" by Gail Fisher (*http://www.alldogsgym.com/content/view/42/*), Keller Breland developed the complete positive-reinforcement training protocol for marine mammals "in a matter of weeks." This was in the fifties, as a result of being hired by Marineland of Florida, an underwater-film studio that doubled as a public oceanarium. His work predated Bailey's with the Navy, which in turn predated Pryor's at Sea Life Park.

someone is called an engine whisperer, the joke is immediately understood. Whisper all you want to, but in the end you either have to clean the valve, or remove two bolts and a hose and remember to hook them back up on a replacement. Controlling behavior has the same narrow range of operable fixes.

A dozen more similarly keen anecdotal lessons intervene in Pryor's account, and then comes the strategy she hit upon for getting an animal to tolerate something unnatural or somewhat uncomfortable. In this case it was a dolphin who would have to wear suction cups over his eyes to show the audience his skill at echolocation: there wasn't a dolphin who would tolerate this affront, not even after a dose of good old habituation, the same technique used on horses so they will accept the scary saddle, or any of us going into a dark basement the first time. The strong and toothy marine mammals had an inevasible way of showing that something was not to their taste: thrashing and threatening or generally pitching a fit. This is what happened at the sight of a suction cup, once it had been placed anywhere near the dolphin's head. Shaping did not work, either. At last, she discovered how to make the demo dolphin agree: by first laying a separate foundation behavior. This would be installed so strongly that the animal was essentially powerless to resist Step II, habituation and acceptance. (This is the strategy that would later be widely used with captive wild animals in zoos so they will not only tolerate, but welcome, procedures like carotid blood draws.)

I trained Kane to press his rostrum against my right hand for prolonged periods, no matter what I was doing with my left hand. I counted the seconds, shaping a ten-second press, a twenty-second press, while I touched, tugged, and poked him here and there with my free hand. When the pressing behavior was well established (we called it "stationing," and learned to use it for all kinds of things) I

*used my hand to stick and instantly unstick the suction cup from his
back. Since he had learned to "stand still no matter what" he stood
for it.*

The definition of elegant: simple, smart, and it worked. And no
harm to Kane. It was all part of the training that to him was a pleasurable game, full of delicious fish. The fortune inside the cookie.

* * *

SHE HAD evidently arrived at all 325 pages of knowledge the hard
way: living it, making mistakes, learning from accident, some of
them painful. By offering these parables of the hands-on novitiate
trainer, she was mapping an invaluable shortcut to enlightenment.

Every trick she dissected, and every *aperçu* she dropped (whether
on the critical importance of timing, or the myopia of adherents to
individual scientific disciplines), could be mined for great chunks of
information on how to apply operant conditioning in the field. It was
just lying there waiting to be picked up.

Not many did.

Perhaps the problem was one of effort: extrapolation is work.
And in this case, it is made twice as hard by the fact that readers
simultaneously had to imagine their way over a formidable barrier, higher than mountains: tradition. Animal training is positively
corseted by tradition.

In a fundamental sense, *Lads Before the Wind* could as easily
have been written by Marian Breland Bailey, its locale changed from
Hawaii to Hot Springs, the animals not spinners and bottlenoses
but pretty much every other variety of mammal, because the moral
was the same: *Here is something new! The key to getting any behavior
you want! Bonus: no coercion necessary.* Furthermore: *It may look like
magic, but it's pure science, and anyone can do it.* Bailey's academic

background was in psychology while Pryor's was in biology; if Bailey had written a similar autobiography for the general reader, it would have predated Pryor's by ten or fifteen years. That is about it for the differences. Two women doing pioneering work, and neither calculating enough to think of turning the klieg lights on herself. Yet.

Looking back decades later on her puzzlement that so few availed themselves of the powerful insights she had gained while working at Sea Life Park, Pryor wrote: "In the words of . . . Keller Breland, we [knew we] could train any animal to do anything it was physically and mentally capable of doing. However, for the next thirty years, to my mystification, our kind of training did not spread beyond the oceanariums. Our fancy applications aroused no interest among scientists and academics."* She finally realized that people had assumed free-operant training only worked on dolphins. Like I said, extrapolating is work.

So, next, Pryor decided to be explicit. In fact, she would write a book about training *people*, so there would be no confusion that if a cat, say, was used to illustrate a technique, it would work only on felines. What then did the publisher (not the author) decide to title it? *Don't Shoot the Dog!* naturally. Karen Pryor, and the spirit of B. F. Skinner now destined to be immured in her, could not escape confinement no matter how hard she tried: first, she was made out to be a dolphin trainer, not a behaviorist; next, she was a dog trainer, not a theoreticist. She wrote one book, but another got read. She

---

* This, and the quote below, are from Pryor's "A Transformation Devoutly to Be Wished: What We Are Beginning to Discover from the Clicker Training Revolution," originally published in 2000 by the Latham Foundation, which promotes education on the humane relationship between animals and people. It is not only a brief history of the development of Pryor's own career, but contains (as do all Pryor's writings) concise appraisals of positive reinforcement's potential for enlarging the experience of both happiness and learning. I will have recourse to this essay at many points.

might have been remystified—"The book came out in paperback [in the mid-eighties]. Sales increased steadily over the next decade. Somebody was reading the book, but who?"—yet this time her stoic acceptance of her restrictive categorization was transformed into the full embrace of whatever possibilities were to occur. The career that resulted gave her an expanding fiefdom over which she would benevolently but single-handedly rule. She became the public face, the de facto owner, of "clicker training." Her company is called, simply, Karen Pryor Clicker Training, and it now encompasses an academy for trainers and shelter personnel, a publishing arm, merchandise including several types of clickers, treat bags, and videos, and the mounting of annual ClickerExpo conferences on both U.S. coasts (and now expanding to Europe) that attract hundreds of amateurs and professionals alike. It was one more of those accidental outcomes that in retrospect could be nothing but foreordained, finding herself before the audience most primed to receive the word with born-again fervor: dog people.*

Pryor mentions, in her thumbnail history of "the clicker revolution," a cardinal reason that operant conditioning was applied with marine mammals early and without opposition from the ranks of traditional trainers: there *was* no tradition of dolphin training. The

---

* Dog people may look like everyone else, but don't kid yourself. They comprise another species, human in physical form but different at the core, from their driving values to their entertainments: everything revolves around their dogs. You might think it evidence of a sly humor when they say the car "belongs" to Rover, or they moved to another state for the sake of Clover, but it would actually be true. They did. And that's only the beginning of it. Their best friends are other dog people (because to these explanations of why the human's day was arranged around the dog's needs and desires are blessedly unnecessary), and their best moments are dog moments. They will be retailed at the end of the day in long emails to, yes, other dog people. Who in kind return the litany of the day's hike, vet visit, training session, or loving or exasperating action by the four-legged offspring.

animals had simply never been trained in any numbers before the Navy (which means Bob Bailey, and thus also Keller Breland, whose work at Marineland undoubtedly informed Bailey's own) started doing it around 1960. Historically, the military innovates much technologic progress; this particular technology, of training, has in this regard proved no different from the development of interchangeable parts, computing, microchips, the Internet, the Boeing 747, and GPS. Only positive reinforcement is used with "their" dolphins and sea lions, according to an official statement of the U.S. Navy Marine Mammal Program:

> *Ever since the Navy realized the amiability of dolphins and sea lions and their potential for working in the sea with human partners, the Navy Marine Mammal Program has relied on the proven techniques of operant conditioning, emphasizing the use of positive reinforcement (correct responses are rewarded while incorrect responses are ignored) to train its animals. The early history of the NMMP coincided with the adaptation and growing use of those techniques among marine mammal trainers and has made a large contribution to pioneering and developing methods commonly used in the industry today.*

It goes without saying (but I am not a trusting soul, so I will) that if another method was as reliable—it is not to be forgotten that lives depended on the performance of these wild animals—the Navy would not have hesitated to use it, no matter what it entailed. A branch of the larger institution whose sole purpose is to come up with ways to kill more, better, faster, does not choose its techniques on moral grounds. That this one manifests a high degree of morality was simply a happy accident of its efficiency.

Another reason positive reinforcement integrated so smoothly into the world of the oceanarium (and the Navy) was that it is, practically speaking, the *only* way you can train a dolphin. Punishment is not available as a tool: try to strike or reprimand a swimmer, and he just swims away. Acoustic reward markers and fish reinforcers—along with good timing and mutual ingenuity, as ever—are the only things that work.

In terms of the history of training other mammals, Pryor explains how the old paradigm is turned precisely upside down by positive reinforcement, as "we operant trainers do everything backwards." Traditional trainers are *enforcers*: they command, and then enforce the fulfillment of the command. (Elsewhere, she refers to a command as "a veiled threat.") If not, then the application of force commences: an unpleasant sound, a shout or a hiss; a smack; a push; a jerk on the trachea by way of a leash pop; worse. The animal learns to perform a behavior in order to *avoid* unpleasantness.

The positive-reinforcement trainer, on the other hand, starts with the outcome: here is the treat. Next, it's paired with, or conditioned to, what amounts to a symbol (a click sound, a hand gesture). It would appear that operant conditioning is indeed as ancient as life itself: it is expressed in the structure of an originary tale.

And then—light and magic. "We let the animal discover that *it can cause the marker signal to happen by its own actions.* [My emphasis.] The dolphin jumps—and makes the trainer blow the whistle. The dog sits—and makes the person click a clicker." This sounds like banner-headline news to me: "ARMISTICE IS SIGNED!"

Pryor reveals the profound implications of this apparently elementary reversal of common order: the animal's discovery that *it* is in the driver's seat is not only "tremendously exciting for the learner"—want to make a dog or a child smile?; one is guaranteed the first moment they twig how this works—but learning new behaviors is "initiated by the learner."

Initiation. ("To begin, set going, or originate.") Nothing precedes.

And *free will*. Its second definition is "the ability to make a choice without coercion."

When positive reinforcement is used to train, you use primarily (but not solely) one quadrant of operant conditioning, that law of behavior discovered by a man who was accused of somehow wishing to deprive us of our birthright, free will. How exactly he was going to do that was never explained. Yet here Karen Pryor describes this technology of managing behavior as based firmly on the *trainee's* discovery that he or she "can make the trainer give signals and thus treats." When that "lightbulb moment" occurs in the mind of the trainee, "real communication" begins, the interchange of meaningful information between learner and teacher. And this "leads to the development of deliberately offered behaviors, which trainers can change or increase without any physical interference, guidance, or restraint at all, simply by choosing when to say 'Yes!'"

I like to sit and think a moment about this—*yes* as a concept. It causes an instant synesthetic response: for some reason I see the sun, feel warmth, associate the word with an intense white-yellow. *Yes* contains light, growth, endless magnitude.

Searching for yes, the trainee *initiates* behavior *without coercion*.

The sound of something grand and brittle breaking, falling to earth from a great height, is the soundtrack to this rather dry explanation. What is crumbling into useless pieces is the mythology that has grown up around traditional training, its rationales of domination and need for authoritarian shows of force.

•   •   •

FOR BEING the Che Guevara of animal welfare, Karen Pryor seems content to see her revolution go where it will, spread or stay local, it's all the same to her. Actually, she is less passive than she is smart: she knows that the discovery of any new way is rarely greeted with champagne and sugared nuts. And that mounting the walls of ancient fortresses only gets you an arrow in the heart, if the boiling oil doesn't fell you first. The thought that she often preaches to the already converted seems to trouble her not in the least, and she seems happy to speak to just relative handfuls of them at a time. (But it is likely she is also quietly weighing the odds of less violent types of expansion.) Her soft but no-nonsense voice, amplified through the mic, heads insistently to the back of a room filled with new acolytes. These are most probably sitting at the edges of their chairs for two reasons: they are in the presence of someone who to them has the status of a lesser god, and they have their dogs lying at their feet. These are almost all, to the last golden retriever, reclining on fleece pads while wearing the blaze orange vest of the service or assistance animal, and watching their people with such concentration you expect something to levitate. The human pupils at this ClickerExpo have come to learn more, whether or not they are already professional trainers. Most are here at the behest of their canine students. (Too, they all have long known what amounts to the second-grade curriculum of R+ theory: your dog is learning all the time; if you don't shape his behavior, then the environment surely will, and usually in ways you don't want.) So, while they listen to the rather slight blond woman onstage put forth theory and observation, jokes and sketches, teasers and stunners, they are reinforcing their charges for lying quietly. The conference hall sounds like a summer afternoon in the country. A noise like a thousand crickets erupts from all over.

Karen Pryor's great role in what she calls "the clicker revolution" is not that of philosopher or fighter, but of an even more important figure in modern insurgency: political propagandist. This is not to say her message about positive reinforcement is spin. It's a little like climate change science at this historic moment, of no doubt to anyone but those who have actively chosen to doubt. In the case of both climate change and the superiority of science-based training, opposition must be retained against both growing consensus and massing concrete evidence. The way this evidence is manifested will be investigated at length later, but we should have no fear: learning about it will be no slog. In fact, we already do it for fun (as millions of YouTube hits attest). Just watch dogs.

The royal road for Karen Pryor to the top of a clicker-training empire led through the succinct and powerful explication of the system that she placed between the covers of *Don't Shoot the Dog!* It is a model of clarity, relevance, and satisfyingly credible explanation. Its validity to the widest category of reader is perhaps without parallel: I cannot imagine, much as I try, the person who would not find benefit or use from its pages.

It is nearly impossible to pull one or two examples illustrating the book's valuable insights about behavior and how it is reinforced, either by mistake (most of the time) or design (if the theory presented is put into practice). I gave up underlining particularly impressive passages midway through the first chapter, because when I looked back I saw there were few sentences that had escaped the pen; the margins were a mess of checkmarks, doubled and tripled.

Here is a representative sample from chapter 1, "Reinforcement: Better Than Rewards," in which basic principles and terms are presented. "The warning buzzer in a car if you don't fasten your seat belt is a negative reinforcer," i.e., "something the subject wants to avoid." (Lest you think operant conditioning is not built into pretty much every system already, man-made or naturally occurring.) Another:

Laggardly reinforcement is the beginning trainer's biggest problem. The dog sits, but by the time the owner says "Good dog," the dog is standing again. What behavior did "Good dog" reinforce? Standing up. [Hence the benefit of using a clicker as a bridging stimulus:

the chance for better timing, hence clearer communication.] . . . We
are always reinforcing one another too late. "Gee, honey, you looked
great last night" is quite different from the same comment said at
the moment. The delayed reinforcer may even have deleterious effect
("What's the matter, don't I look great now?"). We have a touch-
ing trust in the powers of words to cover our lapses in timing.
[Emphasis mine; I hope it can't be emphasized too much.]

Continuing this fascinating discussion—as well as the need for me to
flag continuous passages—on the importance of timing in delivery
of reinforcers, Pryor next dissects the problems that can arise from
reinforcing *too early* as opposed to too late. Workers at the Bronx
Zoo discovered one when they attempted to persuade a gorilla who
had taken to sitting in the doorway between his indoor and outdoor
cage, preventing them from closing the door when they needed to.
They tried to lure him out by throwing food into the next enclosure
or implying he would get the banana they held out if only he would
move, but he would either snatch the food or disbelieve their sin-
cerity and continue to frustrate their plans. A trainer on staff was
consulted; he pointed out the keepers were attempting "to reinforce
behavior that hadn't occurred yet. The name for this is *bribery*." And
bribery is always a bad idea. (The solution to the problem was simply, once again, to wait for the desired behavior or even a move in its
direction and reward that.) In the human realm,

. . . we reinforce children too soon under the misimpression that we
are encouraging them ("Atta girl, that's the way, you almost got it
right"). What we may be doing is reinforcing trying. There is a differ-
ence between trying to do something and doing it. Wails of "I can't"
may sometimes be a fact, but they may also be symptoms of being
reinforced merely for trying.

All of a sudden, it seems like it might be fun to do nothing for a few days but look through operant conditioning's spyglass at virtually everything we do. We would see these mechanisms at work in actions large and small—how amazing science is, to give us new eyes! And not only more insightful, but newly imbued with the power that knowledge is said to give; in this case, the power to effect pacific change in some of our most troublesome communications with others.

It was a power largely left untried, though not because of anything Pryor did. She could not have been more clear or encouraging about the possibilities. If it weren't for the misleading title, the book, brilliant as it is, may not have had any readers at all, even dog trainers. In choosing the tongue-in-cheek and inflammatory title, the publisher sought to do two things: sell books, and avoid any scent of taboo emanating from the true subject, which is actually one of the biggest taboos there is, training people.* Once more, Skinner was whispering sedition from an orchestra seat: *We are not fundamentally*

---

* The reference to dog shooting came from chapter 4, "Untraining: Using Reinforcement to Get Rid of Behavior You Don't Want." She outlines eight different methods of dealing with undesirable behavior and shows how each is applied to one of ten examples. (Only two of these have to do with nonhuman animals, one a continuously barking dog and the other a cat that jumps up on the kitchen table; the others concern situations like a messy roommate, noisy children, or a grumpy spouse.) The methods span the most dire—"Shoot the Animal," which is literal only in part in the scene in which the dog appears; otherwise, the roommate gets changed for another, the children made to get out of the car and walk, the spouse divorced—to the most subtle and thoughtful, "Change the Motivation" (the dog gets exercise, a companion, or brought inside; the roommate is let off the hook by hiring a maid; the fatigue or hunger that is the probable cause of the fractious children is attended to; if the grumpiness is a result of a stressful job, that is what is remedied). Pryor uses an absurd notion—of course capital punishment "always works," since using it means "you will definitely never have that behavioral problem with that subject again"—to point out the superiority of many other methods.

different from other animals. The only place in society where these
principles might be practiced in safety, then, was the neohuman relationship of pet owner and dog. And only the sappiest sentimental-
ists of all, amateur trainers—since many professionals were already
deeply invested in the conventions of their trade—would find
appealing those methods that so thoroughly contravened training's
backlist of classics. Only those who "didn't want to use the choke
chains and dominating tones of traditional training on their beloved
dogs" would take *Don't Shoot the Dog!* as their bible. The revolution
necessarily started small and quiet.

Something like the clicker itself. In the way of the talisman, the
object is both separate from the potencies that are ascribed to it and
peculiarly magnetic to them. There is *something* about this unpre-
possessing noisemaker that makes it perfect, neat: it is incapable of
harm, like the practice in which it is used; it is almost laughably
simple, ditto.

Clickers may still be found at the counter of many toy stores
where there are jars of tiny prizes just waiting to be exchanged for
spare change or the exhausted child's fit (ensuring that the likelihood of throwing one will increase the next time in a store; hey,
knowledge of behavioral science is parental power now). We take
primitive pleasure in activating things, and the sound that proves
the completion is our reward. In fact, we have long clicker-trained
ourselves to play with clickers. Children's clickers might be shaped
like a beetle, but there is always a metal strip underneath that when
pressed emits a crisp sound, so these can be used in training as easily
as an "official" clicker.

You don't need the box clicker on a wristband. The toy works
as well. But any clicker is usually better than a word, say, at least
in the beginning of a training program, in part because behavior
is so fluid and fleeting. The speed with which a click can be made

gives a vast advantage over cumbersome speech, even the small word "yes." Besides, that word happens around us all the time; if we use it to "capture" our dog's correct behavior in a training session then respond without thinking to someone asking "Are you ready to go?" it loses some of its power as a bridging stimulus—now it's just background noise, and the dog's world has a lot of that already.

It is possible, too, that a dedicated noise works better to teach because of its *salience*, that is, it stands on its own to be processed directly and quickly by the reward center of the brain. At least one study and a lot of professional-training anecdotes point to an auditory marker achieving quicker results in learning. It also, some trainers note, seems to make their dogs happier, more eager. One trainer in an online discussion of whether or not a clicker is superior to a verbal bridging stimulus pointed out that it's so difficult for us to unload the emotional freight from our words that we run the risk of starting to believe a *nice* word like "yes" or "good" is a reward in itself, forgetting that it has no such function to a dog, to whom it is meaningless noise unless used as a temporary stand-in for a primary reinforcer. Another offered a more powerful reason for using a clicker, especially by the "crossover" trainer originally schooled in using what are called in traditional procedure "corrections": "I do think having a clicker in one's hand is a great way for a crossover trainer to avoid giving reflexive and/or inadvertent leash corrections."[12]

Pryor perceptively notes that it was precisely the clicker's unthreatening nature that enabled it to work such enormous change on a field that was historically, and deeply, resistant. The toy itself "precipitated" the increasingly widespread acceptance of a novel approach to teaching because there was previously "no tradition of training dogs, or anything else, with a clicking device." Consequently the use of the clicker had accrued no heavy debris of "preconceived ideas."

Push buttons on devices have been available since the late nine-

teenth century, when they started displacing levers. The final tran-
sition occurred around the first decade of the twentieth century.
Buttons represented the first true abstraction of an action from its
result: the action of a lever is instinctively understood as an aug-
mentation of our natural powers, as every monkey knows, while
button pushing requires an intellectual, not muscular, leap to comprehend. The century-long era of the push button is only now coming to an end, supplanted by that of the surface, aka touchscreen.
While it was in play, the push button connoted ease and luxury.
Even magic. This touch of the supernatural fell on the clicker, too.
Watch Skinner teach his pigeon to turn: He holds a wired button
in his hand. It activated the feed dispenser in front of the bird. Yet
our minds are ever primitive, so it is the button that made the bird
twirl. Even if the scientist's didactic voice-over negates what we see,
the eye will not be fooled: the button actuated the bird's will. The
pigeon was more amenable to the truth that it was the grain dispenser alone. There could have been a whole troupe of psychology
professors dancing *Swan Lake* around him, but nothing besides
the food appearing rocked his world. Skinner was here not using a
bridging stimulus but rather direct reinforcement (no click or other
signal preceding it—food only). The bird started to look left: *open
dispenser*, down the throat. "Hmm. That worked before. Let me
look left again." *Open dispenser*, down the throat. A couple more
times, then: "Hey. I'm looking left—it always worked before, why
not now? Maybe I need to turn a little more." *Open dispenser,* down
the throat.

Skinner was shaping the turn he wanted: only he knew what the
final product should look like. His process was to reward successive
approximations in the direction of it. When he saw the bird had
grasped exactly what movement would yield a bit of food and was
offering it reliably, Skinner stopped reinforcing that and asked for

more—in technical terms, he raised the criteria. A more definitive turn of the head; now a turn of the breast; now a full body turn; now a foot moved. Each motion in the desired direction in effect made some food appear.

The bird's behavior was "operating" on his environment to get the goods, remember, which meant he too was training, in this case Dr. Skinner to press a button. There was a two-way flow of communication, which feels deeply (there is no other word for it) pleasant. Positive-reinforcement training itself is rewarding to both student and teacher; it can become positively addictive.

Finally, no movement but the finished product got rewarded. Thus the full turn was trained, to the satisfaction of both customers. And just because some food appeared at exactly the right moment. Direct reinforcement, easy to do with a remote control.

Yet . . . the grain dispenser inevitably made a sound when it began to operate. The sound, although it was not an intentional part of the trainer's arsenal, was certainly not lost on the bird. It was the sound of something good coming, the sound of the footsteps on the front walk when we await the arrival of the beloved and feel an anticipatory excitement that may even eclipse the heat of the first embrace. It became a conditioned reinforcer and quickened the bird's responses. A conditioned reinforcer bears its own gifts.

In that 1951 article in the popular magazine *Scientific American*, "How to Teach Animals," Skinner instructs his audience of amateurs to capture a dog's good behavior with the quick hand of the conditioned reinforcer, although even a whistle was not timely enough, since there was a brief but critical lag caused by the intake of breath. By the time the whistle made a sound, the moment would have passed. One needed a "convenient signal" such as "a rap on a table with a small hard object"—difficult to imagine now as likely to succeed, since practical training really needs to be mobile and active—"or the noise of a high-pitched device such as a 'cricket.'" Ah. That's better.

This is the place to note a prime reason the little "cricket" revealed itself as essentially perfect for the job. It is easy to operate, pleasant to use, ready to the hand. And the more it is used, the more you want to use it. This is because, according to the law of behavior, the happy effect of each click is doubled, since it reinforces learner and teacher both. The click signals two positive outcomes for the learner, those of the rewards themselves and then the chance to learn, which itself opens fonts of pleasurable chemicals in the brain and encourages finding new ways to keep them coming. To the teacher, who has caused all this to happen, the sight of a desired behavior occurring becomes rewarding in turn. Both parties are engaged in a joyful game in which each seeks to make more clicking occur. Thus the genesis of the clicker—as an object of play—is fully expressed in its new use.

Although Skinner may have occasionally used one for purposes of demonstration, Keller Breland is generally credited with being the first to use a clicker (along with whatever reinforcer was determined by the particular animal he was teaching); whistles had to be used with dolphins because the sound carried underwater, while birds respond to color or light, deaf animals require visible gestures, and so on. Yet Breland's innovations remained all but invisible outside Animal Behavior Enterprises, walled off from popular appreciation by a misperception that his work was specialized and the fact that ABE's efforts could not capture the public imagination to any permanent extent—despite innumerable contemporary reports in the popular media about their miraculous feats with animals. (So many, in fact, that a scholarly paper titled "Operant Psychology Goes to the Fair: Marian and Keller Breland in the Popular Press, 1947–1966," running to seventeen pages inclusive of tables, photographs, and references, was published in 2005.) They, like Pryor upon publication of her memoir, thought scientific training so self-evidently exciting and desirable that people were just waiting to jump on the good news. They had initially wanted to launch a dog-training business, but their vision of immediate success was hopelessly naïve. As Marian dolefully related to Sophia Yin in 2000: "We knew there were so many dogs in the country and people always wanted to get them trained. So we thought this would be a cinch. We'd tell people about this new humane way of training and they'd be talking to us by the thousands. Nobody listened to us." It would take the shrewd calculations of a woman with the mind of a scientist and the heart of an entrepreneur to make large numbers of the general public feel that this was what they had been waiting for all their lives.

Karen Pryor gave her first seminar for dog trainers, 250 of whom attended, in 1992 in San Francisco. Her copresenter was a dog trainer and animal control officer named Gary Wilkes. Pryor attributes the idea of using a commercially available box-cricket noisemaker in their demonstration to Wilkes. But she does not mention which of them brilliantly decided to *give everyone in the audience* one as a prize to take home. Like the food reward itself—meaningless to the body, incalculably small, a tiny calorie or two—the receipt of swag proves the expansive nature of the symbolic giveaway. It's the aspect of surprise that makes a small gift large. Pryor walked the talk of positive reinforcement from the beginning.

Anyone who witnesses Karen Pryor onstage would rush to place a bet on her as the one who had the acumen to make an empire of an idea no one else could give away. Twice yearly she now stands in front of a packed conference hall to give a galvanizing welcome speech. She works both sides of the aisle, as evangelist and theologian. Her unassuming demeanor no doubt aids her case;

one is startled into attention by the commandingly brainy message as well as the dry wit that was also in evidence in *Don't Shoot the Dog!* With Karen Pryor Clicker Training, she has made a capacious inside for those who did not even know they had long lived on some lonely outside.

Now that they are here, bathing in togetherness, everything that meets their eyes is a validation of their sense that they have found the place they belong. ClickerExpo is equal parts tent revival, honors course, and secret society for those who have seen the operant-conditioning light. There is a joy palpable the minute the hotel's automatic doors slide open: the very hallways and conference rooms at the exposition fling off the energy of so many happy people and even happier dogs. You only become aware that most dogs you've ever seen are bored dull or displeased with the general proceedings after you watch a dog being clicker trained by an owner who has just gotten out of a seminar where she thought her head might explode she was trying to absorb so much information. The keen delight of open communication is passing between the two of them like an electric current. They have eyes only for each other as the one tries out a new idea and the other as avidly wants to figure out what it is, even before it has begun to be expressed. (This dog has played the clicker game before.) It's become a little bit of an addiction for both of them—and it feels every bit as delicious as one. In fact, they will understand this is both in the nature and the outcome of the practice: they will hear trainer Kathy Sdao advise them to "get your animal to be a gambling addict." Gambling on getting a reinforcer for the *next* repetition of the behavior, that is. ("Shortening latency," it is called, as a result of getting to the stone reliability of a behavior that is always promised by a variable-ratio schedule of rewards—i.e., hooked on learning.)

Since giving reinforcement is reinforcing to the one who does it, then, the dealer himself becomes an addict—addicted to hooking another on his own addiction.*

The gladness that is so thick in the air at a ClickerExpo it can be touched also results in large part from relief: freedom from the dark shame of being a perpetrator. Punishing a dog—which frequently comes from being emotionally out of control, as any dog owner necessarily is before learning those scientific rules of teaching that insert a cool intellectual distance between behavior and cause—is a burdensome secret. First it feels good, with its release of frustration and fear. Just as quickly it feels terrible. Someone was hurt or confused at the expense of an outburst that served no purpose. I have known that shame. It leaves a dark pall on the soul, like a smoke stain.

There is no such anger evident here in these halls. None. Happiness has a slight weight, like humidity, and that's what surrounds you here. You can always tell when someone is being authoritarian for an audience—the father who chastises his frightened, frustrated kids in the shopping center in ever louder tones as his approach repeatedly fails. He's going to make you see it work, even if it takes every decibel he's got—because this is the *right* way. "Isn't it?" hesitantly queries the small voice of doubt at the true purpose of his own insistence, hiding itself within the impressive armor of righteous belligerence. Not a person is striking that kind of pose here. All the people you see, as well as their charges, are expressing curiosity, which is the opposite result of oppressed certainty. To risk chastisement or punishment is to preemptively give up, close down. To know that only wonderful, surprising possibilities can ensue is to remain open, searching, enthu-

---

* "Latencies are addictive," says Bob Bailey, adding another thread to the web spun out of all the ways in which addiction operates in positive-reinforcement training theory and practice.

siastic. Isn't this what we want from life? Isn't this what we'd like to offer our dogs, our darlings?

I was once this excited. I was once standing on the brink of great discoveries—I recognized them, in my gut, as incipient truth—and I walked into the Hyatt, expectant.

My new puppy, Nelly, was expectant, too. As always, she seemed to want to know *why* we had come here, and how best to determine the purpose of this most human of worlds, the carpeted and granite-countered gentility of the midrange hotel. I mean, she seemed to want to understand it conceptually.

What are we to do here? I see there are other dogs. Will I be kept on a leash? You haven't told me if I am allowed to smell these other dogs' butts and then mount the ones I like . . . ? Did anyone leave some food in any of these corners? I think I need to check them out—yes, all of them. There do seem to be a lot, I agree. Wait, you're not going to leave me? Good. Then let me leave you. Eee; you've got me on a leash and I can't get to where I want to go but I'm not entirely sure where I want to go, maybe here? Or there? Whoa! There sure are a lot of different kinds of stimuli here. I can't investigate them all at once. I need to, though. Oh. God. It's all too much. I think I feel a scream coming on.

This was Nelly's general approach to the world: who, what, why, where; who, what, why, where, were the horses of a merry-go-round spinning in her little head, quicker and quicker. When she reached meltdown, because answers were not forthcoming *immediately*, she raised her head and shrieked. It was always quite a moment. People instinctively flinched; some covered their ears.

I had brought her here in part to see if I could teach her how to accept novelty with good grace. Self-control. Maybe I could take lessons in how to impart mindfulness to dogs.

But as always she reminded me, not so gently, she possessed her own agenda. She was made of her own minerals, just as ancient as those that made me. And she decided, midway through a long speech full of juicy maxims by Karen Pryor and her handpicked teachers, each exceptional in his or her field, to become scared of the sound of applause amplified through the speaker's mic. And there was a lot of applause happening. Pages of my little ClickerExpo notebook ("Training with the Stars!") flipped past as I hastily scrawled one note after another. Almost everything had an aphoristic force. Almost everything amazed. But I could tell Nelly was working up to a scream.

I was failing in my effort to create a dog as calm as those all around us, happy to snooze at the feet of their people so they could give all their attention to the country's best minds in animal behavior, onstage before us. Not that every one of these dogs was never visited by malevolent spirits, touched by black urges. A significant number of these people, I knew, had been driven to positive reinforcement by the necessity of love: their dogs had first insinuated themselves into the heart, then showed that they could not live in the community of others. Some were what used to be called "fear biters"; others were resource guarders who bared teeth (or worse) whenever another dog or person got close to anything that represented a valued possession: to a dog this can be a food bowl, the person who fills that food bowl, a beloved toy, or the dirty dishes in the dishwasher. This last I know from personal experience; woe to the visiting dog who dares to walk past Nelly's dishwasher. For these dire behavioral proclivities, traditional compulsion training has no remedy. It leads, in many cases, to a worsening of symptoms. And that leads, in many cases, to the death of the dog. Only scientific training's force-free counterconditioning procedures, confidence building, and strategy of teaching alternative behaviors can manage these lethal anxieties. To the person who loved a disturbed dog, what was being taught in the conference rooms of the Hyatt Regency Newport, Rhode Island, at ClickerExpo in 2006 represented the last hope.

Whatever I was now doing, with my beginner's skills (a little learning is a dangerous thing), was instead ratcheting Nelly up, as she became more and more frantic to discern what I wanted and how she could get *more treats more quickly or maybe not that maybe I just need to get out of here or perhaps I should stay here and explode I am just not sure.* I was trying to reinforce every split second of silence she offered, even if it came from a nervous yawn between incipient whines. This was clearly not the right approach, and I did not know if I was truly reinforcing what I was trying to reinforce, or if my rate of reinforcement was wrong, or if my timing was off. Or all three, plus other things I did not understand yet. (The next day in a so-called Learning Lab, a clinic where we worked with our dogs under the eyes of the all-star faculty, my retarded timing would be commented on by none other than Jesús Rosales-Ruiz, associate professor in the Department of Behavior Analysis at the University of North Texas. I was like a kindergartner whose substitute teacher happened to be a particle physicist: Rosales-Ruiz's "areas of interest" according to his bio "include antecedent control of behavior, generalization, behavioral cusps, fluency-based teaching, treatment of autism, teaching of academic behavior, animal training, and rule- and contingency-shaped behavior.")

I was flipping page after page in my ClickerExpo notebook as consecutive flashes of intellectual light incited me to write so fast my hand hurt. I had not been so excited since Anthropology 101. These constitute most of my notes before I finally had to lead Nelly from the room:

*"Talking, yelling, pleading, don't change behavior—*only consequences do.*"*

"These are laws like the laws of gravity: they are there whether you want them to be or not."

"Training is controlling consequences to change probabilities of future behaviors" (K. Sdao: each word here v. impt.).

"We think dolphins are smart because *they're all clicker trained— no one has ever punished them."*

(But "Many dogs trump dolphins.")

*"The ink coming out of your pen right now reinforces the behavior of note-taking—if it didn't, you would stop—but in itself it is not real pleasurable. It is therefore a conditioned reinforcer, not a primary reinforcer [food, sex, water, sleep]."**

"Pain can be a reinforcer [!] if it has been in the past paired with a primary reinforcer."

"Mistiming of the click and/or the reinforcer is actually punishing to the dog."

"It is not a sentimental foible to train this way, without correction; there is mechanical proof it is the best way."

The trainer becomes *"a road map to hot dogs"*: this is important biological information for the subject because it is not just about this hot dog, but the rest of the hot dogs, for the rest of life.

It is *"more grownup"* to do this type of training, since it drives toward developing trust in your information.

---

* I am here at the educational point where I find it *interminably* fascinating that there even exist such things as primary and secondary reinforcers, never mind what they actually do. I am even more amazed that people have identified and named them. Then there is the yet more dumbfounding disjunction between the almost bored calm with which they are being described from the stage and the electric charge they trigger in me. I am discovering a new galaxy, which practically collapses me but of course has no effect on the stars.

"Training is a two-way street—we get reinforced by receiving what we want, they get reinforced by what they want."

Clicker-training programs in prison give prisoners a nonaversive way to deal with people. (Once you learn how to reinforce, you can't unlearn it.)

Saw one woman whose cue for her dog (pit mix) to lie down was closing her eyes briefly; the dog had quick latency. He dropped like lead.

General Observations. 1. People love to instruct beginners. (Reinforces sense of self-worth!) 2. Instructors afraid of being ambushed [by worshipful acolytes in the lobby or hotel bar who have to tell them personal stories of how their dog/their own lost selves were saved by the video/seminar/book of the teaching trainer]. 3. 90% women here. 4. Timing is everything.

⋆ ⋆ ⋆

THE DOOR closed softly. As I walked away, the sound of applause grew ever more distant. In one of the wide hallways leading from the conference room, some people—more specifically, some women, per my notation—were lolling about, experimenting with their avidly fascinated dogs. Bits of hot dog were in the offing, that's why. These animals looked like they might belong to some sort of . . . pack. Several of them wore red kerchiefs with some printing on them; others sported what I would have sworn were badge sashes, but red. I had had a green one myself, when I was a Girl Scout. My back rode down a wall as I took a seat on the floor an observant distance away. Now Nelly was simply looking around nervously, instead of planning to bolt. Maybe she had retreated along with me to just this side of reactive, able to think and learn; I had been reading about the brain's circuitry and knew it was no use trying to reach her when she was overtaken by fear. She had no access to the part of her brain that could process information.

As for me, I was feeling defeated, looking failure in the eyes as it skulked, famished, toward me. I wondered if I would even be able to go to any of the other lectures I had chosen for my schedule: these were foundation classes that were prerequisites for the Learning Labs I hoped would give me some practical answers to the questions that Nelly shoveled my way by the pound. The talks also promised to be on some of the most fascinating subjects; I could think of nothing in life I wanted at this moment more than to hear the eminent Karen Pryor hold forth on shaping ("Catching, Building, and Repairing the Behavior") and the language of cues, including an introduction to the weird phenomenon of behavior chains. Not to mention the passionate and brilliant speaker I had just gotten a taste of, Kathy Sdao; she had a master's in experimental psychology, had worked for the Navy in its dolphin program, had once trained a 3,400-pound antisocial walrus in a zoo and made him like it. She was as interesting on the subject of ethics as she was on mechanics. Both seemed on the verge of coming together in my head this weekend; the instant I walked into the hotel, I felt more intellectually alive than I had in years. Something soaked in gasoline was yearning for the match. I wanted the big blaze. But I had Nelly, afraid, instead.

Having spent a few years attempting rudimentary clicker training with two dogs, advancing bit by bit into reading, listening in on listservs, and conversing extensively with friends both online and in real time, I now felt exactly as I did when I started to write a book: about to drown. After swimming happily for some time, as soon as the shore came into sight, suddenly I got breathless. The more I wrote, the more I realized I had yet to say. The finish line pulled away faster than I could advance on it. Despair was always the result when I came upon a "good idea" for study; it ended up way too good. Here I was, taking on the implications of poor old Skinner's taking on of implications.

But now it felt a little more life-or-death-ish: it was not just intellectually painful; the impasse meant I was unable to figure out how to train my dog to live in the society of humans. The more I learned, the harder it was to put it into practice: everything was connecting at an alarming rate. A united theory of everything seemed within reach, and so did the inability to teach my crazy dog the simplest things.

I watched as a busboy left the dining room at the end of the hall and positioned a cart a dozen steps away. Then he left. Ergo, a cart full of desserts, unattended.

The next thing I knew, I had locked eyes with one of the women whose dogs wore a red neckerchief. "Cheesecake, or strawberry pie?" she asked, holding out two plates.

More than anything at that moment—more even than dessert—I wanted someone to talk to. Someone sensible. Who better than a member of Dog Scouts of America?

If they didn't exist, someone would have had to invent them: the goal of the organization, with thirty-eight troops in twenty-two states, as well as in Canada and Japan, is to improve dogs' lives through education and training—and to help others. Service is big in the Dog Scouts. So, of course, is camp. There's swimming and crafts. (One of the 60 badges that can be earned—by the dogs themselves—is for painting. Yes, painting: a clicker-trained behavior attained through shaping.)

The woman had certainly done a service to me, and not only in delivering pie. I was in a moment of doubt, the kind that sorely tests one. Dog ownership did that to me like few things in life before or since, including motherhood; on a regular schedule it seemed to cut down to the bone of who I was, in the form of how I handled adversity. This could manifest in being made to stand helpless and alone in a field thirty minutes from home as the freezing night descended while my dog was in her fourth hour of chasing rabbits through an impenetrable briar patch (I was not sure who would drop dead first, me from worried frustration or her from exhaustion and a pelt full of prickers). Or it could arrive as a conceptual and practical conundrum that consumed itself like the Ouroboros: the technology of this training that had at first seemed so simple was getting more, not less, complex the more I tried to practice it. The questions that daily occurred as I tried to follow the first rule—"Set your dog up for success!"; it sounded like one of those Sunday supplement ads that promise you can make $100,000 a year in your free time— ended up starting conversations with interlocutors who expended thousands of words in explanation. When I tried to put the extensive, commonsense, stunningly smart plans into action, something just wasn't right. And five new questions would spring up where one had been before.

This kindly woman, who told me she had joined the scouts in 2000, five years after its founding, becoming one of its biggest boosters, did the equivalent of "there, there" with a soothing pat on the shoulder. She, like so many others here who had come for answers to similar bedeviling problems, had "lucked" into troubled dogs. She felt it was luck, that is, because an easy dog might never have required her to search for a way to reach an otherwise unreachable animal. And finally she wouldn't be here, sitting in the hallway of the Hyatt, helping to change the mood of one unhappy dog owner.

She suggested I sit outside the conference rooms, where I could still hear the presenters but might be far enough away to bring Nelly under the threshold of her fear. The idea of working "under threshold" was big in applied behavior analysis: first you had to be able to recognize the signs of stress, not always plain since dogs' physical vocabulary needs to be studied like any foreign language, and then you inserted enough distance from its source for the animal to be able to think again. The reason fear closes access to the processing parts of the brain is that the reactive amygdala hogs the bandwidth. So often we demand things of our dogs when they are not neurologically capable of doing them, and then brand them "stubborn" when they don't comply; the next step is "showing" them. It's like being spanked because you couldn't complete the crossword puzzle at the same time you're trying to escape a burning building. You physically can't. The technique of "flooding"—of forcing a dog to tolerate the very thing he can't tolerate—is unsound behavior-modification practice. It's also cruel.

The obvious solution now for Nelly's fear of amplified noise— leave her crated in the hotel room—would not work for two reasons: Nelly shrieked nonstop for the first few minutes after I left her anywhere, and, um, I had never crate-trained her. Instead, channeling a Birkenstock-wearing proponent of attachment parenting, I had used our bed as a sort of crate. Knowing that dogs naturally resisted fouling their nests, I let Nelly curl up in sleep between our heads; when she stirred in the night with even a suggestion of a whine or an anxious yawn, I hustled her outdoors. She was completely housebroken in a couple of days. I halfheartedly tried to introduce her to a crate in the kitchen for other purposes, but my terrible inconsistency scotched the possibility of it ever succeeding. A too-lenient parent, I never pressed the issue again. I should have connected my tendency to inconsistency in all matters to my inability to produce the behavioral results I claimed to want with my dog.

Another trainer with whom I would later consult would intone: "You get the dog you need."

This oracular pronouncement would stop me cold. As is the general purpose of such. The truth hit me between the eyes before shattering into a hundred sharp pieces. It was true on so many levels I couldn't attempt to think about them all without going mad. Nelly would direct me to face the particular internal challenge that I most needed to address: the one that, but for her, I would choose to disregard. The one that dogged my heels and tripped me up for as long as I could remember.

Here, now, my new friend—so upstanding, so moral, the ideal expression of the Scout—reassured me we all had our battles to fight. Those at the expo whose dogs appeared perfectly at peace in every situation and whose grasp of training skills made them look like gold medalists in a particularly graceful but strange Olympic sport (a triathlon combining long-range darts, dancing en pointe, and Scrabble in a foreign tongue) had had their own dark nights of the soul, and continued to. Their perseverance was a matter of being unable to let fall the ones they loved most. In finding their way here—I mean both *here*, at an educational conference, and here, to a place of understanding of the patience and thought and, well, yes, paradigm shift it required to teach in a wholly new way—they had gone on a long and wild journey.

Along the way, some of them would do what was said to be impossible. I saw the impossible the next day walking down a hall in the Hyatt.

My eyes had to adjust. It was strange enough seeing multitudes of dogs in a place originally devoted to such pursuits as conversation, cocktails, and checking in—this was not Europe, and the reason dogs in restaurants and on trains were not familiar sights could only have to do with an American brand of fear, possibly concerning unknown diseases and corporate lawyers, if that's not redundant— but the four-legged creature I saw heading into a conference room simply wouldn't compute at first.

The tiny piebald horse walked at the side of a tall, mannish woman, her long hair held back by a barrette and her hand on the bend of a metal handle attached by harness to the animal. It was the kind of rig worn by seeing-eye dogs. Holy shoot. It was a seeing-eye horse. A little one. A mini miniature horse, its back coming to mid-thigh on the woman. They were going the same place I was.

Inside the room—white sheets unfurled over the carpeting, the reason probably obvious, with wood flooring laid over that—the woman and the small horse headed to the chairs lined up against the tall curtained windows. Onlookers. The woman sat, and the horse stood. Which amounted to the same thing.

The horse continued to stand, almost motionless. That was what was really weird about this scene: the fact that the equine digestive system is built to consume forage almost all the time, and to excrete it just as often. This Learning Lab, a beginner's clinic given by Karen Pryor on the process of chaining together cues, building compound behaviors by using achievement in one as a reward for the next, was a long class. Her ability to withstand biological need was quite an achievement. Or perhaps she was something close to what she appeared: unreal. With her impossible little feet no bigger than teacups and her forelock a mop-top in perpetual explosion over her eyes, she looked like nothing so much as what lies across every other four-poster bed in some 12½ million pink bedrooms. But she was not stuffed, and still she did not expel anything on the white-sheeted floor.

Karen Pryor introduced the auditors. The woman was Alexandra Kurland, a horse trainer who was at the expo teaching a clinic in "Zen Leash and Rein Handling" as well as an advanced-level lecture on something billed as "Teaching to Make Smart Choices in Ambiguous Situations."* The horse was Panda, one of the first min-

---

* In a post to a listserv called the Click That Teaches, a writer described some of the content of this talk, as she experienced Kurland giving a version of it at another ClickerExpo:

In it, Alex says that she exposed Panda [the miniature horse she had trained as a service

iature horses to be trained as a seeing-eye guide animal. She can ride in a car or plane or train, climb stairs, lead her owner to the mailbox or to locate a door handle, or navigate the grocery store. She has learned the preeminent twenty-first-century skill: patience. Kurland taught her how to wait. And sometimes wait to wait.

Each step—literally, for climbing is not in a horse's natural repertoire—had to be trained, and Kurland, one of the pioneers of clicker training for horses, animals for whom the method has proved especially and impressively beneficial, used a bridging stimulus and reinforcers at a high rate to attain these difficult behaviors. (One of traditional horsemanship's biggest canards is that you must

---

animal] to a variety of situations where Panda had to make choices once she was presented with a situation where a decision to go forward was not clear and another path had to be taken.

This is because service animals have to be trained to make decisions—to think for themselves. (The very thing resolutely denied to animals: the ability to be rational. That's supposed to be ours alone. Yet every day we are presented with abundant and easily accessed occasions to view animals doing exactly that; we encourage or require almost all of the animals who work for us to use this thought process and to exhibit self-control.)

In the children's book about the guide horse, her trainer, and the woman who uses her as eyes, *Panda: A Guide Horse for Ann*, by Rosanna Hansen (2005), the assistance animal's ability to judge risk is described as crucial. And, difficult as it might be for us to conceive, executed in the absence of self-interest. Take the case of the four-foot barrier, or tree with low-hanging branches: a guide dog or miniature horse can easily pass under them. But the person who is counting on them certainly can't. Even if the person urges them on, probably with a cue they know well, they must possess the wisdom to say *no*. As Hansen notes, there is a wonderful term for this skill:

"Panda, forward," Ann said, and gave her horse the forward hand signal. . . . If Panda had seen something dangerous when she watched the traffic, she would have refused to move when Ann told her to go forward. This skill is called "intelligent disobedience," and all guide animals need to learn it.

Come to think of it, this is what I most aspire to be: intelligently disobedient.

never hand-feed a horse. It only teaches them to bite or get pushy, and when a 2,000-pound animal pushes, you know it. I asked a horse trainer versed in operant conditioning about this, wondering what she could possibly say to a thousand years of accumulated wisdom on handling horses. "Sure, it teaches them to bite if you reward biting. The moment you give the treat is the moment you're rewarding—most people hand it over as soon as the horse starts mouthing or pushing. So the next time they push harder. But give the treat *only* when the horse is standing back, and I give you a money-back guarantee that horse will always, always be polite." It made perfect sense, the kind it seems almost impossible not to have been self-evident from the get-go.)

Clicker training has saved many a horse, in fact as well as manner of speaking: many a horse has been saved from violence. It used to be that a horse with a fear of loading onto a trailer—again, a far-from-natural behavior, entering a small, dark enclosed space—would face only difficult outcomes: force, fear, or pain. Clicker training can yield a quick and permanent turnaround in even dramatic cases of trailer refusal, just as well as in other behavioral problems that have serious repercussions for any potentially dangerous animal.

The very oddness of what I saw, that little horse endlessly patient in the climate-controlled confines of a carpeted hotel conference room, seemed as good a proof as any that clicker training was responsible for miracles. She was one of nature's impossibilities, packaged in huggable size.

I found that specialization offered some hope for us at ClickerExpo: if I went to one of the smaller presentations, where there was not apt to be a sound system to amplify the dreaded applause, Nelly was reasonably fine. She was more than fine in the Learning Labs, with their breakneck pace of hot dog delivery. The wisdom around here was that learning new tasks plus doing so in a new environment filled with distractions (normally you'd choose the most ho-hum familiarity for initial training, adding distractions in stages until fully proofed to the ultimate) required the highest-value treats possible. And the individual dog, as always, chose from the menu: for the very few who were utterly cold to edible reinforcers, there were tug toys for rewards, but it is the rare dog who turns up a nose at hot dogs. That's what I had in the newly purchased "bait bag" clipped open on my waistband to ensure I could provide the quickest delivery possible: a slimy mass of chopped hot dogs, mixed together with tiny cheese cubes for variety.* We would

---

* The element of surprise, and variety, is always an asset to training, as in life generally. It keeps a dog guessing, for one thing. Just as you would be a lot more eager to work for a big paycheck than for a dime, so is your dog: canned chicken—for many dogs the highest-value treat around, although check with yours—can help with focus in the face of distractions. Having a dog who is a foodie certainly makes training easier—it's a no-brainer for the human. Nelly, for instance, is amenable to just about everything she can digest (and many things she can't). But certain items definitely make her step more lively: Vienna sausage, freeze-dried liver, lamb roll, and cheese. Any of these, cubed, stored in a baggie with a handful of kibble, allows the latter to absorb the smell of something a little better.

And now for an interjection prompted by the word "variety" in conjunction with the topic of food: *Hello, people!* Do your dogs a favor. Imagine the entirety of your life, and then imagine having only a single food for breakfast, lunch, and dinner every day of it. Probably best, so long as we're imagining, that it be something like Cheerios with skim milk. Fifty-five thousand bowls in a row.

Why do we make our dogs live without variety—and then censure them when they express interest in something so obviously more tasty than processed kibble? "People food" is a fictional construct, so the idea that dogs are "not supposed" to eat it is impossible for them to conceive.

Now I have to make an interjection in my interjection, on the subject of variety in general. Our dogs are made to live, for the most part, sterile and uninteresting lives. They walk around the same block every day, as if their only need is to eliminate waste. As if they too don't need to socialize, to run, to exercise their minds in learning new things, seeing new places. Because they are in essence our captives—imagine, too, being tied by the neck to another being every minute you're not indoors—it is incumbent on us to provide them as much variety in activity as possible. Let your dogs run

be encouraged to work fast, with a high rate of reinforcement, since as soon as they understand how this whole positive-reinforcement thing works, dogs can't learn fast enough.

In a Learning Lab called "On Target!" we were introduced to a versatile technique called targeting, which has so many applications no one has yet come to the end of them. Targeting is what enables zookeepers to modify behavior in animals who are always behind the bars of a cage; it is used to teach agility dogs precisely where the contact point is on a piece of equipment; it is how service animals are taught to bump a light switch with nose or paw. And a target can be almost anything: a plastic lid, a Post-it note, the end of a stick, or a collapsible antenna that can travel in your pocket.

It took Nelly a few seconds to get it. That's because we were told to dab some *eau de chien chaud* (essence of hot dog) onto the end of our target sticks; as soon as Nelly went to sniff it, which took, oh, a sliver of a second, she got a "click" followed by a treat. This caused a look of mild surprise that didn't last long. She already knew what the clicking business was about, and it was good all around. Do this, get that. She only had to figure out what "this" was. I was told to wait until she had run through the possibilities: Did I get that click for sitting? No? For looking up? No? For starting to get antsy and ready to let out a scream of frustration? No? How about for putting my nose near that thing? *Click*.

---

and play—and I'm not talking about running with you. Jogging to burn calories is not a dog activity. Running with other dogs, chasing balls, and stopping to smell things when they want to, which is often, are dog activities. One more thing, while I'm on the soapbox: buy some enrichment games for your dog when you leave him alone, such as a stuffed Kong; even a knucklebone to chew. Would you be fine for ten hours alone without something to do? Your dog isn't either. And just because he *can* hold it that long doesn't mean it's comfortable.

In a matter of seconds she was reliably running back—we were told to toss the treats in different directions onto the ground nearby, so our dogs were forced to break position, then come back in order to do it again. This way they learned solidly the act that was desired: *going to touch the end of the stick*, not sitting in one place where a stick happened to be in the neighborhood. In a few trials, she was flying back to bump the end of the stick ever more forcefully with her nose. That's my Nelly! As soon as it was abundantly clear she knew what was wanted, I was to add the cue: say the word I wanted to associate with the action. It could be anything, of course; it was possible to get very silly with cues. At the moment, I was feeling as tense as a student before midterms. The word I chose was, imaginatively, "touch." The plan was that henceforth she would *only* touch upon receiving the cue (and it became my job to see it through, by reinforcing only the touch that was cued and no other).

There was something particularly ecstatic in Nelly's response to targeting—as if she had just learned she possessed a sixth sense. Maybe a seventh. Her world had enlarged. Mine had, certainly: The uses of targeting could change a lot of things for the better. If Nelly could be instructed to go to target—a keen way to move a dog nearly anywhere you wanted, including away from you as in championship obedience, or by your side in a crisp heel, or focusing attention on your face, since that is a form of targeting as well—I could teach her to "go to bed," or lie down on a mat in another room. I could think of a dozen circumstances in which lying down elsewhere would be incompatible with an annoying behavior, and all of them included screeching and whining. In the hotel conference room I saw the future: Nelly would be more than happy to do her part. She would never have to be forced to do any of these humanly useful things, but they would each become a variation on one of the funnest games she knew. Just so long as I was willing to do the work, that is. I was human, after all, and sometimes the wish for the easy solution hung like the golden ring on the carousel. Grab it, and all would be well. This was not good karma. Desire for the immediate reward, at least in the teaching process, often cut the ethical corner. Punishments, ironically, were immediately rewarding. Just not to the dog.

I didn't think it was possible to have my mind expanded any more than it already had been, and then my preconceptions were blown up yet again. In the same hour-and-a-half class.

We were introduced to the work of David Premack, professor emeritus of psychology at the University of Pennsylvania. His pioneering experiments with language and the great apes were published in 1983 in *The Mind of an Ape*. I noted it down for future reading. But it was the results of a 1962 experiment published in the journal *Science*, one of those papers with a title you couldn't get to the end of without a yawn ("Reversibility of the Reinforcement Relation"), that made me get down on my knees in the church of science and say amen. Premack had discovered that what is rewarding is fluid. It is relative to what else is rewarding, too, which is both hierarchical and changeable. His lab rats would drink water they didn't particularly need in order to get something they wanted even more—a run on an exercise wheel. When they were genuinely thirsty, however, they would run even when they didn't want to in order to get the water they craved. This finding, that access to a high-probability behavior reinforces a low-probability behavior, became known as the Premack Principle. Apart from the fascinating view on our behavior it offers—one not lost on countless mothers through history, who have told recalcitrant vegetable eaters that if they have their peas they will get some dessert—it can be one of the most powerful tools for training a dog. Suddenly all those things that presented themselves as distractions, the squirrel demanding to be chased, the other dog that needs to be greeted, could be offered up as a reward for an act we preferred: giving us their attention first, say, or the perfection of an Olympics-level down-stay. The highest-value reward yielded the most probable response. Sometimes there was no hot dog on earth that could compete with the absolute doggy desire to chase and hunt—and here was a way to employ those very urges in creating an alternate rock-solid behavior that could interrupt the same when it was a matter of life or death to do so. A sit-stay that could one day save Nelly's life, if she found herself on the other side of a busy road from me, could be built in the safety of our yard. She didn't need to know, even if she could care, that I would release her from that sit to chase that squirrel she'd been boring through with her laser beam eye for the past thirty seconds (*Hallelujah!* her little heart screams) only when I knew there was no chance of either of them getting hurt. It was no skin off my back—or the squirrel's. He was near a tree at the edge of the woods. She would run flat out as her every gene begged her to do, he would scamper to safety, and I would be that much closer to a perfectly reliable sit-stay. All hail Dr. Premack.

Nelly and I slept soundly, dreaming our relative dreams, that night. In a hotel bed, the both.

· · ·

SUNDAY'S LUNCH break offered another surface broken clean through, halves fallen away to reveal a fresh reality newborn and sparkling with dew. We crowded into the Rose Island Room and stood behind a knee-high tape demarcating the performance space. Enter Fly, a black-and-white border collie—the most intense, the most wolf-like, and to me the most heartbreaking of all dogs—and her owner, Attila Szkukalek. Together they are U.K. freestyle (or "dog dancing," for want of a better term) champions. Szkukalek is a Czech-born biochemist now living in England who came by Fly the way so many border collies find their callings: by proving unmanageable to their first owners. They manifest the concept of "driven." They are working dogs, not pets. Their natural herding instinct, which can show itself almost full-blown in the puppy, an almost frightening sight when they "clap," or suddenly drop to earth, or give the famous border collie eye, a stare that can burn holes in skin, is millimeters from outright rapaciousness.* Now Fly's urges had all been bent toward one end: a bond with her owner-trainer that transcended life and death.

There was no entrance into the next five minutes; it was enclosed, and not for us to understand. Something invisible connected the two while they danced first together and then apart, Fly backing, mirroring, leaping, crawling. What she gave was given. It had not been taken, nor could it be. The entire dance was nothing more than carefully built chains of behavior—broken into constituent parts, they were nothing more than that "mechanical skill" writ world-class—but in the finished product the seams were nowhere to be found.† No one would want to say so, but everyone felt the

---

* In *The Farmer's Dog*, 1960, author John Holmes writes, "The young dog herds, not so much because he wants to herd, as because he cannot help it any more than, when he was born, he could not help squirming around until he found where the milk came from." He goes on to describe the utterly astonishing fact that a "well-bred" sheepdog may, *with no instruction whatsoever,* "cast out" in a wide arc from the handler and run a half-circle outward, then behind a flock of sheep, instinctively to drive them toward the handler. (This represents the natural, and complex, prey drive of a social animal that harries quarry toward a hunting mate—in this case the human handler. It's all about the kill.)

† In an interview published on the Karen Pryor Clicker Training website, Szkukalek explained how he built Fly's routines:

> *With the combined use of targeting and shaping and a lot of patience. I observed that if I shortened the backward walk steps Fly occasionally lifted her feet higher. So I started shortening the steps with Fly in heel position, while maintaining the speed/rate of Fly's steps*

same certainty: we were in the presence of a song-length expression of love. Out of science had come pure emotion. So this was alchemy. One thing had been changed into another; we knew it was logically impossible. Yet here it was, gold. I looked around as Fly took a bow. Almost everyone was weeping.

In the end, it was this depth of relationship that had expressed all our hopes for clicker training, and why we had come to Clicker-Expo. We wanted, finally, to make the invisibility of our animal's experience visible to our eyes. This seemed the imperative of love. To get as close to inside as you can.

. . .

THIS THEN was the final frontier. We hoped, privately since it was full of hubris and possibly shame, to transcend our speechlessness. That rarely seems the human's problem, but in the face of love for another species, we suddenly realized it was the true one. We wanted to be "reaching the animal mind," as the title of Pryor's most recent book promises we might.

Here she states it even more baldly than before. Never threatening, but like it is.

> This wonderful technology does not depend on me being able to impress or dominate the wolf. Nor does it depend on making friends first, or on "having a good relationship." That's often a happy outcome, but it's not a requirement: the laws of reinforcement will get the job done.

---

by using the heel commands as beats. Since her energy could go backwards it went into the height and she sometimes lifted her feet high, which I captured by the click. This exercise is difficult for most dogs, since they have to build up the shoulder muscles. Therefore I practiced only short periods—20–30 seconds at most—twice a day to start with. So it took many weeks to teach Fly to do this on cue and in different positions.

Once you know how to build bridges, you can get across lots of different rivers.

We were there, we said, to improve skills. We held our clickers in our hands. We looked for the moment of recognition. We learned about learning, which takes place in the brain. And all along, something was happening in our hearts, or maybe our souls. Since they are the province of religion, it is why we wept.

It is also why we are gripped with the need to proselytize: once you have seen a great light, it feels downright churlish to keep its majesty all to yourself.

CHAPTER SIX

✧

Ask the animals, and they will teach you, or the
birds of the air, and they will tell you; or speak to
the earth, and it will teach you, or let the fish of
the sea inform you.

—BOOK OF JOB 12:7–8

In the darkened conference room, the screen was literally going wild. One of the world's most fearsome predators, the hyena, was visible behind a wire enclosure. Hyenas have teeth that can crush human bone, and have. Made bold in the night, they have sometimes been known to attack people who sleep outside their huts in the hot months. By day, they are quite shy of the equally fearsome predator who stands on two legs. Here was something that was about to contravene both axioms. And almost every other one I knew of, too.

A trainer approached the fence with a large hypodermic needle in her hand. She made a noise, and the hyena came close. He pointed his nose upward, the better to press his formidable neck against the wire. He pushed so hard his flesh protruded through the squares of the mesh; it looked very much like eagerness, or love. He wanted to experience the needle. It entered his jugular. The syringe slowly filled with his blood. He didn't move until after the spike was carefully pulled from its deep embrace. Then he swallowed a chunk of meat. The moment that would stay with me for years, kept fresh by astonishment, was over.

The lights came back up. Out of the dozens of seminars held at ClickerExpo, no minute was more incendiary to the dry tinder of thought than this one. The clip was meant to show one of the ways positive reinforcement had revolutionized animal welfare in the zoo setting, and a revolution it seemed, upending the established order. A captive wild animal had just voluntarily offered up his neck to be punctured. All the beasts who heretofore had to be roped into submission, sedated, or simply neglected until death and replaced—overnight, one body removed and another substituted, for as they all look the same to the public, it rarely knew—could now be taught almost any behavior to enable veterinary and husbandry procedures from blood draws to toothbrushing and willingly entering transportation devices or squeeze cages.

It had saved many a hippopotamus, who when deprived of the opportunity to range and thus wear down the toenails naturally would suffer ulcerations and infection. A hippopotamus is not easily wrangled against his will. Now his will itself, a far lighter thing, could be wrangled. It could be transformed into any shape desired, so long as it did not transgress physical or biological possibility. With an exchange of small bits of whatever the animal deems valuable, cooperative behaviors of all sorts could be taught; few animals do not regard food as desirable, including man, though sometimes he prefers the tokens that in the form of cash stand in for the ability to acquire food or perhaps speedboats or pretty wives or other signs of primate status. The brain is organized to learn in two directions—by way of the receipt of pleasure and its beneficial neurochemicals, or by way of something unpleasant and therefore to be avoided in future. It is theoretically possible to teach a hippo to stand still, each foot in turn placed on a stool for filing, by beating it—though not likely in reality. And certainly not easily or without risk to the teacher. This is because, as a teaching modality, punishment cannot give instruction on what action is desired. It only stops ongoing behavior. You'd have to beat the animal when it offered every option you *didn't* want. And well before that point, you would be the victim of a 4,000-pound beast acting in self-defense. The easy way out (for all) is treats and a target stick. Zookeepers took it. Their animals' lifespan took a leap.

So did well-being. That's a large subject, what makes an animal well. The short answer: being able to practice all that evolution fits a species to accomplish in order to survive. That is also the long answer. No matter how many papier-mâché trees in an exhibit (and the nomenclature of the zoo should be attended closely), the spectator is fooled in a way the animal on the other side of the fence can never be.* The environment in which the species evolved is the only one in which he can fully live. The entire board of directors of the zoo, the preeminent examples of their species, possessing portfolios packed with the equivalent of vast stores of nuts and berries, and emblems of their high rank aplenty in dress and BMW both, are still unable to conjure space. They are unable to order the construction of the unexpected, the hidden and found, the miles, the interlinked world of a million parts. Carnivores, whose every cell is directed to the hunt for prey, are not permitted to catch anything alive because doctrinaire animal rightists would kick up a fuss.† Car-

---

* In the zoo, we draw a frame around existence. In that way, it becomes ours, and diminished to possessible size. The animal's sole value is reduced to spectacle. What is truly experienced by the subject remains invisible.

† There is no one who holds faster to animal rights than I do; I am farther left than your average ecoterrorist (on paper, anyway). Rights are exactly that: They are not granted by anyone—they are already held by individuals by right of birth. We can

nivores whose hunt for prey would normally take them over wide, effectively unlimited, territory are cut off from the aspect of selfhood that defines their essence.

Gus the polar bear lived in New York's Central Park Zoo from 1988, when he was three, until his death in 2013. It was largely a life of frustration. (Unbearable, as it were.) In 1991, I wandered into the glass-paneled room where we had been given the opportunity to watch another being whose life had been sacrificed for the unappreciated privilege of looking, then looking away. This is the sum of the zoo experience. He swam from one side of his small pool, kicked off the side, and returned. Ad nauseam. Even without specific knowledge, the spectator—and to become one of these narrowly constrained constructs frustrated also one of the human's birthrights, that of full engagement with empathy—knew something was terribly wrong. A knowing spectator could name the problem: stereotypic behavior. It is one way the system attempts to cope with extreme frustration. Most of us are familiar with it. When anxious, we tap a foot. When confined, we pace. Carnivores are especially prone to compulsive repetitive actions, because they especially suffer from constraint. When covering their normal ranges, they often follow the same routes on schedule, hitting the highlights on a regular basis like a postman going his rounds. But deprived of their normal ranges (in the case of polar bears' zoo enclosures, likely to be *a million times smaller*), the animal urge to familiarity similarly condenses. This endless pacing or rocking or self-mutilation—"motor rituals," as they are known—is of a piece with all the wondrous variations of obsessive-

---

decide only to deny others their rights. Animals have all the same rights we do as sentient beings.

In the case of captive carnivores, the food we provide them in lieu of live prey must by default be factory-farmed carcasses. The animal-rights activists who prevent live feeding thus contribute to a far greater evil. But none of it makes any sense anyway.

compulsive disorder, morbidly fascinating to watch on reality TV. There's something horrifying in those towering hoards of outwardly inconsequential stuff, which obviously feel central to the people who can't stop amassing it. Like building a bulwark against attack. And indeed, it is: a defense against the burning torment of anxiety.

Watching Gus on his endless Möbius strip of a swim induced such anxiety in me I turned to leave. I felt a panic attack coming on. Some of the emotional mechanisms meant to accommodate faults in the system are imperfect; some solutions create other problems. Such is neurosis. We are not unflawed engines, we animals. We continue to run, but lopsidedly, when our pistons are broken, accompanied by a large grinding sound.

The newspapers laughed, calling him the Bipolar Bear, but no one of any account called for his release from what appeared to be a sort of hell.* Instead, and this is where I finally get to the point of this ride on a hobbyhorse, they implemented interventions that permitted Gus (and his companion Ida) to use the parts of their minds that had been forced to run without purpose. The enrichments they offered the bears were grounded in operant conditioning. It took the Central Park Zoo until 1994 to do so, a gap of many decades between the availability of the knowledge how to stimulate animal

---

* A study published in the journal *Nature* (October 2, 2003, 425, 473–474) by researchers Ros Clubb and Georgia Mason, of the Animal Behaviour Research Group, Department of Zoology, University of Oxford, presented their findings on the cause of these neurotic behaviors in captive wide-ranging carnivores: not primarily that they were prevented from hunting but rather that they were deprived of the ability to roam. Therefore, unless more space could be given in zoos to species such as Asian elephants and polar bears, the researchers' recommendation was that they no longer be held. The unfortunate fact is that it is exactly this sort of animal—the "cute," powerful, or amazing ones—that is most popular with visitors. Such a recommendation, even from the highest authority, is not likely ever to be taken. Animals are kept in zoos not for their welfare, but for that of the zoo.

minds through teaching, and a gap of six long years for Gus. His neurosis was by then entrenched, practiced from youth into adulthood. By that point it could probably only have been mitigated no matter what. The sole condition under which bears like him could avoid it entirely is through the offer of a more natural range. For them this amounts to between 50,000 and 350,000 square kilometers. Since New Jersey (not to mention Pennsylvania and Connecticut) has historically and resolutely defied any land grab by New York, this seemed unlikely.

Both Gus and Ida—the stereotypic behavior of the latter consisted of pacing on land while her partner took to the water—were finally granted the exercise of their natural instincts by finding food at unpredictable intervals or inside puzzle boxes and blocks of ice, which mimicked what their environment would ask of them. They were given toys, such as plastic barrels to throw and crush. They employed their brains when they were taught to target, as Nelly had learned at ClickerExpo: to touch nose or paw to a stick in return for edible reinforcers. This, too, provided welcome echoes of their wild habitat: nature's game is the opportunity to discover *what works.* There is no more powerful motive to learning, or survival, than seeking to fulfill essential needs. The well-played turn wins sustenance, safety, procreation. An error once is less apt to occur when the prize is so great. In fact, neurology is designed to embrace mistakes, since only through mistakes can we learn precisely what it takes to avoid them and thereby tighten our aim on what we want. I trust this is not just the rationalizing of a mother who has to tell her boy *something* when he has bruised himself from a fall either psychic or bone-jarring.*

---

* The cliché offered by parents to weeping children is apparently truer than we know: We learn from our mistakes. Our brains pay more attention for a longer period of time

The bears' stereotypies diminished but did not disappear; these were found to recur more strongly in times of stress.[13] The damage of captivity could be controlled, but never fully repealed.

One argument often used to condone keeping animals in zoos is that they are fed without having to work for food or risk hunger. A fine thing, yes? But one of the arguments against the welfare state for people, conversely, is that it promotes a dangerous passivity. Which then is true? In prison people are first and foremost deprived of a sense of purpose. Futility is the real punishment.

In all cases when we are called upon to decide what is right, the Golden Rule is a good place to begin, and end. There's a reason it is articulated in the tenets of every major religion. Its abnegation is the first sign of a civilization in decay. I have never been in jail, though there's always a first time for everything. I do, however, have a pen pal who has been behind bars for decades. His letters are filled, page after page, with an eloquent, and persistently hopeless, anguish. Restrict physical freedom, and you have voided life. Eliminate mental freedom—nothing to work on, or for—and you have done worse. The voided life becomes a living death that recurs on the minute, every minute.

It has dawned slowly and relatively late that ours is a conflicted relationship with the rest of the natural world. A long-awaited discussion on ethics is at least open, if not yet fully joined. A growing awareness that human rights must be defended continuously against the depredations of power has extended in some quarters to include the rights of other beings. The changing look of zoos, from the concrete boxes in the sad menageries of our childhoods to the green

---

to outcomes of mistaken prediction than correct ones. We absorb more information when we screw up. ("Predictive Learning, Prediction Errors, and Attention: Evidence from Event-Related Potentials and Eye Tracking," *Journal of Cognitive Neuroscience* 19, no. 5 [July 2007]).

and varied landscapes now familiar, reflects that awakening sense
of responsibility. With it has arisen newly sophisticated rationales
for the containment of animals: no more are zoos content to offer
up a tacit explanation that they exist because they can. Now their
purpose is understood as active in a larger good: to save species that
are threatened in the wild. (They are yet silent on the subject of why,
then, they also display a host of animals in no danger of disappearance.) The logic is not unimpeachable, however. The truth is that
the zoo does not hold species in its enclosures. It holds individuals.
Those are two different things. From the point of view of the individual, the act of preservation becomes one of incarceration.

Looked at through this scope, a large question is in the way of
the view. Why do *we* get to determine what price they will pay—
moreover for a concept ("species protection") that is beyond them? It
is certainly a concept beyond any individual's self-interest, and self-
interest is the little gadget installed by evolution in every living creature to ensure they stay that way. Alive.

(And why then try to save the species we almost eradicated in the
first place? In this case the right hand takes from the left, then gives
it back.)

Here is how I have long imagined it, anyway. A godlike creature
tells me: You are one of the last of your kind. We wish to preserve
your species. Perhaps we will give you someone, not of your choosing, of course, but don't be demanding, with whom you can procre-
ate. If we manage to reel back time and restore the ecosystem into
which you might be reintroduced to reestablish a population (let it
be the New York City of 1982! I silently pray), you or your lineage
can once again be free. Until then, you will have to live without family or friends, away from your home, inside this box. (The ceiling
will touch your head. You will never escape.) No music, art, dinner
parties, parades, trips to New Orleans, Christmas, books of poetry,

photography, mountain hikes. No Sunday morning rides. No phone calls, no cookbooks or garden plots or long roads or sunrise over the Grand Canyon. Only walls. Only pacing.

I'd reply: Death. Give me death.

Theft of liberty is universally perceived as an act of tyranny. We rise against it and call the revolt just. How then could it be any less a crime when perpetrated on species other than our own? I feel this logic in my head as something adamantine, something impossible to push through no matter from what angle. I think it is this that is behind the anecdote I am about to retail, in which several zoos circled their wagons. It seems they know their vulnerability intimately, instinctively.

* * *

ALMOST ALL accredited zoos in the Western world (though not private ones, of which there are too many in proof that in legal code commerce always trumps ethics) now extensively employ basic principles of operant conditioning to enrich, expand, and ease life in captivity. The fact that it works, abundantly, confirms to a logical mind that B. F. Skinner really did get it right.

The great improvement in quality of life for zoo animals brought by the widespread adoption of operant conditioning was something to be celebrated, and something I wished to see firsthand. So I approached the Bronx Zoo about a visit. After three months of emailing, as well as interventions by a board member and a former zookeeper, they firmly shut the door. I would not receive permission to witness the zoo behind the scenes. I approached another zoo, and then a third. The way was barred there, too.

I could not avoid the conclusion that this said something quite clear about the entire enterprise: They wanted to keep something

hidden. In their reluctance to let another speak, they spoke everything themselves.

I was to be left only with childhood memories of a trip to the
Bronx in a preenlightened age, when the keys to the zoo were literal
and candy-colored. Insert the trunk of the plastic elephant into the
keyhole in the metal box and it would start the tinny recorded voice
describing the life of the elephant who stood before you, a life he had
been brought here to forget. Funny how all I remember is those keys.
The shapes of animals, made by us.

Then I tried the National Zoo in Washington, D.C. It is a different animal, belonging to the citizens of the country. The welcome was immediate. Maybe it had to be. I would get to spend an
hour (which turned into three) with animal keeper Stacey Tabellario, chair of the Enrichment and Training Committee, and some
of her colleagues.

Trying to make nature where nature has been expunged is like
a puzzle for the trainers, just as they make puzzles for the animals,
to keep life fresh. This is one of the main occupations of legions
of young women—and that this is the case, with animal training
across all categories a predominately female occupation, points in my
view to our perhaps biologically ordained interest in tutelage—who
tend to animals behind bars. It can become so overwhelming for
trainers to come up with novel ideas for mental stimulation (Stacey
says it occupies much of her day) that some zoos outsource the task
to volunteer groups. They rely on the faithful to make the paper deer
that tigers will attack and rip to bits, piñatas and paper-wrapped
boxes, tubes stuffed with straw and bits of sweet potato and burlap
scarecrows hiding fruit, and the next day they will make more and
different ones. The puzzle balls that an animal must work to get
into, the cardboard tubes that must be figured out and dismantled,
are enrichments in the form of "functional naturalism": they don't

look like any food sources found in the wild, but they act as them in the most fundamental way, since for none of us is nutrition easy. Ask the field hand or ask the leopard: our minds were made to figure it out, and our bodies to do the work. Psychological well-being depends on the opportunity to continually engage both.

Khali, a thirteen-year-old, 225-pound sloth bear (*Melursus ursinus*), was indoors, where she was temporarily separated from others of her kind. It was a matter of personality and hormonal cycle. What in other circumstances—namely the forests of the Indian subcontinent—would have been worked out with tools of instinct provided by history and environment now had to be managed by human keepers. We had to be quiet as Stacey demonstrated for me the behaviors she had taught Khali, as in the next completely enclosed room another female sloth bear was denning—pregnant, the zoo fervently hoped.

Stacey moved close to the fence that separated us from Khali, who immediately closed the gap, curious about what was on offer. The appearance of Stacey herself acted as a conditioned reinforcer, her presence associated with good things. Although sloth bears are by nature somewhat aloof, preferring to be solitary or paired, this individual was oriented to attention. She greatly enjoyed having her teeth brushed, and she maneuvered herself up against the barrier so Stacey could gently scratch her back through the wires. "Open your mouth," the human said, with her hand mirroring the action she wished to impel, and Khali opened her mouth. "Give me your hand," and Khali offered what looked like a greeting; she would now agree to place her arm in a plastic sleeve where a blood draw could be accomplished. "Stand up," and up she went. Stacey had previously conditioned the sound of a whistle to the primary reinforcers of food or honey water; later she "faded" the use of whistle and replaced it as an event marker with attention or words. Now her "good" or "good girl"—it could easily have been anything, in any language—made it appear as though the animal knew exactly what she was saying, and found it meaningfully worthwhile. Skinner had suggested we respond similarly to language: that for us, too, the primary meaning of words is as bridging stimuli. In truth, it was almost impossible to view the scene and not think that Khali enjoyed being "good" and even had a concept for so being that cohered with our own, but I suspect that is because we are so enclosed within verbal experience we can rarely rise above it to observe it from any distance. We have a powerful bias toward the belief that words themselves have magical properties (a bias that is further reinforced by appearing to separate us from all other species, as we ardently wish). It is a tough call to see our own vocalizations as nothing more than markers, albeit ones so complexly nuanced it could take a world of time to locate the primary reinforcer back in their history.

Watching the mirroring dance of trainer and bear, I wonder how is it possible for anyone to believe animals don't speak. In the basic meaning of language, that is, as communication, the exchange of information that is *meaning full*. (True, as the philosopher John Gray writes in *The Silence of Animals*, "Only humans use words to construct a self-image and a story of their lives. But if other animals lack this interior monologue, it is not clear why this should put humans on a higher plane." It takes an energetic intellectual stretch to assume they do not engage in similar sense-making narratives. These might be composed of images, or maybe feelings; still, the individual composition of the sense-making apparatus is unrelated to rank. And while we're at it, what's with the human obsession with rank in the first place?) Words are symbolic forms into which information is poured. And information is a conveyance, bringing a promise or a threat of *material* consequence. This is what ties us each to each in relationship: the exchange of information that has real effect. Of the training she does, Stacey said, "This is my way of talking with the animals." Love can follow only from communicating, is impossible without it. There would be no other way to characterize what I saw before me: Khali and Stacey loved each other.

Indeed, it seems unimaginable to not love the funny, wooly sloth bear, if only on aesthetic grounds. They have a melancholic air, which invokes the desire to soothe in the primate manner. We want to hug. For some reason, we find animals with attributes like these to be . . . adorable. (It was hard to write that, but the only other option was "cute.") Their gestures, the way they lumber: I was guilty of a problematic response, since it was the very same that gave these types of endearing, charismatic animals prize berths at the zoo, whether they are a species that can be happy there or not. A zoo composed of snakes, lizards, and turtles, absent pandas, elephants, and leopards, is no zoo at all.

The work that the zookeeper had done with Khali resulted not only in her being amenable to husbandry (she now found nothing amiss in having her tail pushed around so people could determine when she was in estrus), but it kept her mind occupied as well. Ask any high school student after a day of college-placement exams whether or not mental work is physically tiring. A dog in training is little different from a seventeen-year-old or a sloth bear: in need of a nap.

Enrichment is of a piece with positive-reinforcement training done with clickers, whistles, or target sticks: faced with a perforated object in his cage, one that obviously hides food, a zoo animal essentially trains himself, according to the universal principle of learning. The animals puzzle out, from trial and error, from approach and retreat, how to get the reinforcers. Since thinking yields good stuff, thought itself is rewarded—and rewarding.

To the animals, the creatures ministering to them from the other side of the wires are not that much different from the plastic balls that, hit a certain way, eject pellets of feed. They just have to determine how, then act. Across the Western world, animals in cages have turned an army of young women into a lot of grape dispensers.

Looking at Khali's enclosure, it was difficult to tell the garbage from the enrichment tools. A blue paper shopping bag was hung on a branch of a faux tree. Just as I was about to ask what it was, Khali came over to swipe at it with her long claws, whereupon it tore and let a rain of sawdust and nuggets of food fall on her; her breakfast. Other contraptions, plastic balls with holes, also hid food. With one eye on the metaphoric clock, she moved methodically from object to object until all had yielded their treasure; she seemed less interested in eating the contents than she did in showing us how good she was at her job: Come on, keepers—you need to do a little better than *this*, eh? It didn't take long for the carefully contrived devices to be returned to their premanufactured state. No wonder Stacey had to spend so much of her day rigging up new inventions.

The rest of her time with Khali consisted of teaching, which is as much as to say, playing games. Bears are as playful as we are, it turns out, and Khali in particular liked the engagement, both mentally and socially stimulating. She loves the work and the attention. Alone, for a time, she will occupy herself with sections of firehose, strong enough to withstand her long claws, which in her home environment assist her in dismantling the cementlike material from which termite nests are built. Sloth bears are very partial to firehose. But Khali finds both work and attention calming; when sequestered, she found the disappearance of her human upsetting. So they angled a mirror in her cage in order for her to see other trainers walking by. The zoo, and especially those there who have come to know her as well as each denizen in particular, considers the psychological welfare of its animals deeply important. This represents a sea change from prevailing attitudes a few short decades ago. So many profound advances have been made in the zoo ethos that a fleeting thought occurs: If this is the case, perhaps an equal amount of progress is still to be realized. That captivity brings certain unhappiness to animals has now been understood to the extent that efforts to relieve it, if not prevent it wholly in the first place, are seen as imperative. (The day of that extreme will be the liberation at zoos everywhere: for now a dream but not a hope.) It is possible that in the future similar oversights will be discovered, then remedies devised. In fact, as one of Stacey's colleagues, animal keeper Mindy Babitz, put it, "There's been quite an evolution in awareness of animal needs since the seventies. It's still evolving. In fifty years, we'll look back and go, I can't believe we did that then!"

Babitz is sitting in an office with several other zookeepers, all of them apparently well trained in the behavior of attentive screen watching on evidence of the monitors in front of each. In turn, they are watched by an image of the bear in the next room, quietly tending to the fetus invisible inside her, by way of the denning cam trained on her isolated space.

Babitz relates the story of François the sloth bear, a sad case. All caregivers, including parents, can make mistakes that only later reveal themselves as permanently lasting. Philip Larkin famously said it: Your parents, um, mess you up; "They may not mean to, but they do." His poem "This Be the Verse" boils the twenty-four-volume collected works of Sigmund Freud down to four stanzas that stand as the ultimate truth on the sorrows of humanity. François's human parents realized their mistake later, at the same time they learned he may have had a propensity to obsessive-compulsive disorder (some of us do) that they inadvertently exacerbated. Babitz is unusually forthcoming in admitting it. She, too, very evidently loves the animals in her charge, as does her colleague Stacey. I sense it has led to an inadmissible wish that the animals they have come to know so intimately did not have to be here. They know they would be happiest back in the forest-border grasslands of India. But now that they're here, they're going to do their best to fill the deficits. If pure love has a definition, it is this: I will do everything in my power to make you happy. The beloved's happiness is molecularly inseparable from yours.

François, twenty-one years old, was paired with a female named Hana. They clearly bonded. Let's call it love, shall we? But because the humans had to intercede, this being in fact a human-created simulacrum of the bears' world, they had to control access to the full expression of that love. It is, nonpoetically, called SSP—a species survival plan, engineered with genetic diversity, not love, in mind. A Kodiak bear literally came between them. His enclosure was placed between theirs. When he died, they rotated in another bear, a sloth bear named Merlin. Now two males of the same species were in competition, and François fell into a terrible funk from which he never recovered. His stereotypes bloomed. He paced all day, wouldn't eat or drink. The activity that to his brain felt like a remedy for his trauma was going to destroy him, like an adolescent girl's anorexia. His coping method for a buried anguish was itself inducing anguish. The little gift packages of enrichments were left unopened. Finally there was nothing more to do: they moved him to a facility in Little Rock. This further freaked him out. As it might do to you, too, if you suddenly woke up and found yourself in Little Rock. When he returned to Washington, they finally conceded he needed a pharmaceutical intervention, the same one humans in the grip of OCD are often prescribed: Prozac. But with a familiar unfortunate side effect; he would desperately try to masturbate and couldn't.

François was then permitted special dispensations in an effort to throw a wrench in the works of his self-preserving habits, the ones that were simultaneously self-destructive. (Damn the wily brain that is not quite wily enough!) He was given the ability to choose whether he wanted to be indoors or out, and "howdy access" to females—not the full monty, as it were, but a certain contained closeness. It worked, although François will forever remain a fragile individual, which some of us can understand. Sometimes only the provision of free choice—that which the Western world considers a basic birthright—can circumvent a freefall into neurosis.

In practical, and less lofty, terms, choice also provides lessons our brains find it harder to forget. Seems like evidence that we were made always to learn from making choices, rather than being told. (Perhaps that is why I retained little from public school education, and why a preachy program like Drug Abuse Resistance Education, or D.A.R.E., is a miserable failure and waste of taxpayer money.) Say you want to teach your dog to sit quietly in front of the door when you open it to go for a walk, instead of knocking you over to get out first, jumping up and scratching the finish, or forcing you to wear earplugs against a volley of barks. Wait. Let the dog figure it out. He will, eventually. He'll try everything, and finally hit on Sit. That's the minute the door opens, and only then. It will take anywhere from one to three trials, max, and you've got the behavior. Commanding him to sit is a much longer road. And possibly not even then. Making the choice for himself lets him own his actions, and in one small way, his life.

The availability of choice, or a constructed semblance thereof, can be considered a baseline arbiter of happiness. Perhaps a Tibetan monk could find nirvana in prison, but the rest of us animals mainly find abject misery. This is why the mere sight of the National Zoo's brilliant solution for its orangutans, the world's first "Orangutan Transport System," or O Line, induces a sense of happy relief in the viewer. It is the opposite of the sick despair of so many visitors faced with visions like Gus the polar bear's desperate merry-go-round of neurosis. The arboreal orangs—natural brachiators—are able to choose if they wish to stay "home," in the Great Ape House, or visit the Think Tank, an exhibit 490 feet away that focuses on all aspects of animal cognition. There they can participate in activities that resemble those of their evolutionary betters filling café tables at any Starbucks around the world: using their fingers to hit spots on touch screens that give them a certain thrill. As they do, their faces exhibit the same combination of slack-mouthed addiction and thoughtful attentiveness of the privileged eight-year-old girl with an iPad. The orangutans can decide, in the way we can decide whether or not to stay home and putter in the kitchen or go out for a walk, if they wish to climb a 50-foot tower and swing on plastic-covered wires over the intervening zoo walkways and exhibits (prevented from detours to visit the tigers by wire "skirts" under the platforms armed with electrically charged surrounding grid collars that give a sharp little zap well before the point of injury) and come down in the Think Tank.

All of the orangs, by the way, except one—a female named Lucy, who for her own inscrutable reasons has never climbed the tower that leads to relative freedom—choose where to go. It is never to where they truly belong. But that place, in Indonesia and Malaysia, has been made perilous by man and arguably worse than any zoo, certainly one that routinely provides grapes proffered by loving young women who are interested in knowing what their captive relatives know.

. . .

INSIDE THE Great Ape House, a volunteer tells me about some investigations into metacognition ("What is it that I know?" or awareness of knowledge itself) done with lowland gorillas. The blue cup sometimes contained two grapes, sometimes none; the yellow cup always contained one. When the "sure thing," the yellow cup, was placed next to the risky choice—maybe two, but alas maybe none—the gorilla would sensibly choose the sure thing. This is an animal that would surely find a bank that offered free checking with interest. But when the risky choice sometimes offered *four* grapes— ah, then matters changed. The possibility of hitting the jackpot was too powerful to resist. Blue cup it was, then.

Nature provides the opportunity to hit the jackpot sometimes, too. This is why we are programmed to take risks. This is why we stand in long lines to buy Powerball tickets mainly when the jackpot has risen to irresistible (if statistically improbable) heights.

On the way out of the Great Ape House, I pause before a portrait wall picturing all its denizens. They look back at me, frozen. Each one is so vastly different from every other. This startles me momentarily. I feel as though I am looking at a school yearbook. Partial accounting of humanity though these are—all the high school yearbooks in recorded history might number in the hundreds of thousands, with hundreds of people in each of them staring out with the same slightly pained smile—they represent a certain knowledge: each one of us, incredible to contemplate, has never been repeated. Every blonde looks different from every other blonde. The series of secret thoughts they think in the night before sleep is utterly unique. Unique times 108 billion. Now here was the suggestion, irrefutable through the means of side-by-side portraits, that every gorilla is also very, very different from every other one. All thoughts, all features, reconfigured and never to be repeated. Through all history, back down to the beginning, inconceivable.

Just before leaving, my son stops to take a digital photo of an orangutan who has similarly stopped to look at him through the glass. Only when we get home do we look closely. The reflective membrane that separated us has in the picture borrowed a telling statement from over a door in the hallway behind. Across the fore-head of our kin now reads in mirror reverse EXIT ONLY.

* * *

WHEN ASKED what about positive reinforcement made it most useful in laying the groundwork of behavior acquisition—and once laid, increasingly effortless to build new behaviors upon, as *training itself* becomes a reinforcer, a bit of happy magic that will be revisited anon—Stacey replied, "I could do more overall, and do it quicker."*
I wanted to know if it was possible for any of these behaviors to have been taught any other way. "I *could* maybe do it with punishment," Stacey said, hesitantly, "but I wouldn't." Here I heard dislike, pow-ered by regard for these individuals. Every time a request yielded a positive outcome for the bear, "I put a deposit in my trust account with her. Asking her to go in the squeeze cage is a withdrawal from that account." This sounds a lot like justice, a philosophical construct that is an outgrowth of a natural consequence of under-standing the way organisms learn. "Now we have a basis for valu-ing cognitive ability; the practice is respectful," Stacey agrees. The National Zoo has been conducting the first test of relative cognitive ability ever done on sloth bears. Since September 2012, the three adult bears there have been playing a matching game. The aim is to see whether or not they will transfer the concept of matching a sample—*The sample is coconut, got it? Now here is coconut, and here is peanut: which one is the sample, Khali?*—to new pairs. This would demonstrate a level of intelligence we have so far not been able to attribute to bears.

---

* "Clicker is quicker" is one of the taglines of the methodology, and the impres-sive speed with which behavior can be taught using a bridging stimulus is on view everywhere the training is.

Then again, it begs a larger question about whether or not humans are intelligent enough to discern nonhuman intelligence. I mean this seriously. Only in relatively recent years have we thought to devise tests that are appropriate to the species being investigated rather than to our own; certainly sloth bears are smarter at being sloth bears than we could ever hope to be. (It is likely that termites would find us sooner than we would find them, and moreover we would be real failures at sucking them up with the impeccable table manners of the bear.) Primatologist Frans de Waal, writing in the *Wall Street Journal* in 2013, describes how scientists had decided that elephants lacked the ability to use tools, since they refused to pick up a stick to help them retrieve food that was out of reach. It was only when someone twigged the fact that the act of grasping something with his trunk caused an obstruction in the elephant's crucial olfactory sense was it apparent that the type of tool was at fault; asking an elephant to use a stick was like "sending a blindfolded child on an Easter egg hunt." When a different tool was offered—a box that could be kicked into position under a high branch on which food hung—the elephant rapidly put it to use.

(After this heartening news of so much progress beyond an anthropocentric approach to the rest of existence, in the same article some ground was lost when De Waal betrays an elementary, and common, misunderstanding of Skinner. He describes him as a Cartesian who believed animals were "soulless automatons." Behaviorists, De Waal goes on, thought that animals "might be capable of learning . . . but surely not of thinking and feeling." It is true that Skinner disavowed the existence of the soul—in man and animal alike—or specifically those mysteriously unlocatable "inner agents" that people often believe direct their actions. But thinking and feeling: never. He couldn't have terrified people with the suggestion that rats and people were fundamentally the same, otherwise. What

Skinner remained resolute about was that the *feeling* that some "little man" inside us caused us to act was quite separate from the *fact* that outer agents of reinforcement provably direct our actions. Contrary to De Waal's assertion, it was the *human* animal that Skinner believed could be fully described without recourse to the mythological "homunculi" to whom we attribute inner agency. That an eminent scientist like De Waal is ignorant of Skinner's ideas but pronounced upon them anyway—in a major news organ at that—is a perfect illustration of how pervasive misunderstanding of Skinner truly is. Far from being unusual, such examples are quotidian. My file folder of examples, drawn from accidental sampling of the general press over the course of only a few years, is full.)*

Creativity and problem-solving were, like use of tools, once considered solely the province of homo sapiens, and evidence of our superior intelligence. Both have now been observed in multiple species, and the list is expanding constantly. According to Tabellario, sloth bears have joined it. Or at least the one named Khali: She actively engages in conceptualizing. She tries to figure out the rules of the game—if the prize was located behind Door Number 1 the first time, let me try it again; oops, no; my new strategy will be to try Door Number 2; if that doesn't work, I need to try either Door Number 1 *or* Door Number 3—and appears to have gone through "a few phases of decision making." She also plays a game with her human called Create. When given the cue ("Create!"), she must offer

---

* Another one, from a momentary vacation to Googleworld, the all-inclusive resort that offers the weary writer all the procrastination she can eat: Hey, cool, an excerpt from a newly released book on dogs! It detailed some new findings about dog vocalizing, which is apparently more complex and variable than previously thought. One of the first comments under the piece read: "Finally puts the lie to that old behaviorism crap once and for all, as it should!" The research had no relation to behaviorism whatsoever.

a novel behavior, not given before in the training session, before she earns a reward. In order to do this, she must reflect. It could only be by a process of intelligent analysis that she could come up with something new, something she knows she has not already done.* This is the act of a being who is doing something not very different from the all-too-human who has forgotten the house keys on a dark night and stands in the rain cogitating about whether she could actually fit through the second-floor bathroom window.

In addition, Khali has learned a counterintuitive maneuver that is practiced by crows, believed by us to be superintelligent creatures: she will pull *down* on a string in order to *raise* a treat hung outside her cage until it is within reach. The dog who has figured out how to get to the enticement on the other side of her fence by moving in the other direction, finding the place where the fence ends because her benighted owner "thought" it was safe to fence only half the yard, is doing the same thing. Ask me how I know.

A group of cognitive scientists, neuropharmacologists, neurophysiologists, neuroanatomists, and computational neuroscientists meeting in Cambridge, England, in 2012 signed "The Cambridge Declaration on Consciousness," which states in part:

> *Convergent evidence indicates that non-human animals have the neuroanatomical, neurochemical, and neurophysiological sub-*

---

* Thanks to the burgeoning growth in the field of cognitive ethology, animals' creativity is being tested in all sorts of, yes, novel ways. Scientists are putting many species through their paces to see if they can solve complex problems (they can) and "make and revise inferences and decisions" (they can). This last is conveyed in a paper by Irene M. Pepperberg, best known as the researcher who had a thirty-year relationship with the African gray parrot Alex, whose verbal and cognitive skills earned him the dubious distinction of being called "smarter than the average U.S. president" by the delightfully wiseass *Guardian*.

strates of conscious states along with the capacity to exhibit inten-
tional behaviors. Consequently, the weight of evidence indicates that
humans are not unique in possessing the neurological substrates that
generate consciousness. Non-human animals, including all mam-
mals and birds, and many other creatures, including octopuses, also
possess these neurological substrates.

If one bear, in one zoo, has exhibited intentional behaviors, largely
because she has been given the opportunity to do so, it would be
lunacy (or at least not very smart) to presume that others—perhaps
all—are not similarly capable. And then it would be unethical,
unkind, and inhumane to continue to prohibit the exercise of a
natural ability.

Tabellario comments on the potential outcome of her work:

The ultimate goal of the study would be to prove that the bears
can recognize objects and communicate choice to their keepers (dur-
ing the tests the bears blow at the objects they're choosing—a very
natural behavior for a sloth bear!) [since they alternate blowing and
sucking to dislodge dirt and vacuum up food termites]. We hope to
use this to give the bears more choice and control in their daily man-
agement. For example we could give them a choice of enrichment
foods for the day and instead of us choosing, they would be able
to choose. The idea is to give them as much choice as possible. We
take away many choices from the animals when they are put under
human care and we are trying to find ways to give those choices
back to them, especially with a species as smart as we believe the
sloth bears to be.

This, too, sounds like love.

• • •

THE PHILOSOPHER of geography Yi-Fu Tuan writes about the construction of love in *Dominance and Affection: The Making of Pets* (1984): "[A]ffection itself is possible only in relationships of inequality." This sounds startling, impossible. And then you run over your relationships in your mind—children, crushes, teachers, parents, the friends you secretly wish you were like but daren't admit you envy— and darn if it isn't true, if the admission doesn't bother you too much. But an imbalance of power bears down with a deadly weight: "Contact with power often ends in death. What was once alive becomes inanimate matter. Thus trees turn into tables and chairs, animals into meat and leather."*

Yi-Fu describes the history of zoos, which were once the private holdings of nobility. "Potentates demonstrate their power by appearing to sustain a cosmos. One element of that cosmos is the menagerie." Often power paraded itself, as in ancient Greece, where ornate and seemingly endless processions of collected animals—every sort imaginable, including arboreal species in dismembered trees carried by slaves (themselves not on display, but they might as well have been)—could take all day.

The very structure of the zoo expresses the coaction of the pow-

---

* A professor of agriculture, Brian VanDelist, cheerfully recounted to a reporter all the inanimate matter the once-animate can become: "It takes 2,000 cows a year to keep the NFL in enough leather for one season." Sixty percent of the cow's body, the portion we don't eat, finds its way into lipstick, piano keys, asphalt, ball bearings, and chewing gum. The wool of sheep cleans up industrial spills. Pigs give us their skin for grafts, their insulin to diabetics, their heart valves for our own failing ones. Dry eyes? Artificial tears are well named: they are what we cry for the rooster whose comb gives us the means. "There is not an industry in the world that does not depend on agriculture," he says, pride obvious. The word "agriculture" functions here as a clever dissimulation.

erful and powerless. Upon entry, two classes are called into being: the spectator and the spectated. The wall between the two can be invisible even as it remains unbreachable, as it is for female persons in most cultures, whose freedom to exist unwatched or verbally unmolested has been appropriated. The gaze is a form of invasion, even ownership. (Critic John Berger, in *Ways of Seeing,* observed, "Men look at women. Women watch themselves being looked at.")

Or the wall is very real, as it must be for the wild animals collected from their homes and brought to relative immobility so they can be readily viewed by those powerful enough to enact the theft. To gaze presupposes a primary purpose of the existence of the viewed: to be looked at.

In a scathing essay titled "Zoos and the End of Nature," Steve Best, associate professor of philosophy at the University of Texas, El Paso, captures what might be called the dialectic of watching and watched, and what becomes of each in the process:

> *Zoos speak simultaneously about the animal objects they dominate, and the human dominating subjects. The abomination of zoos is a projection of the horror that haunts the human spirit, its utter revulsion from its own psychic roots and animalic origins. When we stare through the bars at confined animals, at the hirsute commodities imprisoned for entertainment value, we peer into the face of our own alienation. Simultaneously, we see our past sins and our future mortifications, as we ourselves decay with the death of nature. As we gaze upon our genetic brethren who never look back at us, we demean ourselves. The fact that—as insipid parents claim—their children "enjoy" the zoo is not an argument for it, but a disturbing indication of an early stage in the warping of a young mind. Apparently, Schadenfreude—the delight in the suffering of others—is good fun for the whole family.*

One might take exception at his tone (the frustrated cry of one who has looked into the face of infinite misery without being able to do much about it), but any attempt at refutation turns into a proof of the alienated finality of which he speaks. The inuring of small children to suffering—an empathy that is inborn but that can be and often is extinguished through systematic desensitization—might be seen as one of the functions of the zoo. They are preeminently entertainments for the young, and no childhood is complete without a visit, or as many as possible, to the zoo. When the first and only animals beyond pets or backyard squirrels are encountered in these living tableaux arranged for the ideal view, children learn quickly the function of animals: to provide us with something interesting to look at.

Thus looking does not promote respect, as zoo dogma has it; it teaches disregard. It is a neat lesson in the ways and means of becoming a proper colonialist. Researchers in the field of human-animal studies have found that the average time a zoogoer spends looking at any given exhibit is 99.31 seconds.*

We have the right to watch—and to do whatever it takes to enable a good look-see—those we consider less powerful, or in fact just "less." Those on equal footing wouldn't dare: to test the theory, provided you're a man, go to the nearest bar, stand before another man, and just stare.† Sociologist Erving Goffman, in 1963's *Behavior in Public Places,* noted how the status of the watcher can allow "one

---

* One's lifetime behind bars to provide another's minute and a half of amusement.

† We are not the only species to experience the direct stare as a challenge: bears, cats, and many other animals issue threats by way of the unblinking gaze. And dogs. It is so threatening to a dog that the "lookaway"—often fleeting, a flick of the eyes, but loud enough in their language to defuse even incipient aggression—is one of the most common canine appeasement gestures, of which dogs have a particularly rich vocabulary. A dog that doesn't blink, and especially one who goes very still at the same time, should be taken at his word.

person to stare openly and fixedly at others, gleaning what he can about them while frankly expressing on his face his response to what he sees—for example, the 'hate stare' that a Southern white sometimes gratuitously gives to Negroes walking past him."

It was not so long ago that it was socially permissible to display other humans, provided they were classed as essentially different: as animals. Human zoos became quite popular in the nineteenth century. P. T. Barnum exhibited—there's that word again—a black slave named Joice Heth in 1835, claiming she had nursed George Washington. In the human zoos of the great and civilized capitals of the western world, the display of differently colored people was often dressed up in scientific costume, including ethnographic explanations of where the types fitted in the Darwinian line (usually just above apes, and naturally a very safe distance from the whites who came to view them, nodding in interest). As major attractions at world fairs, the humans were placed in dioramas as if they were merely more lively upgrades to what one saw behind glass at the museum of natural history.

In 1906, a Mbuti Pygmy from Congo was put on display at the Bronx Zoo, where he sometimes inhabited the Monkey House. Ota Benga reportedly befriended an orangutan there, one presumes primarily due to the lack of other companionship. His face in a rare photo of him holding the primate—pinned doubly by the gaze of the photographer's eye and that of his lens—expresses such discomfort and disgust it is almost stomach-churning. An educational sign in the style of those for the zoo's other animals was posted for the viewer: it gave his provenance and the helpful information that he would be "Exhibited each afternoon during September." The Reverend James H. Gordon, superintendent of the Howard Colored Orphan Asylum in Brooklyn, protested, "We think we are worthy of being considered human beings, with souls." (Shades of Shylock:

"If you prick us, do we not bleed? If you tickle us, do we not laugh? If you poison us, do we not die?" The next in the logical progression for Shakespeare, at least in regard to the dispossessed human being though not yet for the animal, would not be expressed until a nationwide wave of race riots that began shortly after Ota Benga's captivity and built in intensity through the first half of the twentieth century: "And if you wrong us, shall we not revenge? If we are like you in the rest, we will resemble you in that.")

The *New York Times* rejoined:

> *It is absurd to make moan over the imagined humiliation and degradation Benga is suffering. The pygmies . . . are very low in the human scale, and the suggestion that Benga should be in a school instead of a cage ignores the high probability that school would be a place . . . from which he could draw no advantage whatever. The idea that men are all much alike except as they have had or lacked opportunities for getting an education out of books is now far out of date.*

Ota Benga was removed from the zoo, but his true freedom was never restored. Sent to Virginia to become Americanized, he yearned to return home. The outbreak of world war scotched the dream, and one March day in 1916, in the depths of despair, he aimed a gun at his heart and pulled the trigger.

. . .

JUST AS evolution drives changes in the organism toward the betterment of survival, so does ethical evolution toward the betterment of conscience—or so it sometimes seems. On the one hand, in less than a century, what was acceptable enough to be defended in the newspaper of record became morally insupportable. On the other, we may have only turned these destructive, imperialist impulses elsewhere. Genocide based on spins of propaganda, for instance toward entire countries peopled by those of foreign religion, looks increasingly possible; after all, in the time it has taken me to write this sentence, my own country has killed unnumbered children and other innocents, and at a drone's cool distance. Then there are all the other countries and other tribes doing the same to their chosen enemies.

Yet in some small corners, where change always begins, in some small fraction of the world's zoos, which have long been nothing more than prisons for animals who committed no crime except to have been born powerless, ethical progress is apace. It is B. F. Skinner's baby, this respect for the emotional needs of the animals we are not yet ready to yield fully to their own lives. That might be coming. It came too late for Ota Benga. But the Stacey Tabellarios and Mindy Babitzes of these enlightened zoos, in full possession of science and of the hearts it encourages to beat, are signs that hope may not be without warrant.

CHAPTER SEVEN

⋎

In one case, the corpses had joined with the furniture, slowly sinking into the fabric of the chairs. Some were found up the chimney, as if escape were a dream from which their waking actually was death. Over three hundred cats in one house, if one counts both the quick and the dead, of which there were 87 in the latter category. But who could know, at any moment, what was living and what was not?

In most cases of animal hoarding, the dead and dying coexist with the living, a spectrum of the beginning and the end stretching from one end of the experience to the other like a fatal rainbow. There is always filth, starvation, thirst, disease; the excrement is high enough to wade in and the ammonia vapor burns through skin. One dog crawls under the skeleton of the couch to die. How can he be noticed, when it has become impossible to count? More are born every day, while some disappear. There are two more desiccated bodies, unageable, already there.

How do people live like this? They do not, or at least not to their mind: they are in another place, one not alarming, not sadly sick. What is patently there is not there for them.

Our inborn capacity for denial may have originated as the primary shield against unendurable pain: *will it away*. But the very complexity of some of our most astounding abilities—the circuitry a compact tower of uncountable parts—means it easily comes untuned. In some people, a defense becomes a very grave offense.

Psychologists are only now starting to examine the phenomenon of animal hoarding, so they have yet to arrive at solid conclusions. The disorder—how pertinent the term!—shares most with the general outlines of obsessive-compulsivity. The person lives in incredible dirt and disarray, prisoner of possessions that somehow feel necessary to survival but that have an uncanny resemblance to trash. To him, everything seems just fine. The towering mess is not a problem, because it's not really there. One woman was busted for having 552 dogs on one small farm, and attempting (but naturally failing) to care for all of them. Was it possible for her truly to have known how many there were? If she could have numbered them, would she have known the scope of the problem and perhaps come to the conclusion that there was a problem in the first place? Not likely. None do, or can. Most of them claim to love, and to have saved, the animals they then go on to destroy.

Nelly spent her first day of life in a plastic kiddie pool in the basement of a Barbour County, West Virginia, animal shelter volunteer's house. The previous evening, her mother and another pregnant bitch had given birth in one of the many temporary wire pens set up in the woods outside the shelter, which had no room for so many dogs all at once. (*Nelly, babe of a wandering Mary who could find no room at the inn* . . .) At their place of rescue—a relative term, given the conditions from which they had been taken—they had been "packed in like sardines, [we] not paying any attention to sex, etc.," explained the volunteer. The newly born had to be taken to marginally better situations, like kiddie pools in a basement. The volunteer's house might have begun to look a lot like the hoarder's from which 69 dogs had finally been sprung, after waiting far too long for legal recourse. She had two litters of puppies (as well as a bunch of other dogs) to care for all of a sudden. Is it any wonder chaos happens?

Unimaginable as that scene was, all these border collie/Australian shepherd mixes, crossbred and crossbred again, came from a place of which the rescuer said, "You would have to see where they came from to believe it." She says by the time the county gave them permission to remove the dogs, several of the males had killed each other.

Nelly's father—at least I am convinced it is hers—stares at the camera in a picture. He looks just like her, except that his eyes seem to be spinning backward. It would appear he's just smoked crack. His name is Houdini, since he was apparently adept at climbing over tall fences in order to visit the ladies of the neighborhood, at least one of whom was now in a temporary pen on the shelter grounds. Eight feet was not a problem for Houdini. Later he'd head home and climb back in for dinner, as if nothing of much interest had happened in the meantime. If my suspicion is correct, he had his way with a bitch they named Cassie, a fearful thirty-five-pound border collie mix who was never socialized (hoarders don't have time for the niceties), but who was plenty fertile: she had nine puppies, the most the volunteer had seen. Before they could get Cassie (and another new mother named Blue, who had three pups in the pens the same day) to a safer place, "the other dogs were carrying off" her puppies without a protest from the terrified mother. "Two were so tiny I could hold them in my palm. Looked more like mice." The smallest died within four days.

There were too many dogs. Most of the time, there were too many dogs, and each of the volunteers that comprised Animal Friends of Barbour County was strapped to the limits. A 2007 newsletter from the nonprofit says the organization "is in desperate need of volunteers." Fifteen of them were caring for 70 dogs; if another hoarder should be called out, as was seemingly inevitable, another Nelly situation would occur: simply too many at once. The animals would be removed from fiery hell to an interim that was still quite hot. This would not have been a problem prior to 2001, when every few days the county pound had gathered up all unclaimed dogs (and virtually every cat that was unlucky enough to have passed through its doors) and pushed them into the gas chamber. It still sits outside the building, looking like a concrete beehive, its opposite in purpose. It is impossible to look at this inscrutable shape and—perhaps because of its eerie generality—not imagine in garish images exactly what went on in there. Ever since the organization was formed, its aim to make the pound into a no-kill shelter, a few volunteers had struggled to care for, then place, thousands of animals. In 2006 alone, they rescued 535 dogs and 250 cats. (Multiply that by over 3,100 counties, and you get how there come to be up to 8 million dogs and cats entering U.S. shelters every year.) The county provides no workers on weekends and holidays. Without the volunteers of Animal Friends, the dogs and cats inside would have been left without care.

In parts of America over which tenacious poverty holds seemingly permanent sway, especially some rural swaths so expansive it is strange how invisible they can be, homeless dogs roam the countryside. A few found themselves quite suddenly without owners when they were tossed onto the road from a car that barely slowed before hurrying on. Where many residents lack either money or incentive to spay and neuter their pets, a wild ecosystem of rampant procreation and just as richly spreading death forms. A place called Square One. I followed the trail of Nelly back through space and time, from north to south. A year after she had made her way to us on the underground railroad of breed rescue from West Virginia to Pennsylvania to New York, I reversed the drive. The first thing

I saw after crossing into Barbour County was a dog in the distance attempting to cross four lanes of divided highway. Up ahead a black figure feinted with the traffic. No one slowed. By the time I got there he was only a shadow on the retina.

The volunteer had reported two curious things about the population of canines rescued from the hoarder, and in particular Cassie's large litter: many of the dogs had the sharpest screaming voices she'd ever heard, and some of Nelly's littermates had the same crooked tail she did. The only idea she could offer was that with so many puppies mashed together in one womb, some of their tails got bent. It was not the first time it happened. In *King Lear*, Shakespeare describes a dog having a "trundle-tail."

After Mercy's death, my only comfort was the absorption of searching for her. Late at night I sat for hours haunting Petfinder, and in its hundreds of thumbnails I read the promise that her brown eyes would soon be looking at mine. Then I could simply go get her from wherever she had escaped to. I was certain that if only I continued looking, I would eventually find her.

When concerned family members sought to convince me that my belief that she still lived—I had only to search harder and harder, longer and longer without sleep—was a sure sign of insanity, not perseverance, my shame caused a slight change of course. I was now looking for a *new* border collie. One night I found her.

Breed rescue is conducted by equally unstable people, many of whom are no doubt also looking for a love departed obscenely soon. These dog lovers have spun great nationwide webs along which dogs are passed, person to person. For some, the call that a German shepherd needs transport to his new home half a country away will have them driving six hours to Maryland for a handoff in a Home Depot parking lot. There another person will be waiting to carry him onward. The halfway house on Nelly's northward route was that of a border collie rescuer in Scranton, Pennsylvania. We drove a couple of hours, with an umbrella and a half-baked plan.

I was determined, though subconsciously, that I would not leave Scranton without a dog. I know that now. Then, I imagined that I was mentally sound enough that I would carefully consider whether any of the dogs we met were "right" for us. To give the plan a gloss of sane consideration, I had triangulated from several dog temperament tests to arrive at a ten-point list of pop-quiz questions I needed any dog of mine (who would be entering a household with a young child and the prospect of visits from many of his unruly friends) to answer correctly. One was "What do you do when an umbrella is suddenly opened in your presence?" Of the three piebald puppies we met, two looked at me in shock. Only one stared down the umbrella to say, "Yeah? Then what?" She didn't give a shit. We brought her outside where she proceeded to investigate the grass and pay us no more mind. This was the one I then determined should be Mercy's successor. I knew enough to know that a frightened dog was a project dog, outcome uncertain. A lot of remedial counterconditioning—time that amounted to a second (or third) career—would be called for to make such a dog safe around children, of whom dogs are naturally suspicious. Children have a tendency to do things like hug; an arm over a dog's shoulder is a grave threat. They stare protractedly into a dog's eyes; ditto. They speak in high squeaky tones and move in jerky lurches. And so they get bitten in the face, conveniently presented at muzzle level. After the dogs have done due diligence with protest—the quiet lip lick (Please . . .), the quietly bared tooth (Let me repeat . . .), the low growl (I've asked twice now . . .)—the unheeded pleas are backed up with action. There is no such thing as a dog who won't bite; the only question is when. Different dogs, different whens. *It came out of the blue, we had no warning!*

Actually, warnings aplenty. They just weren't heard. (Poor dog. Poor child.)

We must give the dog the same allowance we would give ourselves, and so if you think about it, there is also no such a thing as the person who won't hit back, either. Backed into a corner, pummeled on the last day at the end of the world, even the staunch pacifist throws a punch. Every organism comes with an instinct for self-preservation. It either takes more or less provocation, but it can always be found.

With dogs, it's all about what they call bite threshold. Because I had a toddler, I had to find a dog whose threshold was as high as possible. (I also prefer friends whose punch threshold is high.) I had three items on my shopping list: a dog who didn't mind riding in a car, a dog who got along with other dogs, and a dog who was not fearful. The last was the kind I feared—one who lived temperamentally in a zone with no options. Teeth would be both first and last resort. Border collies already tended genetically to fear: a subsection of a wide study conducted at the University of California, San Francisco, into the genetic basis of phobia concentrated on border collies with an intense fear of noise. It can be severe—unto death. Dogs have been known to throw themselves out of windows. One dog I heard about, as soon as Fourth of July really got lit, launched himself into the Hudson River and didn't come out till Rhinecliff, a mile away.

My little test had been designed to assess confidence. Some of it is inborn, some is habituated through socialization and proper maternal influence before weaning—I had my doubts that Nelly was allowed to stay with her mother for the ideal eight weeks (significant behavioral problems are noted in dogs separated earlier than this, which used to be the usual practice)—but I just knew we stood a better chance of winning dangerous-dog roulette if our puppy presented as confident. This one did.

Nelly was placed on the backseat of the car. Test notwithstanding, I had no idea what I was getting into, for the second time. She was as small as a teacup. Yet somewhere in me was the certainty she would attain fifty pounds and full border-colliehood. She was white and black, whereas Mercy was black with white, but this was merely surface! I knew that!

She would go on to resist every attempt to make her into Mercy, physically and intellectually. She would stop skeletal growth at twenty pounds, though she did get chubbier when I continued to feed her rations for a much bigger dog until onlookers pointed out that she was not growing taller, only wider. I would occasionally look at her with an inner sigh: You're not terribly bright, are you? Compared to a canine Einstein like Mercy, no. She was as smart as she needed to be in order to be Nelly, though. She would, always and ever, be herself. She was, without trying, the Grand Canyon of life lessons.

When her Nellyness resolutely asserted itself—she would every day slip through the wide gauge of the wire fence (far too small for Mercy) between us and the psychotic neighbor's many allurements, including feeding stations for both deer and coyotes, as well as their own small dog and several cats—I started to wonder about her past. This was beginning to look like a thing, needing to know about the origins of whatever beast I was falling for, two-legged or four.* I emailed the volunteer in West Virginia, and made plans to visit. I wanted to meet Nelly's long-lost brother, the only one of her

---

* What in her character I could only explain as belonging to an infusion of genetic material from another breed—the terrifying tenaciousness of the terrier, say—and what in her looks other people attributed to something like Papillon (immediately and condescendingly dismissed by me) were both dispatched by the volunteer. There were

remaining seven siblings I could locate, most curious about how they would react to each other. Would it be a tearful yet joyous reunion? It turned out she and Dusty, who was now so grossly obese I could only imagine he was so overstuffed in his own skin he just wanted out, growled at each other while I sat uncomfortably in some strangers' kitchen, almost as eager to leave.

I wanted to follow Nelly's trail, back and back through time. I got only as far as a few months before. Pets that come out of rescue share something with history's vast immeasurable peasantry: official invisibility. Birthdates, like names, are fluid; many of our Ellis Island forebears lived their whole lives not knowing exactly when they were born or what they were named—two of our heaviest anchors. They are considered to signal—at least to us, the inordinately privileged—that we matter. We have *registered*.

She will have to remain forever mysterious, the creature that is to us (probably secretly) the vector of all love. Our dog. Where, oh where, did she come from? It is so frustrating: when it comes to something this elemental, all should be clear as a lens at Palomar. Love instills this itching desire to know. This minute with the beloved is not enough. Buddhism has nothing to say to biology; it's good with generalities, but it appears to reject the defining yearning for complete possession that is enfolded into the experience of romance. *Phthooey.*

I will never know much more about Nelly and her closely avoided fate, here in her homeland along the Tygart Valley River, on the Allegheny Plateau where the western Allegheny Mountains roll toward their end. Almost a quarter of the county's population lives below the poverty line. The passenger train stopped running in

---

no Jack Russells or Papillons anywhere in the vicinity of the hoarder's place. Nelly was fully herself: Houdini's daughter in both literal and literary terms.

1956. There is not a whole lot to do, a bit of coal mining and farming, the rest service jobs at minimum wage.

That a small handful of West Virginians, preeminent among them the woman who brought Cassie and Blue into her home because they needed her to (not because she had the ability at the moment), thought to save the throwaway dogs and cats of Barbour County is pretty much a miracle along the lines of divine images appearing on toast. How can I say I am horrified at the conditions these dogs sometimes endure at the homes of their kindly rescuers—the ones who have taken them from *much* worse? Nelly's mother had been living with a mass of parasite-infested dogs on a property hidden far off the road. Some were in a trailer, others in an abandoned house on the grounds, heatless, its windows broken. A couple of dogs called a derelict car home. Dogs everywhere. Filth everywhere.

Another dog this volunteer had rescued another time, she was telling me, had been chained to a tree in the woods without food or water. The cops found him, somehow, through one of those strokes of crazy luck, maybe only a day later when (*And then* . . .) it could have easily been a week later. What constructed the person who would do that? Condemn a dog to a slow death of thirst and starvation? What punishment to mete out to this animal?

Here I am in one small corner of the world, and it contains a whole universe of dog misery. Compound it a millionfold, and you approach the totality of suffering of "man's best friend." It is horrible stuff. The dog who gets hit on the highway and dies instantly is one lucky dog.

. . .

IT WAS part of Nelly's grand plan never to reveal what she was. A hunter, certainly, but then all dogs, being genetically virtually indistinguishable from the gray wolf, are hunters in the bone. In fact, their mitochondrial DNA sequence differs by only some 0.2 percent, which caused the American Society of Mammalogists and the Smithsonian Institution in 1993 to reclassify dogs (*Canis lupus familiaris*) as a subspecies of wolf (*Canis lupus*). But Nelly was especially tenacious as a hunter: more than once the only part she left one to grab was the final three inches of tail before she disappeared forever into a hole she was energetically excavating in search of some rodent or other. Usually this was directly under some massive stand of briars. I cursed colorfully as it cursed back, taking blood. Time lost all meaning to her as she hunted for hours, well past dark, past hunger and thirst and aloneness. (How many times I drove away from her, heart in throat, because I had to go pick up the child that to me was the only creature more important; I would talk to myself as I went, streaming justifications and hope and resignation, and when I returned, I would find her in the parking lot waiting, confused, anxious. Then I felt other emotions mixed, like incredulity, relief, anger, in equal measure toward myself and her.) It could be pointed out that I lost something, too: my mind, since I persisted in walking her off-leash several times a week along the edge of the cornfields by the river. Giving her the freedom to be herself, even though it came with head-spinning risk, seemed my half of the bargain: you will be mine to love, but I will give you a taste of who you are at heart. Run, Nelly, run.

The risk (in my head, if not always in reality) was mitigated by choosing to walk only in areas deemed far enough away from roads. Not that she never managed to pull off the impossible, easily overcoming human engineering without even trying, *so there*; with her hundred lives, she has managed to cross a hundred roads. Forbidden fruit is sweetest not only for you and me. . . . Unsettlingly often, Nelly would decide what was across a road so far distant I hadn't even known it was there was of greater importance than anything in the twelve square roadless miles I amusingly thought would satisfy her.

How it is that she is indisputably over there on the couch while I write this, splayed in late-night sleep and well into her tenth year, is a grand mystery.

It was an unfortunate piece of luck that the best walk closest to home—and to the two dog friends who shared my bad habits and thus became fast friends and the center of my society—was the cornfields. And cornfields are where the hedgerows between fields always become boisterous with briars and the rabbits that call them home. I have a photo of the closest of these close friends, Janet, who was kind (or ill advised) enough to offer to care for Nelly when I went away. She stands in the darkened cornfields holding my dog— or at least I think it is her, under all that wet, dirt-blackened fur— after an epic hunting expedition. My dog seemed fully capable of reenacting *The Odyssey* in full length at will. To Janet, anyway, this one night might well have lasted twenty years. During the time Nelly was gone, day became night, dinnertime came and went. Her caretaker was alternately terrified she was lying somewhere mortally hurt, perhaps in an ankle-hold trap, and livid to be made to undergo such fear and dark-night waiting in the cold. She should have long before been home sitting in front of the fire with a postprandial cocktail, her own dogs lying happy at her feet. (Her Labradoodle rescue, Willy, Nelly's paramour, was cut from the same cloth as his wee girlfriend—with whom he shared many NC-17 moments—but even naughty Willy only went AWOL during the day, for an hour or two when he disagreed that his walk was over.) In the picture, Janet makes an expressive gesture with the finger of one hand. She wrote a poem about that night, the first line of which goes, "We stood where you left us" and continues on with several "I hate you"s and an "I'm going to fucking kill you" with a stop at a plaintive "Are you hunting or the hunted?" But this is the poem all of us who live with dogs will finally write. Containing both scream and sigh.

It ends, "My good girl. We love you, Nelly. / Houdini's daughter." "Good," I wasn't so sure about.

Sometimes she was, of course (keeping me on a variable ratio schedule of reinforcement, so I never did end up in front of the grocery store with a sign begging FREE TO GOOD HOME). I was good a few times myself when Nelly was young, notably when, conscious of the few and minor problems Mercy had manifested because of my pre-Polly ignorance, I set about forestalling their like in Nelly. Of course, my first dog was so utterly *perfect* in every appreciable way, I would have her back under any circumstances. In memory she could do no wrong, in reality, eh . . . I was having the prickly sensation that perhaps Nelly was, in one signal characteristic, the reincarnation of Mercy. Where anything edible was concerned—and she would be the judge of that—she would stop at nothing. For all of my ten years with Mercy, one sensation prevailed: that of the sinking feeling upon leaving the kitchen. I *never* learned before I left the room to remember anything on the counter was fair game; I only recalled this salient fact when I was fifteen paces away. By the time I gasped and ran back, whatever it was—lunch, dinner, cookie dough—was already history. Why did I expend the energy to run back, again and again? That's the definition of unteachable. The sound of her front paws hitting the floor as I skidded around the corner, coupled with the sight of her licking her lips, a "What's the problem? I handled it already" look in her eyes, is burned into me. Only because Nelly is too short to reach a counter was I released from another decade of *Oh, shit!* Then again, she learned fairly quickly how to use a chair to further her aims: I have had my share of expletive-laden moments upon realizing I had neglected to push the kitchen chairs fully under the table. I would race back to find an animal looking much like a miniature Holstein, standing on top of the dining table and grazing from the plates.

I think dogs must experience a rush exactly like that of the criminal attorney who wins the dismissal, the journalist who gets the Pulitzer call. It's not easy to take down a whole dinner party when you're a twenty-pound mixed breed. Especially one who was considered so worthless that if she had been born only a few years earlier she would not have lived out her first year before ending up in a mass grave. Or wherever they put the bodies of the millions of pets put to death every year.

After the score, you see it in their eyes. It's a dopamine dump. It's what we all live for, probably. Nothing better. Nothing.

Nelly is about the age at which Mercy came to her untimely end. (I had gloated at every chance about how healthy I kept her, with her superior diet and other boons to long life which I in my enlightenment had provided; I wondered later if "pride goeth before a fall" had something to do with it, and felt sick.) But I know now that I am not powerful enough to either vanquish death, or promote life: both are well out of my hands. Nelly will go on as long as the dozen critically balanced aspects of life and death decide she will. I can mitigate or I can hasten risk—and sometimes, inadvertently, I do both—but I will never fully own it. I had no idea of all the factors that were playing upon Mercy as her death stealthily drew near.

In ten years, I have spent time teaching Nelly and learning from her in equal measure. We've gone to agility class, made friends, barked at each other. We've stayed in motels and for hours upon hours in a car. We've gone to the vet, to the pet store, to the library and the hospital and street fairs. We have slept in the same bed. We have been mad at each other, and we have kissed each other. Mainly we have walked. At some point in most of these mostly gorgeous hikes, I have deeply regretted it. She has put me through the mill. Afterward she pilloried and then guillotined me for good measure.

Just before Mercy died, I remember thinking, I have finally gotten her to where I want her! After ten long years. We understood each other implicitly. I could predict exactly when she would embark, in what circumstances, and what were the penalties (for me) of her bad behavior. It was always good, to her. We were both creatures of habit, together. Her habits became mine and vice versa. Now the good stuff could begin. And then she went and died.

I have almost gotten Nelly where I want her. Time and tide have assisted: like the spouse twenty years into marriage who doesn't particularly care to have sex anymore, Nelly seems to be less in thrall to her hunting-and-roving hormones now. She makes half-hearted efforts to chase, but she doesn't go far. She knows she's no match for the deer or the squirrel. The rabbit—well, it now has to make an effort to meet her halfway. A couple of weeks ago, she seemed very interested in something under the deck of the house. When she stayed insistent, I knew I had to investigate. I knelt down to see a very large cottontail gripped by rigor mortis lying behind the latticework. How the heck did a dead rabbit get there? Well, at least Nelly can't get in; I have to figure out a way to get that out! When I turned from the garage, where I had gone to look for some tool that might be of help, Nelly was trotting away toward the woods with the body in her mouth.

But that rabbit came and bit her, not the other way around.

Or did it?

Now I simply don't take her to briar habitat on a rainy day— something about the wet intensifies the scent of rodents—and that is that, pretty much. I have her where I want her. Or she me.

We're both getting old.

• • •

I HAVE a vague and shameful memory of myself from the days of callow youth. This was the time in which I made sweeping observations about whole swaths of life I could not understand but believed I did. Believing I did, in other words, was the sign that I did not really know the first thing about what I was so ready to pronounce upon. Perhaps I had some foreknowledge of what I would become, or I became what I did because I had once condemned it: the lonely person who "substituted" the affection of a dog for the presumably superior love of the human. Oh, how could I have known the far more intricate biology of truth! The creature I sneered at—my own future self, who knew that the relationship with a dog took place in its own cosmos, untouchable, sui generis—I in some way made. Maybe so I could then turn around and, down the years, chastise the arrogant unkindness of the outsider I used to be. "I don't ever want to sink so low as to have to rely on *a dog* for companionship." *Pathetic,* I might have added, but could not even whisper it to myself. It became necessary, then, that I would someday be made to experience the sole companionship of my dog for years. As well as at last knowing a longed-for and perfect peace: I rested in the absolute knowledge she alone among beings would never, ever suddenly decide, *You know, I realize I don't like you anymore.* She was constitutionally unable to reject, to unlove, to leave, to reconsider. I had become familiar with the most extraordinary circumstance life can ever offer, if we're lucky.

Another amusing memory comes at me from the haze of long-ago. Another pronouncement. "If I ever have a dog, I won't *train* him. We'll have a *natural* relationship." If the paradigm outlined above holds to explain how purpose works, this is why I had to spend more than nine years working on a thesis about dog training: to rebuke myself.

Yet in this case it's not that, really. That pronouncement was born of an era in which training *did* mean coercion, not relationship. I knew I wanted no part of that then, and I want no part of it now.

Now we do train, and we do have a natural relationship. The most natural there can be, in fact. But first we had to come to terms with pain.

CHAPTER EIGHT

> From being an art of unbearable sensations
> punishment has become an economy of
> suspended rights.
>
> —MICHEL FOUCAULT, *DISCIPLINE AND PUNISH*, 1975

There are days when the drive-up teller at the bank seems like the right thing. It is certainly the American thing. If we could only manage to procure our haircuts, our groceries, and our dentistry without leaving our cars, we would finally have arrived at a yearned-for destination: complete pod-life. No face-to-face intercourse of any sort.

Then again, the pneumatic-tube delivery of the checks to the teller behind the window is nostalgically Jetsons, a lovely reminder of a time so simple it strove to appear complicated. It also brings back another cherished memory, the Jules Verne–ish system at the New York Public Library. I could not help but imagine it as the circulatory system of a great sleeping giant: call slips vanished by tube—state of the art in 1911!—to be delivered to what had to have been a race of strange gnomes, scurrying to fill requests in this vast underground of books. At the bank, I reach out the car window and fit the plastic capsule into its launcher and push the button. *Fshoop.*

It always gives the body a brief jolt of pleasure *to actuate* something. Ancient desire fulfilled.

By this time, Nelly is halfway out the window, using my lap as a stepladder to get closer to her goal. Which is the capsule. Look, here it comes. Arcing overhead. She waits patiently, breathless. This has everything to do with the fact that once upon a time, something arrived for her. Alongside my deposit slip, there was a suspiciously colored (hmm, green?) biscuit in the shape of a bone. It probably tasted like chemicals and sawdust. But it was an unexpected gift, and she has never forgotten. Even when we pull up at the ATM instead, her hope springs eternal. She does not know that here, no human has been watching our arrival through plate glass to spy a little black-and-white dog alert in the backseat. Even at the drive-through, there are times when the teller is not as attentive, or sometimes the bank is out of dog treats. But that first gift has marked this place for all time. Nelly has memorized what a bank looks like. Or maybe she knows what a bank sounds like, smells like. Because even when we go to a different branch, still she knows. All of her senses become hyperaware; the magic that tube once delivered seems to stir her to feats of metacognition. She seems to have arrived at a notion of *bankness*. And it is all caused by the unexpected appearance of something highly valued. Indeed, both Nelly and I feel a similar heady anticipation upon arriving at the bank, even though the money I get is about as wonderful as a no-name dry biscuit; it is mine already, and also there is less of it all the time. No matter. It arrives as if it were a prize.

This shapes the experience for both of us. Nothing of substance separates dogs and people in the ways that count. That is why, I suspect, we are able to love each other so deeply, in what feels like a meeting of true minds. Our mental worlds are essentially identical. To show this I offer my own biscuit-at-the-drive-through example.

One day, I had—in fact, coincidentally—gone to the bank for some cash. I arrived home after dark, on a windy night in deep winter. As I got out of the car, the purse into which I had stuffed the bills fell out of my lap. When it hit the ground, the wind pulled five twenties across the yard, where they skittered along the ice-crusted snow and into a depression dense with honeysuckle brush. And beyond that was thirty acres of cattail-filled marsh. I called off the search with a flashlight after twenty minutes; it was like looking for a couple of sequins lost in a Gobi desert sandstorm.

Months later, it was May. I was wandering about in this section of the property, a place I rarely went not only because of the impenetrable honeysuckle, but also the thickets of sharp-thorned wild rose. Still, I was meandering around in my mind, musing on whether it might be possible to clear the brush and plant some fruit trees, make a little orchard. As I scanned the half-acre, my eye caught a flash of dull green. We are all conditioned to this color; it causes an immediate uptick in heart rate. Money! For a moment, I thought it was these vile invaders of the landscape that had finally decided to cut me a break—I had fought with honeysuckle and their roots of the damned for years in every place I had tried to garden for the past fifteen years. Now, it seemed, the very earth had paid me back!

That's when I remembered the night months before. In that moment I knew, consciously, that all I had found was my own lost money (which moreover was only a secondary reinforcer). It had no meaning itself—was only printed paper; try to eat or cozy up to that—but what it represented to me, and to most of us, was enough to forever imbue this bit of earth with a force field of hope and joy. For years afterward, anytime I approached this corner of the property, I felt a flutter of excitement. I knew it was impossible for that experience ever to be repeated, but the one brief shock of a moment in which my brain mistook the visual information as the best sort of luck left a permanent indentation on my memory. Indeed, no cash was ever to appear there again, either mine or anyone else's. But like Nelly at the bank, giddy, every time I neared the place I was overcome with the sensation that I was just about to get a free biscuit.

This is the power of the conditioned reinforcer. The dopamine in Nelly's brain—triggered by the anticipation and not the receipt of biscuity goodness, as you recall—starts flowing as soon as we pull up to the bank. The approach, in fact, is better than any biscuit ever tasted. It is the biscuit of dreams. These are the treats (the anticipated kiss, or the anticipated rush of heroin, apart from the real kiss or the real high) that become the engine of behavior. Nothing feels better. Nothing feels more like hope, or more like eternity is in our grasp.*

---

* Does dopamine explain everything about us? It seems impossible and the only possibility in equal measure. The autobiography of *Homo sapiens* is dense, rich, full of narrative surprise. *No* great tale we believe, whether of gods or demons, is as powerful as the inexplicable profundity of us. Then, imagine—suddenly negated, all of philosophy from Plato to poststructuralism! Surely the story of humanity could not be one word long, The End.

Yet . . . yet . . . Nothing else so fully answers the most fundamental question: Why are we, so smart and built of compassion, also so vile and destructive and cruel? *Humans, the self-canceling species.*

One night, through the portal leading to the vast interwebs, in which you can find nothing and everything and then nothing and everything again, I find what appears to be the answer. It is a piece of hay in a stack of needles. TheDopamineProject.org. One individual who has sewn together all the specialists' widely strewn patches to make a uniform blanket that explains it. I felt like I'd been socked in the gut. No one really wants to know this. No one wants a picture so big it makes you dizzy. (No one at first wanted Galileo or Newton, and no one wants their descendants either.) In fact, in support of this guy's prime contention, no one wants anything, including his discovery, to interfere with our plug in the socket of the ultimate drug. He says we get it from all our addictions, which we already knew, but he vastly expands the category. Now it contains all the primary reinforcers, like sex and food, that hook some of us all too well, the chemical triggers of the bliss hormone, such as drugs, and the most alluring of the secondary reinforcers, like money and symbols of status. When he adds in the rest is

• • •

THE ALARM is set for 7 A.M., far earlier than I—procrastinator par excellence, effective bohemian for whom the 11 P.M. bourbon is as coffee for the productive workingman—would like. But the school bus waits for no malingerer.

At 6:30 my eyes fly open. Damn. I could sleep, need to sleep, another half hour. But my wheels have hit a rim-cracking bump.

---

when it starts to look like dopamine is the definitive philosophy of humanity: the rush-inducing rewards inherent in seeking power, safety, the certainty of belief systems including religion, the infinite number of ways we punish others, as well as the good stuff we do. His theory that dopamine is the single unifying element of all human behavior and misbehavior—his belief that he has found the core of the universe in one substance—is both compelling and crackpot. It is Skinner's overarchingly complete law of behavior updated and deepened by the inclusion of current neurochemistry.

My name is Charles Lyell and I'm not a scientist. That doesn't mean the information on this site is wrong. Instead, it means that I'm free to extend what is known about dopamine to areas that established researchers dare not explore.

I've spent over 40 years trying to figure out how a species with so much potential could end up in the predicament we're in. My quest began with a suspicion about something being seriously wrong with Homo sapiens. The symptoms of our insanity include child abuse, human trafficking, slavery, bigotry, wars, destruction, pollution, lying, cheating, stealing, and venal leaders selling out the human race.

I set out to answer two questions:

- *Why do we behave so irrationally and inhumanely?*
- *What's behind the rampant self-deception that makes it possible for even seemingly rational, highly intelligent individuals to ignore and deny their undeniable, irrational, inhumane behavior?*

I was convinced that there had to be a book, teacher, teaching, discipline, something offering a plausible explanation.

Needless to say, he never found it. So he became an autodidact in neurobiology and started connecting the dots. Perhaps only a nonspecialist would attempt a unified theory of humankind. Perhaps only an outsider could get there. What if he has? Talk about implications.

It is the expectation of unpleasantness. My brain would do anything, even deny myself the bodily necessity of sleep, to avoid it. The ugly little beep of the alarm, small and relatively painless though it is, is so powerfully aversive its anticipation is enough to wake me from a sound sleep. So think of the avoidance effect caused by something truly painful. When I do, it makes me suddenly sick.

Psychologists, in my fond imagining, are a class of people devoted to welfare. I hear the word and picture a man wearing a slightly shapeless tweed jacket and a salt-and-pepper beard looking earnestly into my eyes, no needs of his own but to listen patiently to endlessly unspooling tales of woe. He wants nothing more in life than for me to feel better. And he believes I can. He believes I *deserve* it. Thus his belief is almost enough to get me there: Valhalla. Mental health.

In actuality, psychologists have proved themselves some of the world's coldest, most persistent sadists. Hidden behind the windowless walls of academe's labs, the unspeakable goes on. There, animals are our stand-ins: they are at once considered enough like us that results can be extrapolated to us—the pertinence to our well-being is the justification for anything-goes experimentation—but different enough that what could never be countenanced toward humans is routinely visited on our proxies.

The fact that these screamingly exclusive notions can calmly coexist in the minds of scientists, society's prime exemplars of Smart, is testimony to the power of desire to eradicate anything that stands in its way.

Although we might like to believe that only a few times in recent history have laboratory experiments been carried out on human subjects, the facts are quite different. The Nazis were not alone in demoting to subhuman status their subjects in order to perpetrate an obscene quest for "knowledge." The mentally ill, the indigent, the black, and the incarcerated until startlingly recent years composed a large pool of voiceless test subjects—and "voiceless" was the critical feature of their fitness as subjects.* It also marks their essential kinship with the rabbits, rats, monkeys, pigs, and dogs whose use in our research has yet to raise an actionable question. The psychological experiments are no less terrible than the ones involving scalpels and corrosive chemicals. We know, thanks to brain imaging, that emotional pain lights up the same areas of the brain as physical pain.†

Is it coincidental that one experiment that shed great light on how "normal" people can become, well, like experimenters was itself censured for being unethical? Yale psychologist Stanley Milgram theorized that Nazi cruelty was neither aberrant nor specific

---

* Over the course of some two decades, ending only in 1972, mentally disabled children at New York's Willowbrook State School were used to research development of a vaccine against viral hepatitis—by being intentionally infected with it. In 1963 over 200 prison inmates had their testes irradiated by researchers from the University of Washington. Until 1974, prisoners at Holmesburg in Pennsylvania were paid to undergo extensive chemical experimentation, including injection with dioxin and topical application of blistering compounds. Nineteen sixty-one saw the infamous psychology experiment conducted by Stanley Milgram at Yale, discussed below. All these are failures of the notion of informed consent, and some of them thus contributed to the formation of subsequent codes of ethical conduct in research. These have helped reduce experimentation on humans, because it becomes too difficult to accomplish in the presence of specific narrow definitions of informed consent. No such regulation pertains to nonhuman animals.

† Any argument that pretends to justify experimentation on any living being is flat-out specious. Its illogic has been put to rest by people whose intellect and morals completely align. The most eloquent, perhaps, spoke over a hundred years ago: George Bernard Shaw, perhaps one of the most humane and most eloquent men ever to have lived. (And is it possible the two do not spring from a common source?) "If a guinea pig may be sacrificed for the sake of the very little that can be learnt from it, shall not a man be sacrificed for the sake of the great deal that can be learnt from him? . . . I would rather swear fifty lies than take an animal which had licked my hand in good fellowship and torture it. . . . If you cannot attain to knowledge without torturing a dog, you must do without knowledge."

to the German soul but rather was the product of circumstances. In 1961 he set about seeing if he could replicate these circumstances and influence normal, noncriminal people into behaving cruelly. The answer was yes, fairly easily. In the lab, his student subjects delivered potentially lethal (actually fictional) electric shocks to *their* test subjects (actually actors), simply because they believed it was expected of them as "scientific researchers." The results remain stunning.

Yet into the next decade, far worse—irradiation, infection, pain—continued to be visited on throwaway humans: the poor, the black, the imprisoned, the mentally disabled. Then, it seems, we suddenly woke up to our depravity. (The Nuremburg Code, issued as a result of the Nuremburg Trials of Nazi criminality, is credited with ushering in a new era of sensitivity, which was nonetheless not so spiritually profound that it didn't need nearly continuous further legislation, for instance in codes of ethics regarding human experimentation issued in 1964, 1966, 1974, and 1975.) Or we did at least as it affects human animals.

The history of dog training is a story of two elements bound together: a classic conception of teaching as inseparable from threat and compulsion, and a woeful though historically understandable ignorance of how animals learn most effectively. A necessary corollary, in the form of icing on an already caloric cake, is the thorough misunderstanding of their expressive language. This history does not make for pleasant reading.

Until dogs were relied upon for specific tasks during wartime, most training of working dogs was a homegrown affair. In fact, for centuries we took the more laborious approach—building a better dog through genetics—to getting our jobs done. Traits were selected for and bred into types with different natural abilities, such as for herding, retrieving, ratting, and guarding. It is possible to train a shih tzu to retrieve dead ducks, but without recourse to scientifically based teaching, the means of which were unknown prior to Skinner, it is a lot easier to breed a Labrador retriever instead. The dogs that proved to the farmer most adept at rounding up the sheep were kept and bred with other farmers' good herders, while those who did not perform got sent to the bottom of a pond in a weighted burlap sack. Eugenics 101.

Although dogs had proved themselves helpful in war for centuries, it was during World War I that their exceptional usefulness found formal employment in large numbers. The list of their roles alone is heartbreaking, the sound of an endlessly tolling bell marking the arguably pointless loss of 9 million lives: sentry, scout, messenger, mercy, mascot.* By 1918, Germany was employing an estimated 30,000 dogs, mainly Doberman pinschers and German shepherds. The Allies (apart from America, which was slow to adopt the movement) together used another 20,000. Military technology advanced swiftly in a terrific fight that demanded every advantage, and dogs, with their unparalleled senses and instinctive loyalty, represented a prodigious arsenal of ability. They still do, even in an age of automation that means the increasing replacement of traditional military personnel in every sector: the U.S. forces still use over 2,000 dogs to perform functions that computers can't.

Whatever we felt about the Germans as our enemy in two destructive conflicts, we approved of their model of dog training. Colonel Konrad Most, who in turn-of-the-twentieth-century Berlin trained dogs for the police and then for the army when war broke out, published *Dog Training: A Manual* in 1910, although it was not translated into English until decades later. Instead, his methods were disseminated by students who emigrated, to the United States and

---

* My dog's namesake, the mercy dog, was also known as a casualty dog: these were trained to seek the wounded and dying on the battlefield. They bore kits containing medical supplies, to which a casualty could help himself; if he was beyond such help, the dog would stay with him, sole comfort in the face of approaching death.

other countries, and down the line again by their students. With the onset of World War II, when America found much wider use for canines in combat than previously, and later in the postwar period when increasing suburbanization meant dogs' role changed from working animal to pet, "obedience" training became commonplace. The most influential of the military-model trainers advocated harsh, often lethal maneuvers (hanging until near asphyxiated, "helicoptering," leash pops with spiked collars, and later electric shock), moreover promulgating the idea that "kindness" in most forms was morally weak. Who wanted to be weak? Certainly not anyone who had seen firsthand what weakness in the face of the Germans could amount to.*

---

* In *Training Your Retriever,* 1949, "The Classic Work in Its Field," Most's follower James Lamb Free has recourse to the stern lesson offered by opting to join the weakest of the weak. How does one sink to this level? By having undue sympathy for animals. He can think of nothing more despicable. His book dedicates a whole chapter to punishment alone, apart from its role in training many of the maneuvers that are the book's purpose, even though he knows he will have to bravely face "the chorus of shrill, outraged screams from some of the more hysterical unclaimed maidens of the SPCA." He can imagine no fate worse than being "unclaimed"—he is circumspect about what this entails. At any rate, it must cause so much sad frustration it leads directly to the unfortunate circumstance of caring about others.

The book was updated in later editions, but not by much, and recent reviews of it on Amazon perfectly mirror today's schism in training: one of only two negative reviews is headed "Vicious and Outdated." I should hesitate to remark on the fact that all of the comments on this review are themselves rather vicious and outdated. They combine vitriol and personal attack. And they follow a predictable path of all remonstrations against pain-free training: *no other training method works,* and if you say one does, you have "obviously" never trained a gun dog (etc.).

But people can, and do, train to the highest levels using positive reinforcement in virtually every sport and working field. For retrieving, there is the Positive Gun Dogs Association and its online forums; three books on the subject are *Motivational Training for the Field,* by Lorie C. Jolly, *The Clicked Retriever,* by Lana Mitchell, and *Positive Gun Dogs,* by Jim Barry.

The most popular of all these trainers, one whose disciples would continue his legacy of using film and TV to propagate a perfectly edited message of easy-to-attain dominance and control, was William Koehler. He worked for Walt Disney Studios for more than twenty years and trained animal actors for such films as *The Shaggy Dog, Big Red,* and *The Incredible Journey.* His book *The Koehler Method of Dog Training,* published in 1962, remains one of the best-selling titles of all time in its category. It comes with the impregnable bulwark of its own fully articulated religion, one which most closely resembles that of the Catholic Church during the Inquisition. Its adherents are vocally savage and demeaning to those whose views they most despise—those followers of "modern, scientific" training. Why the whip and the mace? Well, because punishment not only headlines the theoretical basis of their training style; as we will soon learn, it feels good.

Koehler's telegenic progeny include Barbara Woodhouse ("Walkies!" on choke chains); Captain Arthur Haggerty, U.S. Army trainer of the Vietnam era and later Hollywood, whose canine charges appeared in hundreds of commercials and movies, and he himself on shows like David Letterman's ("We have a nation filled with sissy dogs," he informed an interviewer two years before his death in 2006, and proclaimed with certainty that those who "kissy face nice-nice and click a clicker" with dogs do not achieve results). Then there are the Monks of New Skete, who despite their good-karma name do not promote anything we are used to considering such. Finally and most famously, Koehler figuratively birthed the irrefutably charismatic Cesar Millan. His hit *Dog Whisperer* show on National Geographic has made him the Mason-Dixon Line of dog training. The channel received letters of protest from individuals and organizations, including the American Humane Association, which wrote, "As a forerunner in the movement towards humane dog training, we find the excessively rough handling of animals on the show and inhumane training methods to be potentially harmful for the animals and the people on the show." Millan's appearance on a British talk show, during which host Alan Titchmarsh accused him of "barbaric" treatment of dogs, caused a furor and prompted the RSPCA to issue this statement read on the air: "Adverse training techniques which have been seen to be used by Cesar Millan can cause pain and fear for dogs and may worsen their behavioural problems. The RSPCA believes that using such techniques is unacceptable, nor are they necessary to change dog behaviour for the better when other dog trainers use reward-based methods to train dogs very effectively." A Facebook group called Beyond Cesar Millan has over 10,000 members.

The conversation between pro- and anti-Millan camps is more of a firefight; thousands of heated words have been flung across space without any resolution except for a definitive escalation of name-calling. Very few minds, according to an informal survey of representative online commentary, have been changed despite hundreds of well-crafted rebuttals, complete with scholarly citations and referrals to further work by experts in the fields of behavior analysis, neurology, ethology, and veterinary behavior. When those fail to rouse reconsideration . . . let the yelling commence.

It's clear the TV personality makes a lot of people mad, in both senses of the word. What appears onscreen is so polarizing it is as if two alternate universes coexist: in one, lives are changed through the miracle of invisible interspecies communication; in the other, confused dogs who have been pushed to their limits are treated to wrong-headed, unnecessary harm. To those who see the latter, it's in the form of traditional dog training's same old intolerable, misguided story: we punish them after *we* misunderstand their communications.

To some it is all eye-closingly hard to watch: they can barely restrain themselves from reaching into the TV to try and stay Millan's hand (especially when it forms a claw to jab unprotected necks). Knowing they can't leaves them writhing in empathic distress. This group—separated by an intellectual Iron Curtain from those who revere the telegenic trainer—are most likely to have studied behaviorism, read a lot of science, and steeped themselves in canine body language. What they see paraded across the screen is a lot of dogs who are stressed, unhappy, afraid, or shutting down; dogs who are offering every gesture of appeasement, "calming signal,"* and protest in their vocabulary, to no effect. In at least one case, a dog lies on his side, tongue blue, partially asphyxiated. These dogs are the soldier who calls out "I surrender" to a foreign enemy that doesn't understand and shoots. And those who make up the anti-Millan ranks are themselves analogous to the animals who have made their quiet protests and now, ignored, feel pushed to bite.

On the other side of the impenetrable barrier, the believers are ferociously loyal, slinging back their morally loaded criticisms: You

---

* Norwegian trainer Turid Rugaas studied dog-dog interactions and with a colleague compiled a lexicon of dogs' conflict-avoidance gestures. Their language is particularly rich in them, for the same reason Eskimos purportedly have many words for snow. They are a social species bearing as a birthright some particularly sharp knives, as it were. They have had to develop many ways to say to one another, *Whoa, calm down; I'm not a threat here.* Rugaas's brief 1997 book, *On Talking Terms with Dogs: Calming Signals*, is a glossary of one of the most important subsets of canine body language. Anyone who reads it will immediately see all of these communicative devices displayed by the dogs on Millan's show: the lip lick, the look-away, the yawn, the quickly waving tail, the ground sniff, all of which signal a certain amount of distress and are meant to deflect aggression (and may at the same time function to lessen stress in the dog who offers them). They appear subtle to the unschooled human, but it does not mean that they are not loud and clear, both to the individual who is expressing them and to the others to whom they are directed. They are, in Rugaas's words, a canine "life insurance policy."

are intolerant; you *must* show dogs who is boss; who do you think you are to tell us what we should and should not do? After reading hundreds and hundreds of comments in the flame wars over Millan's techniques that erupt wherever his work is discussed—news sites such as Slate and the *New York Times*, Amazon listings and clips on YouTube, training and animal welfare pages—I take a moment to distill the main counterarguments and arrive at those three suppositions. I immediately hear an echo. But from where? Then it hits me: These are exactly the same charges that were leveled at abolitionists. Replace "dogs" with "negroes" and you have the prime arguments of those who supported slavery.

For his part, Millan has said the hissing sound he employs to interrupt a dog is harmless. There's a backup in the logic drain, though. If the hiss did not in fact alarm the dog, it could not fulfill its function as a punisher: to stop whatever the dog is doing at the moment.

How do we know if a hiss or a leash pop or "just" a "gentle" swat is truly punishing or not? Terms in behavioral science are assigned solely by their effects: in this case, if an action results in a temporary cessation of ongoing behavior, it is a punishment. This definition also forms the main objection to its use. Since it has only one function, to suppress ongoing behavior, it necessarily does nothing to teach an alternative. It just feels *unfair*. Its metaphysical nature is to offer no out, no way forward. This is why the dogs on the show often look aimless, confused; they know what they were doing earned them a punishment, but they have no idea what they were to be doing instead. What's the *right* thing? According to the law, it's what gets you something good. And here, nothing good ever made an appearance: there was an annoying sound, a sharp jerk on the windpipe, a hand pressing on the spine, a terrible zinging pain to the throat, yes. But the good thing that tells you "That's it!" and makes you want to do it again? No.

A split-screen comparison of two dogs being worked in the different modalities would (if the warring sides would ever consent to permit usage) immediately make evident how dramatically different the dogs' experience of the teaching is. One—and I'm using real examples, from clips available online, mentally but not cinematically united—shows a Jack Russell terrier at ClickerExpo. His tail wags so furiously his body vibrates. His head is up, ears forward in anticipation. His eyes are focused in absolute attention on his partner; every time she clicks him for something, he scooches forward in his sit—it's like he can't get close enough to this font of goodness, and he'd like to actually get *into* it somehow, but he knows he's supposed to be sitting. He'll just bend the rules a little, then.

The other dog, on the second half of the screen, a Rottweiler, is pacing nervously, looking away, giving quick lip licks (the latter two are signs the dog is under stress). An alien from another galaxy who has never seen a dog would probably assess the scene correctly: he's confused and nervous. He is on an episode of *Dog Whisperer*. The contrast could not be more clear. The Rottweiler is in avoidance mode, ready to bolt or attack; the terrier is happy and ready to learn.

A dog who is told in a comprehensible way what he is to learn, and shown that it is a pleasant process full of meaty goodness (literally and intellectually), will always be seen moving toward. A dog who is unaware that someone holds expectations of them but who has experienced the failure of meeting them in the form of a zap, kick, or jerk will evince surprise. They take to cringing, lest the ax fall again. When or why to them is utterly mysterious.

As to the innocence of the *ssst,* it certainly sounds that way to us. But empathy, if not science, asks for any such assertion to be considered first from the dog's point of view. With a hearing acuity far greater than ours, sensible to an additional 20,000 Hertz on the higher end, the noise that to human ears sounds unoffending is to theirs more like a car horn at close range.* To all animals loud noise is a stressor: from falling trees to roaring lions, most catastrophes announce themselves with noise, so it evolved as one of the main triggers of the sympathetic nervous system, which is what moves an individual to prompt, self-preserving action. In turn, stress activates all sorts of deleterious consequences inside the body. The hormone cortisol, released in reaction to stress, starts a cascade of effects in the brain that effectively derails the retention of knowledge; neurologically, the stress caused by pain—or the anxiety of its expectation—closes access to those areas of the brain responsible for reasoning and learning. Not anything you would want to happen when ostensibly trying to teach.

And the less said about electronic shock collars, another tool in the popular trainer's kit along with choke and prong collars, the better. They are twelfth-century devices of torture. No one would condone their use on children; what is the practical difference between a child and a dog? There is no question that anyone who seeks to use one should first be made to wear one around the neck while someone else, under instructions not to divulge what in the behavior will be "corrected," should decide arbitrarily to hit the button. The injustice of unwarranted attack is its first injury; that pain is mental and emotional, but no less distressing for that. Especially when you have no idea why. (Such is the status of the dog, who furthermore

---

* In *How Dogs Think: Understanding the Canine Mind*, Stanley Coren explains why dogs' hearing is profoundly affected by things that don't trouble the human ear:

> *The fact that dogs have greater sensitivity to sound than humans do, especially in the higher frequencies, helps to explain why some common sounds, like those made by a vacuum cleaner, motorized lawn mower, and many power tools, can cause great distress in many dogs. Many of these types of equipment have rapidly rotating shafts on motors that power fans, blades, or bits. This arrangement can produce intense high-frequency "shrieks," which for dogs can be painfully loud, while our less sensitive human ears are not bothered since the shrieks are at much higher frequencies than we normally hear.*

is denied the chance to escape the source of torment—because it is attached to him.) Then there's the truly peculiar pain of electric shock, which even at half the lowest level of strength is enough to make you feel vaguely ill. The unconscionable escalation in torture represented by, say, ten levels above that must go without comment. There are videos floating around that depict dogs being electrocuted into helpless submission during which they mentally and physically self-destruct; it is preceded by their screams of pain. Among the wonders of the Internet age is the ready availability of imagery of any kind of torture the mind of man has conjured; shock-collar training lies somewhere midway on the spectrum between sickening and consciousness-obliterating.

In one of Millan's sessions, he uses an electronic collar on a German shepherd dog who reacts to the shock with obvious confusion and surprise. He first seeks escape, stopped by the back wall, whimpering. Egress closed, he rounds back and, shocked again, in an instance of redirected aggression bites the nearest thing—the arm of his owner, sitting near by. Millan seems unaware that the most common result of frustrating the instinctive drive to retaliate against a source of pain or threat is its redirection to some safer target; this can occur immediately, later, or become ingrained habit, triggered by similar circumstances at any future time.

The salient point is that the dog had never been offered the chance to alter his behavior, no effective lesson in what was desired of him, before he was punished. There can be no better definition of injustice.

And counterproductiveness, too: a recent study by veterinary behaviorists of people who used confrontational, coercive, or painful techniques on their dogs found a notable increase in aggression.[14] Another study examining the effects of using shock collars discovered the signs of stress regularly exhibited by dogs undergoing training—

lowered body posture, yelping or squealing, panting, lip licks, redirection aggression—persisted even after the training session was over
The dogs appear to have been permanently impaired.[15]

Wales has banned the use of shock collars, including electronic
fence systems, and has prosecuted violators of the law. At the moment
I write, similar legislation is being considered in Canada. There is
too much money at stake for this idea to gain traction in the United
States, however. We guard our freedoms too closely, including those
which openly bring others into mortal danger: any discussion about
the legality of shock collars in this country is likely to follow the same
trajectory as that of the Second Amendment. (Interestingly, those
freedoms that also come attached to multimillion-dollar industries
seem to be most vociferously protected.) There is currently a strong
movement to ban shock devices throughout the United Kingdom.
The opening of the Kennel Club of Great Britain's issue statement
on shock collars reads: "The Kennel Club believes that electric shock
collars have no place in a civilised society. The majority of dog lovers
and the welfare and veterinary bodies hold similar views."

Most people either do not understand the behavioral implications
of positive punishment (the direct application of an aversive) or do not
possess the infinitely precise timing that is required to make it work.
Neither are they likely to have read widely or at all into the severe
behavioral fallout that can occur (a situation tantamount to failing to
understand basic gun safety). Most tellingly, they use it as a first resort
rather than a last. In so doing, they risk a failure that is often more far-
reaching than the original problem requiring solution.* It is like hand-

---

* When the problem has been misdiagnosed, it's doubly heartbreaking. A current
trend labels much of normal dog behavior as aggression. Most commonly, these are
displays of resource guarding, or "please don't take my valuable stuff," as well as typical
responses to threat, such as biting or growling. All of these can be positively handled

ing the controls of an F-35 to someone whose sole experience with flying was once watching a twin-engine plane come in at the local landing strip. Not exactly qualifications to operate the most complex aircraft ever.

Perhaps the most open question raised by Cesar Millan's traditional style of training concerns a vaunted and abstract notion, exactly the type that we humans hold dear as defining our nature as superior beings: fairness. Are dogs here to do only what we say, or to be themselves? If the latter, then fairness demands we fulfill a responsibility to study what a dog is. For when what a dog *is* conflicts with what we force him to do, we punish his very nature; we nullify him. We tell him what we don't want of him, but we neglect to inform him of what we do. The exercise of what we believe is our freedom to coerce denies the dog his own freedom: to express and meet fundamental needs.

The belief that he is somehow a "whisperer" persists among Millan's loyalists. He does indeed appear to magically transmit ideas to dogs, although, metaphysics aside, it seems clear to me (as to many others) that Millan's program is less rehabilitative than simply abusive.*

---

with a program of counterconditioning and desensitization that aims at reducing reactivity, fear, and stress, and teaches alternate responses to defensiveness. Treating these with the counterpunch of aggression is similar to hitting a child who bed-wets or cries from a nightmare: the exact wrong thing to do. In effect, anxiety that is handled with painful measures bears a known risk of deepening and widening the fear and also the self-protective reaction.

* Of the many measured discussions of Cesar Millan's techniques (most of them collected at the site BeyondCesarMillan.weebly.com), one stands far above all the others: Prescott Breeden's article "Dog Whispering in the 21st Century." Breeden, a trainer, ethologist, and president and cofounder of the Society for the Promotion of Applied

Only when the film is slowed down enough for discrete motions to become visible does much of Millan's technique reveal itself as less magical than the fast-moving, well-edited segments appear on TV. A little Googling will lead to instructive slow-motion clips where Millan's "foot tap"—a seemingly benign, gentle nudge—can be seen for what it is: a swift, sharp blow to the unprotected belly and the sensitive organs within. The dogs have already indicated that it is genuinely painful, since in the shows they often either cry out or startle and freeze. Dogs are not capable of the sort of elaborate dissimulation required to yelp "as if" in pain if they were not actually in pain. One hears this claim often.

Research in Canine Science (SPARCS), methodically dissects every aspect of Millan's approach to working with dogs.

To take one example, he discusses an episode in which Millan attempts to treat common resource guarding—nonviolently modified with desensitization and classical conditioning—by confrontationally pressuring a dog to guard her food. Then he hits her in the neck with what he calls "the claw," claiming it is how bitches discipline their pups. (Breeden notes it could not be as painless as the trainer asserts, since viewed in slow motion it becomes obvious that, given the way he directs the hit, force is concentrated in the knuckle and contacts the most sensitive area of the neck.)

Ultimately, humans lack the morphological and hormonal traits required to reproduce maternal behavior towards a puppy and thus using occasionally observed maternal behavior as support for a highly confrontational technique on a broad scale is behaviorally flawed. Confrontational methods which involve pain, fear and intimidation increase the probability of owners being bitten by their dogs, damage the owner-dog relationship, and decrease a dog's willingness and ability to obey commands (Weiss & Glazer, 1975; Reisner, 1994; Hiby et al., 2004; Schilder & van der Borg, 2004; Herron et al., 2009; Beaver, 2009; Arhant et al., 2010; Rooney & Cowan, 2011). Not only do we lack an understanding of which degree of corrective maternal behavior, in all of its wide variance, actually produces the best offspring but it is also impossible for us to physically replicate the jaws and teeth of an obligate carnivore and swift strikes with our fingers can teach dogs to be fearful of hands—another significant factor for dog bites (Rosado et al., 2009).

(http://prescottbreeden.com/dog-whispering-in-the-21st-century/)

* * *

IN THE Swiss psychoanalyst Alice Miller's 1983 book *For Your Own Good: Hidden Cruelty in Child-Rearing and the Roots of Violence*, she examined the tradition of "poisonous pedagogy," or child-rearing customs that were fundamentally dishonest and hurtful, but projectively titled "for your own good," which notion finally augured itself so deep in the psyche that it could only be regurgitated, unknowingly, onto others later. She explained, "Beaten children very early on assimilate the violence they endured, which they may glorify and apply later as parents, in believing that they deserved the punishment and were beaten out of love."

A dog owner who him- or herself grows up in a culture where violence and coercion is visited on children because its practice is accepted, widespread, and rationalized, can only grow up blind to the truth: that such treament was painful, harmful, and unethical. Wikipedia describes the retrospective identification of the condition: "A relevant criterion in defining poisonous pedagogy is if a manipulative approach reveals behavioural issues in the parent such as a blindness to feelings, cruelty, or a tendency toward violence, or if strong negative emotions such as anger or hate are being discharged, emotions against which the juvenile or infant psyche, with its age-based limitations, cannot defend itself."

This may go some way toward helping to understand why the Cesar Millan loyalist cannot see the patently obvious inhumanity of his maltreatment of creatures who are unable to conceive of why they are being hurt. Miller's theory offers the Occam's razor of explanations: one need change only a few words in her definition. "One reality, two views. Pain and torment, impossible to look at. Or fine. Just fine. Admirable, even.

• • •

WHERE DO politics come from? The tap water? Our genes?

Recessive traits never caused fisticuffs that I am aware of, no clashing rioters in the street, denunciations fired from one side of the protest parade to the lemme-at-him on the sidewalk held back from a bloody pummeling by only the taut jersey of a shirt hem, or the preelection bloodletting on millions of social networking pages where old friends are summarily vanished because it came to light that they hold abominable views on what are perceived to be not issues but truth. Being left- or right-handed is never the object of vicious ire. Being left- or right-wing is.

Nothing is so dear as a belief. Our lives inside our skins, blood and juice racketing around unseen and unconsidered, rarely seem as imperative as the bodiless thoughts that somehow formed inside our brains and now guide us in tandem with the serotonin and testosterone, the instinct and the desire. But how did they form? Bequeathed along with the mashed pear and bedtime kiss? Heard from the living room as we crouched in our jammies on an upper stair while ice made lush, low clicks in glasses of bronze liquid and adults laughed and murmured inside clouds of smoke from an entire pack's worth of Tareytons? You became Catholic because your parents were, or the girl you married, but your tennis team pal who was confirmed Episcopalian can remain your friend forever. And you would never rather fight than switch, except for sides in the gun debate. Then you'd punch your friend, because she tried to show you a statistical study. When she was on the floor, you'd pull out another one that proved her wrong.

Science can't find it, this most powerful of urges. It is equal to thirst, revenge, copulation, greed, but exists only as thought, as electrical impulses in the brain. The need to hold political beliefs can almost certainly be found in our biological evolution as cooperative social animals. But where does the origin of *particular* political beliefs reside? There can be no left without a right. One view posits a way society and all its factors—psychological, material, and theoretical—work and the other contradicts it. Where, then, is truth?

Like political parties, two prevailing schools of dog training oppose each other in fundamental assumptions of what dogs are, how they learn, and how we should teach. There is the traditional and the scientific, the nostalgic and the new. They cannot coexist, because their fundamental assumptions and their final applications are utterly divergent. The basis of acceptance is not a matter of theoretical belief; it is a matter of truth. Acting upon traditional beliefs has both ethical and practical implications. This is not just a problem about dogs. It is a problem, first, about us.

. . .

MY MOTHER was a Democrat, my father a Republican. My mother voted a straight ticket, while Daddy took each candidate on individual merit, dubious though his considerations sometimes ended (he voted for Nixon—twice; in 1972 in my first public act as a newly socially aware teen I leafleted for McGovern). He would sometimes vote Democratic, sure, especially if the Democrat was a personal friend—but only, I hasten to add, a friend of sterling character— or if the opposing candidate held insupportably heinous views. Our habitually recurring discussion, from as early as I can remember, concerned whether or not it was the nature of man to be warlike. Young, naïve, hopeful, unschooled, and violently pacifist, I argued the learned-behavior line. He quoted Shakespeare in return, and that shut me up, as it must. But we always began again the next day. Another common topic was the existence of God; he was agnostic, which I considered certainly good enough for a deep-thinking person until I went all the way over the beam in tenth grade and "I don't know" suddenly appeared the mark of a person who had either just poured himself a drink or who didn't like to follow logic to ultimate conclusions if they might interfere with going to St. Paul's to listen to its excellent choir. We discussed anthropology much later, when I took a freshman gut course in college and discovered the anthropology of Marvin Harris, who developed the notion of cultural materialism; my roommates must have been curious as to why I kept shouting "Yes! Yes!" behind my closed door even though no male visitor was present. My belief that I had found the definitive closer to our earlier speculations was itself foreclosed: I made my father read Harris, convinced he, too, would jump up and down over what appeared to be the absolute, impregnable logic of a form of human history that is, I see now, the historical analogue to behaviorism. *Follow the resources!* But he didn't, just quoted more poetry.

The family joke was that he and Mom went to the polls to cancel each other's vote and they might as well have spared the mileage on the cars.

*   *   *

DOG TRAINING, as a direct result of B. F. Skinner's introduction of a new way of thinking about how the brain learns, has become politicized. Party lines have formed where before there was only concord. Or perhaps it is more pertinent to say it has become sectarian: religious war has broken out in a formerly peaceful land. What was a place with a unified mythology of behavior—all Athenians one in their regard of the night sky full of gods—is now the globalized world where Muslims, Catholics, Buddhists, and Hindus all visit the same market square (and argue). The folk traditions handed down from generation to generation have been interrupted by the appearance of a prophet who preaches a new system of belief. And, as in the story of the one whose teachings were reputedly rejected two thousand years ago in Nazareth but who later became the unquestioned leader of billions, the new doctrine is always a hard sell: "No prophet is accepted in his own country."

But the divisiveness has also allowed a true philosophy to emerge in the area of the treatment of dogs. The Greek φιλοσοφία (philosophia) means, simply, "love of wisdom." The quest for truth in the field of behavior has given rise to some astute thinking on the essential questions of learning, ethology, traditional training, and the nature of divisiveness itself.

The only question is, who doesn't love wisdom?

CHAPTER NINE

❧

It's unendurable. It is the moaning of the world, it
is the martyred creation, wild with anguish, filled
with terror, and groaning.

—ERICH MARIA REMARQUE, *ALL QUIET ON THE
WESTERN FRONT*, 1929

Dog training is both exquisitely simple and achingly hard. Just like tearing down an engine. (Notwithstanding the fact that dogs are engines with brains and emotions, hence exponentially more complex, with the infinite mysteries of biology, the manifold interplay of chemicals, and a few hundred thousand years of pushmi-pullyu evolution at work as well.) I love to watch someone wandering thoughtfully through the deeps of a mechanical system like a motorcycle or a furnace, with their looping systems within systems, all communicating, interdependent, one small wire hiding inside a bundle of other wires as able to bring down the curtain the same as a burnt valve. The person who is able to leave a trail of bread crumbs and come back alive from the inside of a machine has, to my mind, just figured out the universe.

Dog training is simple because, like the purposeful arrangement of pistons and crankshaft, it operates predictably. To manipulate it requires no inborn gifts or casting of magic spells. It requires only the same scholastic understanding of universal learning principles that apply to anything with a brain stem. But at the same time, it is hard because it requires unaccustomed dispassion. The trainer must map procedure, display patience in application, and embrace the necessity of problem-solving on the fly. The trainer must first question his or her technique, without recourse to emotional voodoo, when assessing progress. A failure to obtain results is never attributable to Fido's desire to get over on you; it is a failure of the person who devised the program to create one that works with Fido (which is only marginally different from the program that works with Rex). Blaming is such a familiar path for most of us it does not come naturally to take such a hard left off its track.

Dogs are not stubborn, spiteful, or withholding. They either haven't been adequately taught and the behavior sufficiently proofed, or they have not been motivated to act. There are no other options.

In a related development, training in the scientific manner also requires that massive and personally challenging thing called a *paradigm shift* (with apologies for resorting to a cliché, but it is the only shoe that fits here). One must get out from under historically weighty beliefs, which also happen to be utterly wrong,* of how dogs work.

As with a bridge, though, these conceptions of dogs amount to pilings that are sunk deep, through multiple geologic layers of belief. You have to pull them out from the sucking notions of free will. And beneath that from wishful thinking. And beneath that from bedrock beliefs of what we're all doing here in the first place.

Oh, is that all? Just change the worldview bequeathed to you by

---

* In the past thirty years, such an enormous amount of research on a vast number of relevant, interlinked subjects—wolf ethology, neurology, psychology, macrobiology, behavioral analytics—has been accomplished that the world itself might as well have tilted a few degrees. And its spin increased, too.

thousands of years of Western thought, and you, too, can get your dog to come when called.

If Karen Pryor is the Henry Ford of dog training, then the ex-pat Canadian Jean Donaldson is its Wittgenstein, its most passionate philosopher and formidable thinker. (As I mentioned, dog training has lately spawned an awful lot of brainy theoreticians.) Her seminal 1996 work, revised in 2005, *The Culture Clash,* is delightfully impatient. Of the mutually exclusive views of why dogs do what they do—she calls them "Walt Disney vs. B. F. Skinner"—she asks, "How is it that this can even be up for discussion in 1996?" (In the later edition, she posits: "If people's knowledge about driving cars were similar to their knowledge about 'driving' dogs, they'd try going across lakes and then sue the manufacturer when the thing didn't float." "Sue" here is an analogy for getting rid of or killing the dog, the frequent result of a serious misunderstanding of one species by another—one that happens to have all the power.)

There is simply too much information available today to simultaneously accept as true the two predominant interpretations of single behaviors. Donaldson uses a common example to illustrate: the dog who chews furniture when the owner is out. In the first view, the dog acts out of deliberate malice, somehow guessing that destroying a difficult-to-distinguish category of wood is "wrong" and so expresses visible guilt when the owner returns; a punishment is obviously deserved if this is the case. In the second, the animal realizes from past experience that the natural and anxiety-relieving pursuit of furniture chewing is safe only when the owner is out. His look of "guilt" is actually the look of fear combined with a well-documented appeasement routine, performed to "avoid or turn off the punishment he . . . knows" is about to come. "He doesn't know why."

Only one of these can reflect the truth, Donaldson maintains, and which truth it is makes a lot of difference to dogs themselves. Dogs, like all of us, do what is safe and what is rewarding. She believes it is time to abandon the Lassie myth: it attributes far too much to fictional motives and to a wishful consonance of intelligence between species. This insistence on dogs' intelligence (a theme binged on of late)* does a dual disservice to dogs: it denies them their "dogginess," their mode of being that is different from ours but no less valuable, at the same time "we set them up for all kinds of punishment by overestimating their ability to think." She points out an interesting paradox: "the so-called 'cold' behaviorist model . . . ends up giving dogs a much better crack at meeting the demands we make of them. The fuzzy-wuzzy [Disney] model gives dogs problems they cannot solve and then punishes them for failing. And the saddest thing is that the main association most dogs have with punishment is the presence of their owner." Saddest and hardest, too, since dogs, like humans, learn through operant and classical conditioning; unlike humans, they don't have full access to learning much through observation and insight. Associational learning is all they have, and we too often give them painful associations. These are all the more powerfully experienced for being pretty much it for their learning repertoire.

In short order, she goes on to dismantle some of our most precious fallacies. (Why, she opens, do we refuse to use "the window which is opened the widest" "of all the windows which exist to communicate with dogs," operant conditioning? The proof of its efficiency and ability to minimize "wear and tear on the dog and on the dog-human relationship" is long proved beyond a shadow of a doubt. It's so *frustrating* that no one gets it. Now she's getting mad.) The idea that dogs do things out of great regard for what *we*

---

* Studies of canine intelligence suddenly abound, with new research presented almost daily, it seems. Yale cognitive psychologist Paul Bloom believes we are entering the age of the dog: "For psychologists, dogs may be the next chimpanzees."

think, all the while orienting to our internal states, which ought to be somehow immediately accessible to dogs because we are so much alike—not!—is a "vacuous, dangerous" one. In traditional obedience training, dogs are asked to work for praise as a primary motivator. But what in their evolution could possibly have imbued human speech with any intrinsic value? Dogs can't possibly find "Good dog!" rewarding in any but the vaguest way, as perhaps connected once upon a time with the delivery of something truly desired, like some food or freedom or the toss of a ball. Otherwise, it is sometimes accompanied by a pat on the head, something the dog is biologically constructed to find only more or less unpleasant. "Attention" is likewise a concept that mainly reflects on our self-regard—*I am so wonderful, merely to be in my sight is reward enough!*—or was once accidentally associated with something the dog truly desired and so stands in rather palely for a reward.

What the dog who is traditionally trained is really working for, Donaldson maintains, is avoidance of pain in the form of leash corrections. "Trainers who make claims about dogs working 'to please' or strictly for praise seem oblivious to the main motivator they employ: pain." These trainers actively opt not to use positive reinforcement, and then refuse to claim the only other operational possibility: either positive punishment or negative reinforcement. One or the other *has* to be happening, or else you would see no change. No matter your *claim* that the animal is working for praise, the sound can only be functioning as a weak secondary reinforcer conditioned by the cessation of pain; no matter what you say about the moral superiority of withholding primary reinforcers "you end up, like they all do, using aversives and announcing that your dog is doing it for you. Pathetic."

She perceptively points out that what is couched in a moral objection to training with "treats" (positive reinforcement trainers are often demeaned as "cookie pushers") is actually an unconscious aversion to the sight of "the intensity with which dogs will work for strong primary reinforcers like food." And there is, it is true, nothing quite like the sight of a dog working for food or a fetch toy. I mean nothing. It is an energetic focus so pure it could singe your clothes; it is the intent gaze of a dog who is trying to learn what it takes for you to give up one of life's great prizes. Nothing knows watching like a dog does.

The sight of this gaze clenched life-tight on the notion of food: not pleasant for anyone who wishes to feel more important than a biscuit. *No. I want to be everything to my dog! How dare he so boldly show how little he cares?*

So, take away what works with such alacrity and precision. Take away our companion's enthusiasm, his ability to expand his horizons and brainpower. Take away a source of a primitive happiness. Do away with a reciprocal channel open to true communication. Crush the free exchange of trust. And turn our dogs into nothing more than slaves—*Do it or else*—because we can't tolerate the notion that another being desires anything other than to serve us with precious little in return.

How much of what we wish would be, as opposed to what reality provides, is sunk underneath how we conceive of our dogs! It's the nest of dirty socks beneath the teenager's bed.* Or, for that matter, under what we think of reality, too: It can take a young girl a whole lifetime of fumbling dreadfully, operating from a hope that love is structured as a meritocracy of personality (as opposed to a brazen marketplace of youth and looks), before she discovers the pastel-hued story she was

---

* And it ends up this way because dogs are such an ideal blank screen for the projection of human social drives: we are fundamentally alike, as predators; they are our complete dependents, reminding us of our children.

told so long ago has nothing to do with the way things turn out. By the time she does, it might be too late to do anything about it.

Relatedly, I also think I know what cherished belief is threatened by accepting that a dog naturally works most avidly for a desired reinforcer, over the affectionate approval of the pet owner. This is the unconscious yet profound desire to be loved *unconditionally* by a significant other. For "who we are." These are catchwords for a sensation of absolute trust, that which meant nothing less than life itself during the period of the infant's complete dependency. Thus does unconditionality—the sense that the provision of life-giving necessities occurs on no basis other than mere existence—become one with the human imperative of feeling lovable.

Anything that even hints at the unsavory notion that obeisance does not come naturally to a dog—like getting close enough to observe that training with "treats" actually works better than anything else— is summarily derided. It should be noted that as great a dog lover as Donaldson (she is founder and director of the Academy for Dog Trainers, for ten years operating under the aegis of the San Francisco SPCA and now a two-year online course of study) is quite happy to admit that her dogs appear devoted to her "because I throw a mean Frisbee and have opposable thumbs that open cans. Not to say we don't have a bond. *We are both bonding species.* But they don't worship me. I'm not sure they have a concept of worship. Their love is also not grounds for doing whatever I say. It is, in fact, irrelevant to training." (Emphasis mine.) What is relevant is control of resources. It sounds cold, perhaps, but that is the way it works. Feelings of love, companionship, and who's on top are quite apart from successful training. A knowledgeable stranger can teach your dog a dozen tricks and the beginnings of a rock-solid recall in a portion of an afternoon. If you have not previously succeeded in these tasks, must you then impute to your dog a greater desire to please the stranger than yourself? It's a rather queer idea.

All the consternation over "why" dogs do this or do that—always a "red herring" in Donaldson's eyes—would disappear with the acceptance of one overarching truth: "Dogs are completely and innocently selfish." Like us, and the rest of Creation, they ask one question about pretty much everything: What's in it for me?

Even altruism of the sort exhibited by numerous mammalian species (humans included) may have a rather large element of self-interest in it; does this make us "bad"? Or does it, instead, give us a gold skeleton key that would permit us to change a lot of antisocial behavior without resorting to fines and jail? Sure. But we'll take the mythical legend of Good vs. Evil, please. Prisons are a booming business.

Donaldson takes care of the next fallacy in short order, too. This is "the dominance panacea," where every conceivable type of behavior is interpreted in terms of dominance or pack leadership. This framework was derived from a single more-than-half-century-old study of captive wolves that has now been thoroughly debunked by research biologists and veterinary behaviorists.* A study for another

---

* In an article titled "The History and Misconceptions of Dominance Theory," on the forum Clickersolutions.com she moderates, trainer and author Melissa C. Alexander explains why this research from the 1940s is flawed. And gives an example of how badly a misunderstanding can spin out of control:

1. *These were short-term studies, so the researchers concentrated on the most obvious, overt parts of wolf life, such as hunting. The studies are therefore unrepresentative—drawing conclusions about "wolf behavior" based on about 1% of wolf life.*

2. *The studies observed what are now known to be ritualistic displays and misinterpreted them. Unfortunately, this is where the bulk of the "dominance model" comes from, and though the information has been soundly disproved, it still thrives in the dog training mythos.*

For example, alpha rolls. The early researchers saw this behavior and concluded that the higher-ranking wolf was forcibly rolling the subordinate to exert his dominance. Well, not exactly. This is actually an "appeasement ritual" instigated by the SUBORDINATE wolf.

day is why it retains such amazing persistence in popular media—
"a great example of a successful meme," in Donaldson's words.*
The idea that dogs are "supposedly staying up nights thinking up
ways to stage a coup" is "too stupid for words." (Don't worry, she
does not only swiftly dismiss; she backs up the charmingly phrased
objection at ample length.) It also ensures that you have to put the
hammer down hard, and often. This is a choice we actively make,
and it's one that has great repercussions for dogs. Either you have
aversive control, she says, or you use "the direct-access means to
modifying behavior," based on the understanding that since all

---

The subordinate offers his muzzle, and when the higher-ranking wolf "pins" it, the lower-ranking wolf voluntarily rolls and presents his belly. There is NO force. It is all entirely voluntary.

A wolf would flip another wolf against his will ONLY if he were planning to kill it. Can you imagine what a forced alpha roll does to the psyche of our dogs?

* Many scholarly and general papers refuting the popular but unfounded theory of wolf pack dominance are available (including Melissa Alexander's, cited in the previous note): they cover its origin, the status of current research, and the behaviorist views that counter its use in any sound training program. The following list contains just a few (references taken from the Association of Pet Dog Trainers' website page, "Dominance and Dog Training").

American Veterinary Society of Animal Behavior. 2009. AVSAB Position Statement on the Use of Dominance Theory in Behavior Modification of Animals.

Bradshaw, J. W. S.; E. J. Blackwell; and R. A. Casey, 2009. "Dominance in Domestic Dogs—Useful Construct or Bad Habit?" *Journal of Veterinary Behavior: Clinical Applications and Research,* May-June 2009, pp. 135–144.

Herron, M. E.; F. S. Shofer; and I. R. Reisner; 2009. "Survey of the Use and Outcome of Confrontational and Non-Confrontational Training Methods in Client-Owned Dogs Showing Undesired Behaviors." *Applied Animal Behavior Science* 117: 47–54.

Mech, L. David. 2008. "What Ever Happened to the Term Alpha Wolf?" *International Wolf,* Winter 2008, pp. 4–8.

Yin, S. 2009. "Dominance vs. Unruly Behavior." *APDT Chronicle of the Dog,* March-April 2009, pp. 13–17.

organisms' behavior is oriented toward obtaining what they want and need, the most powerful tool we have is to control those things and offer them in return for what we want. The bonus is that the individual who feels encouraged, by being positively reinforced, is happier, eager to learn, and able to process and retain information, while the one who is under aversive control is none of these. The misguided belief that we "have" to punish in order to get the behaviors we desire, or that dogs are always scheming about rising up and so must be put back "in their place," leads us to close a golden door between one world and another. It leads us to lose out on a lot. It leads to an essential unfairness: bringing misery to the uncomprehending.

. . .

IN *THE Culture Clash,* Jean Donaldson takes on every important question of dog training at the turn of the millennium with verve, incisiveness, and just a soupçon of well-deserved bad temper. And she does all that in the first chapter. Her book as a whole, one of the greatest ever written on the subject of dogs, is an ontology of dogism (as it is counterposed against people-ism). The titular culture clash is one where people's ignorance of dogs' essential state, refusal to accept what is normal for them, and inability to properly teach the manners that can enable canids to live in a world made by another species means they are too often discarded. After that, in many cases, they end up "summarily put to death." Someone who has worked for an SPCA is in a particularly good position to witness this sad and unnecessary state of affairs. Donaldson is pictured on the back cover with her chow, Buffy, whom she adopted from the shelter. The greatest number of dogs who end up in shelters are those whose behavior failed to be successfully modified by people, not those who are naturally bad dogs. Is it not incumbent on *us* to figure out how to teach dogs, when they must live in our world, not us in theirs? When their lives hang in the balance?

The many and far-reaching reasons why a punishment-based system of dog training is bad behaviorally—which may also amount to morally, although good behaviorists are allergic to that word—are presented most forcefully in a book that is not about dogs in the least and mentions them only once in an illustration of general principles. Yet I came to it as a foundation resource of training methodology. The only people outside of academic psychology who are reading one of the most important books on social theory, it seems, are dog trainers.

Coercion and Its Fallout was first published in 1989 and revised in 2000. Its author knows a little bit about coercion: Murray Sidman, a psychologist who has taught at Harvard Medical School, Johns Hopkins University Medical School, the Walter Reed Army Institute of Research, and is currently professor emeritus at Northeastern University, gave his name to the phenomenon of "Sidman avoidance" (also called free-operant avoidance), which he discovered in experiments using rats. The animal subject would receive electric shocks to the feet at closely spaced intervals until he learned, usually by accident at first, that pressing a lever would suspend the jolts for twenty seconds. Continuing to press the lever, he was able to avoid them indefinitely. Hence lever pressing was assiduously pursued.

The importance of this experiment, unlike prior tests in which a signal indicated that a shock was impending, was that here the organism learned to switch off the stimulus in the absence of any warning whatsoever that it was about to commence.

The psychologist who devised this experiment became something of an authority on how pain, or simply the threat thereof, can powerfully mold behavior. And so he became an authority on its strange and unforeseen effects: A rat who is working for food suddenly hears a warning signal followed by a shock he can do nothing to avoid. After it stops, he goes back to working for food. But soon, even the sound of the signal is enough to stop him from seeking reward. Even though he could continue painlessly during this interval to obtain food, he seems crushed by the anticipation and now "crouches tensely, trembling, defecating, urinating, hair standing on end." The animal is, in scientific terms, scared shitless. He can do nothing to control his fate, and that is untenable.

·   ·   ·

IF THE astounding, alluring science behind how behavior is built is filled with light, the expanding glitter of fireworks brightening the sky with rich color (watch a hundred videos tagged "clicker training," all the dogs sparkle-eyed and tail-wagging), the science that explains how behavior is squashed by punishment is commensurately dark. The light goes out. It is every bit as fascinating and necessary to know, even if it hurts.

Coercion and Its Fallout condenses the history of behaviorism, and thus its problems, from Thorndike and Watson to now in a few sentences:

> *The science of behavior analysis had its roots in philosophy, then separated itself off as a branch of the emerging discipline of psychology, and is now in the process of disengaging itself from psychology. . . . Much of what we know about coercion, the control of behavior through punishment and the threat of punishment, has come from the experimental and the applied sciences of behavior analysis.*

That's one of the problems: the evidence—often enough derived from taxpayer-funded studies—simply has not been communicated further. Knowledge downstream of the dam becomes the river reduced to a trickle that barely moistens some stones. Behavior analysis, for all that it concerns the most essential aspects of being human (and isn't it just too cool to know why we do the things we do?), is not well understood. There are more misconceptions than there is solid grasp of it. Equivalent, perhaps, to what was known of combating viruses during the Dark Ages: not a whole lot. Even though it was a matter of some importance.

If behavior analysis is to be believed, then—as the law of gravity three hundred years earlier was also to be believed—one fact conveying implications of grand scale emerges above all others: "self-control is really environmental control." Just as Skinner did, his student Murray Sidman has taken what could only be the next possible step after long steeping in a pile of data from a thousand experiments in the lab: the scientist's version of jumping up and down and emphatically waving semaphore flags warning of imminent danger on rocky shores and unseen shoals. Or, writing a book that tries to get us to *see*. Society is sliding ever faster down a slope of self-destruction. Appreciating the true causes—which means changing our understanding of ourselves—is the only hope of reversal. It is no less imperative in the eighties, when Sidman felt pushed to write his first book for the general public, than it was when Skinner did the same in the sixties: things are degrading too quickly for them not to have undertaken the effort. "[A]ltering some of the critical relations between environment and behavior is the only practical route to travel if we are really to change our conduct before it is too late," he writes. The words contain more than a slight echo from *Beyond Freedom and Dignity*.

Yet Sidman also had the benefit of twenty years' hindsight on the convoluted misunderstandings that together damned behaviorism. He describes the conceptual fuse on Skinner's unwitting bomb: the older scientist believed "the concept of freedom would be unnecessary, and even without meaning, if our society could eliminate the conditions from which we were always seeking freedom." In other words, society must have been designed to fetter, since we continually yearned for freedom; ergo, eradicate the chains and no one would think to talk about breaking them. Sensible, yes? The behavior analyst knows, from his data stream, that animals look for relief only in circumstances where it is routinely denied. And that is how Skinner arrived at his assumption.

There was one unbridgeable gap between the glaring obviousness of it and people's ability to see it, however. At this distance, Sidman understands what Skinner could not: the idea we could live in a coercion-free world was "so incomprehensible" at base that most people thought he was attacking freedom itself. (He is also able to observe that as the scope of Skinner's work widened, so too did the attacks on him.)

This colossal a misunderstanding of a benevolently reparative prescription for humanity is itself a product of living in a punitive society. We instinctively know that behavior is controllable, changeable. But most people believe *all* controls are necessarily coercive, and they don't know any different because they've rarely experienced positive reinforcement. If society were a child, he'd be the one who never gets any notice from his father outside of being beaten. So he does whatever he can to bring down the fist. It feels like love.

"Supposedly our sense of right and wrong, our conscience is really only a sense of wrong; it develops, initially, directly from coercive control." That is, our laws tell us only how we might escape punishment, not how we might be better people; we are so steeped in punishment from such an early age—children are hit, sometimes literally, early and often for wrongdoing of all kinds but rarely receive rewards for doing right—we know nothing else. The very idea of justice itself becomes perverted, synonymous with punishment:

Rarely do we invoke Justice as a reason for giving something good
to a person who has behaved well. . . . The principle "Justice will
prevail" makes us feel secure to the extent that we know punishment
will be handed out to others who misbehave. To the extent that the
principle applies also to us, it is a threat. The warning that we will be
treated with justice serves as a crutch to self-control. . . .

So, in the behaviorist's view, we have a system so intricately bound
up in punishment that no one could become aware enough to ask
critical questions: But *should* we? Does it in fact work? Both Skinner
and Sidman studied the mechanism of punishment in the lab and
knew it intimately; by virtue of what they had seen and graphed and
replicated—had *proved*—they answered emphatically no.*

* • •

IN 2006, a fourteen-year-old named Martin Lee Anderson collapsed
during a forced run on his first day at a Florida juvenile offender
"boot camp." Five adult guards restrained, beat, and kicked the child.
After that they attempted to revive him by forcing him to inhale cap-
sulized ammonia; thing was, they happened to be suffocating him
at the same time. It took them a rather long while to realize the boy
was no longer in a state from which he could be revived, and the

---

* Yet "no" was not enough. "No" went unheard. So, next, both felt compelled to raise
their voices in book-length alarms. Society would self-destruct if we could not see
what we were doing to ourselves and fix it soon. (Sidman: "Without a science of behavior, humanity will not last. . . . Without one to show us how to change the ways we
conduct our affairs, the world is going to die either from neglect or by suicide.")

Skinner's plea was widely read and loudly denounced, misunderstood for the reasons Sidman saw clear-eyed from the vantage of decades later—decades during which,
of course, exactly nothing had changed. So he, too, sat down to write his own scientist's
warning (a popular genre). Sidman's plea was neither widely read nor denounced.

The effect was the same.

nurse who stood by seemed unaware of certain elementary medical facts. None of them were aware of elementary humanitarian facts. The video from surveillance cameras (which is the only reason Martin's death came to light and forced prosecution of those responsible, though they were acquitted, after which the *New York Times* ran a report headlined "Acquittal Fits the Pattern in Boot Camp Deaths") is available on YouTube, provided you can stand watching it. It is extremely rough going.

Two years before this boy was stripped of his most basic right, to defend his life—the offenses for which he received the ultimate punishment consisted of taking his grandmother's car on a joyride and petty thievery—a panel of experts convened by the National Institutes of Health had already reviewed the extant research on the prevention of youth crime to conclude that programs like the boot camps, organized to deliver fear, threat, punishment, and rough treatment, "do not work."* They may, in fact, make presenting problems worse.

At this point, is it possible to avoid questioning the ethical status of all penal institutions? Is punishment in fact morally supportable—never mind behaviorally—when it is perpetrated on the victims of childhood abuse? For these are who, it is increasingly evident, fill our prisons and detention facilities. A study by the Justice Department's Bureau of Justice Statistics in 1999 found that more than a third of the women in state prisons and jails had been physically or sexually abused as children, twice the rate of child abuse reported

---

* Listed on a website promoting nonviolent treatment of children (http://www .nospank.net/boot.htm) are citations to 212 studies, reports, and books all detailing barbaric abuse of children—sometimes for profit—in juvenile boot camps. In the aggregate, it is disturbing to an almost paralyzing degree. It makes it appear almost certain that out of the public eye, brutal, medieval treatment of children is not only tolerated but cannot be stopped by any means, judicial or otherwise.

by women overall, while the number of male inmates who reported being the victims of child abuse is also about double that of the overall male population. Some researchers believe the percentage of the prison population that suffered neglect or abuse as children—at a time when the powerlessness of defending against such assault can only trigger mechanisms that cause the later compulsion to repeat the trauma, upon others or oneself—may well comprise the majority. A 2012 survey of sixteen- to eighteen-year-olds in the jails of New York City, the nation's second-largest system, discovered half of them had suffered brain injury prior to incarceration. It says something about our staunch commitment to punishment that we do not question its propriety as a treatment for even victims of physical and emotional trauma. Mental-health care is viewed as a reward for the undeserving. Prevention is a nonstarter.

It is difficult to find solid evidence that juvenile boot camps work; we remain faithful to an extravagantly failed methodology that does not work, either particularly or at all. Rather more to the point, they are so blatantly harsh they may even result in death.* In a 2008 paper titled "Advocating the End of Juvenile Boot Camps: Why the Military Model Does Not Belong in the Juvenile Justice System," lawyer Jaime E. Muscar presents an extensive study of the available facts. "Despite the boot camp model's potential, there is little evidence that it reduces recidivism or has other lingering effects on participants once the residential phase ends. . . . Upon close examination of the four most commonly cited goals of juvenile boot camps, it now appears that juvenile boot camps do not truly

---

* The exact number is not known, in part because there is no mandated government reporting on deaths that occur in privately funded institutions; many boot-camp–style facilities are for-profit. At least one website claims that 115 youths, some as young as nine years old, have died while in public and private residential treatment centers, psychiatric hospitals, juvenile detention centers, and special purpose programs.

fulfill any of these goals," he writes. The conclusionary section of the paper bears the title "Argument: Military Boot Camps Do Not Work and Should Be Abandoned."[16] Why, then, do we not? The question is simple enough.

For a hundred years, patients of everything from fevers to infections were treated to a "bleed, blister, and purge" therapy promoted vigorously by Dr. Benjamin Rush, one of America's Founding Fathers. He believed wholeheartedly in the efficacy of bloodletting as a cure for a variety of ailments, and rarely hesitated to open a vein: "I have found bleeding to be useful, not only in cases where the pulse was full and quick, but where it was slow and tense. I have bled twice in many, and in one acute case four times, with the happiest effect. I consider intrepidity in the use of the lancet at present, to be necessary" in the treatment of yellow fever. He wrote a treatise on this necessity, buttressed with facts. Yet there is no basis in biology for the efficacy of which he spoke. In fact, the calomel and tartar emetic used for purging was highly toxic. Not only was the therapy not helpful, it was actively harmful. From this remove, it is hard to see why the cause and effect was not abundantly clear. Still, thousands were subjected to the treatment even when it continued to have no positive effect, except by accident.

This is merely another example of persistence beyond the bounds of reason, not an answer to the simple question posed above. But in its own way it is the only answer we will have: a reminder about the importance of asking questions.

*   *   *

STEVE MARTIN, a preeminent parrot trainer, in a paper delivered at the Association of Avian Trainers Conference in 2002 in California, shines some light on the consternating problem of why we are prone to these systems of aversive control even when they don't work—and furthermore why they *seem* to work on dogs but not birds.

> *Humans are genetically adapted, and culturally conditioned, to use aggression as a tool for shaping and modifying behavior. Aggression and force are rehearsed from very early ages and are kept close at hand through most people's entire lives. . . .*
>
> *Experience with training dogs may also contribute to a person's use of aggression on other animals. Humans have more success in training dogs than any other companion animal. This success is partly attributed to a dog's willingness to submit to a human's forceful training techniques. Even the most inept dog owner can have some level of success teaching a dog to obey a command in order to avoid physical aggression. This is due to the dog's ability to learn and adapt rather than the training skill of the owner.*

And, he might add, success breeds success: naturally, we like the feeling when something achieves its aim so we're likely to do it again. Dogs' native proclivity to defuse acts of aggression—remember the extraordinary depth of their vocabulary of propitiation—ironically (tragically) contributes to our tendency to continue it. They fight back less often than they submit, unlike the parrot, who simply says, *To hell with this crap*, and bites the hand that hurts him.

Author Stephen Budiansky aptly describes how dogs, and the wolf progenitors who first figured out that we are "compulsive anthropomorphizers" always on the lookout for anyone who can hold a mirror to our narcissistically admiring gaze, "exploit" this characteristic in their human partners for their own ends. Reading

> *social cues adeptly, down to such details of body language as a flick of the ear or the angle of a tail, is the most basic of canine instincts.*

"That's what dogs do for a living," Gregory Acland says. "They figure out what's expected of them in a social situation and do it."

Even people who are very bad animal trainers can usually make themselves understood to dogs. If you shout at a dog, it cringes. Does this mean the dog feels sorry for peeing on your Oriental rug? The fact is that it doesn't matter, as far as the dog is concerned, whether he feels sorry or not. The cringe is a successful technique for deflecting aggression. Millions of years of wolf evolution have selected such behaviors because they are socially effective; thousands of years of dog evolution have fine-tuned such behaviors so that they are socially effective on people. Just as we are genetically programmed to seek signs of love and loyalty, dogs are genetically programmed to exploit this foible of ours.[17]

Unfortunately for dogs, we are also genetically programmed to not see what we wish not to see.

* * *

AFTER DR. SIDMAN observed what punishment did to rats, he did not feel it necessary to look farther to find what it did to us. Instead, he went looking for all the places we controlled one another with the threat of disagreeable outcomes, assuming our response to be analogous to that of the broken rat. He found them—in abundance.

The dean of pain defines coercion most broadly as the "use of punishment and the threat of punishment to get others to act as we would like, and to our practice of rewarding people just by letting them escape from our punishment and threats." Sometimes punishers are subtle little demons. They don't always wield bloody swords or leave us a quilt of yellow-blue bruises. We are exquisitely calibrated to feel the mere nick of a sharp word, a humiliation or show of unavoidable strength. The state trooper hiding in the median's hollow, the threat of the F or the pink slip or the spouse's silent treatment, the doctor's brusque *don't*s: our daily behavior is run through a maze whose walls are made of frustration, fear, unpleasantness. It is almost fun, in a horrifying sort of way, to discover—hiding in plain sight!—how pervasive is our fixation on punishment as a first resort.

Let him count the ways.

In the family. Physical or emotional isolation; various means of "laying down the law"; "taking away possessions and privileges"; "intellectual or sexual disdain": "The common meaning of 'Behave yourself' is 'Do what I want you to do.'" The result? The home becomes a place from which escape is often desperately wished. But not before those under control learn potent lessons in how to become tyrants one day themselves.

In schools. Students are punished for *not* learning, rather than rewarded for learning. School is, let's face it, a hated place for most kids. Does it occur to us to ask why? Simply, these practices have been repeated for so long they appear inseparable from the very institution. It has become hard to conceive of any other way to organize instruction.

In the workplace. It's a dance of mutual coercion: workers, pressed, threaten to strike, and employers threaten to fire. The "good stuff," productivity and pay, are reduced to bargaining chips.

In society. In a nutshell, "A system of justice that is based solely on punishment for breaking the law does indeed keep many people on the straight and narrow, and provides satisfaction for those who seek revenge on lawbreakers. A coercive legal code also generates evasion and defiance by many who are subject to the system, and brutality by many who administer and enforce the system."

In the larger world. The threat of war, emblematized by the arms race, is a form of coercion based on veiled threat of the ultimate retaliation for getting out of line. In turn, this promotes "jealousies, animosities, and emotional countercontrol"—of which terrorism is the most potent and extreme manifestation.

That for many of us the first reaction upon hearing such a recitation is not "Oh my God" but rather "What would he have us do instead?" is perhaps the final proof of how completely informed by coercion is the dream world in which we live: we cannot imagine it otherwise.

As suggested before, the truly odd thing about coercion is that, as a tool of behavior modification, it *doesn't even work very well.*[*] Its cost-to-benefit ratio is higher than any reasonably smart businessperson would permit. Even "when coercion accomplishes its immediate aim, it is in the long run self-defeating," Sidman writes. One does not have to accept this claim on its face: the science called behavior analysis can diagram it up and down the line. The fallout lands over a wide territory, and keeps falling for a long time.

It is true that we sometimes use noncoercive means of control; alas, Sidman maintains, we generally do so "unskillfully." Our more thorough practice is in the realm of coercion, and practice makes perfect. We do it so well the technique is on autopilot.

Still more intellectually engaging than the list of places where

---

[*] Even the ostensibly gentle reprimand of suspension from school does not work on any level, and demonstrably makes things worse, as a multitude of studies has shown. But that's not going to stop kids from getting sent home. "While suspensions are intended to improve student behavior, research shows otherwise, said Russell Skiba, professor in counseling and educational psychology and director of the Equity Project at Indiana University in Bloomington, Ind. 'There isn't any evidence that suspension improves student behavior,' he said. Even controlling for poverty and wealth, Mr. Skiba said, 'If you have higher rates of suspension, it's associated with lower achievement.' Mr. Skiba, who was a member and lead author of the American Psychological Association's Task Force on Zero Tolerance, noted the American Academy of Pediatrics has drawn similar conclusions." (*Pittsburgh Post-Gazette*, "Schools Finding Suspensions Ineffective for Changing Student Behavior," September 3, 2013.)

coercion has insidiously inserted itself is reading of the mechanism by which it functions. And learning how its operation loops around and around perfectly explains why it is so pervasive.

We have seen how positive reinforcement acts in both theory and practice: to the behavior of our canine friends the hot dog effect is powerful, as well as fun. The receipt of good stuff always is. It motivates us to learn how to get more of it. But how does it happen that bad stuff sometimes becomes good? In learning how punishment gives *pleasure* to the punisher, we have the key to understanding the otherwise incomprehensible persistence of punitive systems that are neither effective nor kind. Remember the last time you lashed out in anger or fear.

Two feelings wash through like a fast cold stream, unbidden. Here is a split-second charge of illicit release, the taste of something delicious. Followed immediately by, *I can't bear the thought*, which is when we discover we are each two people. The one who does things, and the one who later tries to make sense of them.

(A cartoon makes light of this internal battle: a couple of businessmen are enjoying the prerogative of martinis at lunch while one muses to the other, "Positive reinforcement may be more productive, but, dammit . . . it's just not as much fun.")

How do we know this unsavory assertion is true? (Still looking for an out.) If a behavior recurs, it has been reinforced. Punishment, indeed, alas, recurs. It even gets to be a habit.

From the horse's mouth: "The only way to tell whether a given event is reinforcing to a given organism under given conditions is to make a direct test. We observe the frequency of a selected response, then make an event contingent upon it and observe any change in frequency. If there is a change, we classify the event as reinforcing to the organism under the existing conditions." That's Skinner, from *Science and Human Behavior*, 1953. The bricks into which we run.

When I first heard it, from a dog trainer who knew her behavioral science, it was a stunning moment. I remember where I was standing, what block of Brooklyn's streets. It was like holding a piece of polished obsidian in the hand, feeling its weight and irreducibility. And its fathomless blackness. *Punishment is reinforcing to the punisher.* Of course. It fit the science, and it also fit the hidden memories stored in a deeply buried, rusty lockbox inside me. The people who walked down the street arbitrarily compressing their dogs' tracheas, to which the poor beasts could only submit in uncomprehending misery; the parents who slapped their crying toddlers for the crime of being tired or hungry: These were not aberrantly malevolent villains. They were not doing what they did because they thought it was right, or even because it worked very well. They were simply caught in the same feedback loop in which all behavior is made. Their spasms of delivering small torments relieved their frustration and gave the impression of momentum toward a solution. Most potently, it immediately stopped the behavior. No matter that the effect probably won't last: the reinforcer—the silence or the cessation of the annoyance—was exquisitely timed. Now. *Boy does that feel good.*

.   .   .

PUNISHMENT IS a dangerous thing. Not for the obvious reasons alone. As behavior analysis in the lab has shown, pain is really the least of it.

"In addition to suppressing unwanted conduct"—punishment's only accomplishment, aside from that psychically expensive kick of pleasure received by the punisher—"punishment's success in getting rid of behavior will seem inconsequential. The other changes that take place in people who are punished, and, what is sometimes even more important, the changes that take place in those who do the punishing, lead inevitably to the conclusion that punishment is a most unwise, undesirable, and fundamentally destructive method of controlling conduct."

Sidman's authoritative explanation continues with pointing out just how much unintended, and uncontrollable, fallout we endure due to "society's nearly universal orientation toward coercive control" of behavior. We *could* engineer our systems differently, building them deliberately from the ground up using a positive reinforcement blueprint. (*What a wonderful world this would be . . .*) For all that we aim for behavior we deem desirable—remember, we are modifying others' behavior always, everywhere—employing positive punishment and negative reinforcement to do so is coercive while "control through positive reinforcement . . . is not coercive." To be clear: Positive reinforcement does not issue Do This or Else commands, leaving one without options. It opens up, not closes down. The learner finds he is situated in the one area where he *chooses* to act.

Using the click, or any signal that says essentially "Yes!" is a form of handing the reins of control over to the subject—exactly the opposite of the common fear that engineering our social systems will render us mere automatons in the hands of dictators. Our social systems already are constructed to employ the two "nasty" quadrants of operant conditioning, positive punishment or negative reinforcement (threat). *Something's* going to get used, as there are only four possibilities. Better, from neurological and existential standpoints both, to opt in every event against coercion. If only on scientific grounds: we retain knowledge and are quicker to perform if a behavior is acquired through positive reinforcement.*

---

* "The behavioral experiment, therefore, showed that only reward but not punishment enhances the implicit learning of sequences. This finding is at odds with previous studies of reward and punishment on learning, which, however, were generally confined to associative-learning tasks. This result provided us with an opportunity

Since punishment is capable only of suppressing behavior, when it is employed as the predominant mode of teaching, your student exhibits . . . nothing. In the absence of instruction on what should be done (what should not is, alas, clear), the best course of action is to sit tight. Coercively trained dogs look a little, um, stupid. Their inquisitive lights have been dimmed. On the other hand, clicker-trained animals (and positively reinforced people) do plenty of the following: offer novel behaviors—in other words, create, which makes them not much different than an artist or philosopher; show elastic intelligence, because thinking has a history of being rewarded; are demonstrably happier and more confident; know how to problem-solve, since doing so opens the door to new chances for good stuff. Their actions, freely given, control the click, not the other way around.* And *this* is why "control through positive reinforcement . . . is not coercive."

Sidman immediately points out that "[m]ost people understand negative reinforcement and punishment without difficulty." They are the flyswatter at hand, the angry word that leaps from the tongue. But practicing positive reinforcement takes thought, con-

---

to test the neural substrate of the reward and punishment effects during procedural learning." From T. Wachter et al., "Differential Effect of Reward and Punishment on Procedural Learning," a study published in the *Journal of Neuroscience,* 29, no. 2 (January 14, 2009): 436–443.

* "Training through operant conditioning results in purposeful behavior, while training through classical conditioning results in habitual behavior. . . . The difference between an animal that behaves with purpose, rather than by habit, is vast. Clicker trained or operantly conditioned animals try to learn new behaviors. They remember behaviors even years later because they were aware of them as they learned them, rather than acquiring them without awareness. They develop confidence because they have control over the consequences of their actions. They are enthusiastic because they expect those consequences to be pleasurable." Win-win-win. (From Karen Pryor Clickertraining.com.)

scious distancing from our reactive emotions, in a word, mindfulness. As tough to reach as a peak in the Himalayas. To most of us,
instinctively, others' good stuff appears most useful only as things to
take away upon misbehavior. Or else they are deployed with unfortunate bad timing: the cookie finally surrendered to the child who
has escalated his whining to intolerable levels has just guaranteed the
future production of increasingly epic fits. But the cookie bestowed,
unasked, in a moment of calm produces a child who will happily
and endlessly search for ways to be quiet. (Just be sure to reinforce
it periodically with things the child values—attention and games
work particularly well with children, though the former is less interesting to most dogs—or else you will extinguish the behavior you
most wish to have.)

How many of us speed when we have reason to suspect there
are no gendarmes in the vicinity? Another way to ask this rhetori-
cal question is to inquire into the robustness of the market for radar
detectors. When you were young, was your first toke of mary jane
taken at home with your parents in the living room? Is a kid more
likely to steal a candy bar while the clerk is looking?

We are as watchful as our dogs to the perceived safety of a situation in order to receive what are known as environmental rewards,
those pleasant sensations that are simply on offer, the gifts of the
universe. Engineering rewards that are as valuable takes a lot of
thought and control of the environment, so it does not pull rank.
Much as Nelly loves Vienna sausage—and oh she does, as much as
I did in my prevegetarian youth—if I offer it to her when a cat is
lurking, it might as well be sawdust. Very little in her hierarchy of
value sits above cat chasing. Unless it is rabbit hunting. She wants
her rewards, and she wants them now, in the order she prescribes.
If she were caught every time she chased, her desire to chase would
go undiminished. She would simply become very perceptive about

what conditions foreclosed the possibility of a dream fulfilled. And she would learn to avoid them. She is wily, that one. Learning how to circumvent punishment (and negative reinforcement) is an evolutionary necessity: "stuff that hurts" is the category head under which both punishment and potential death are listed. We're naturally quite sensitive to danger.

So it is that the dog who has not been fully housebroken—or, more precisely, not fully proofed for housebreaking, since the concept of "house" belongs solely to humans, and dogs need to be shown in detail the apparently arbitrary lines that inscribe "house" from "nonhouse"—learns through experience where it is safe to relieve himself when he must. He quickly figures out that the middle of the kitchen is generally not (there, he gets a nasty high-pitched shriek that hurts his ears or a swat on the rump), but a distant corner of the basement almost always is. (He is able to make absolutely no connection between using it as a toilet area and the inexplicable occurrence of being dragged down some hours later and having his nose shoved into his own excrement. From this he gleans only one fact: that his human is bizarrely unpredictable, so he is left only to cower—his native tongue for forbearance—or attempt to escape the fearsome hand.)

"Sensitivity to the likelihood of punishment will either restrain or encourage personal and even international aggression," says our authority on coercion. That sensitivity is composed of heightened awareness to the signals of either safety from harm or incipient pain. The light in the lab rat's box goes on for ten seconds before the electric shock commences; the parent shouts "No!" just before smacking the child on the behind; the door opens at 5:30 P.M. and shortly thereafter the dog gets yelled at and dragged down by the collar for an unhappy encounter with his waste. At around 5:10 most days, therefore, he starts to feel very anxious.

The light, the particular soundwaves of *nnoo*, the door opening: none of these is intrinsically punishing, but once they have been paired with an aversive experience, they become one with it. In the brain, in the electric impulses shot across neurons, the contextual environment becomes a conditioned punisher, too (in the way the sound of the clicker, itself meaningless, becomes a secondary reinforcer and cause for celebration, because it is temporally connected to a happy event). This can happen quickly, in one or two trials; we are primed by history to read all sorts of signals with alacrity. (We had better.) Symbolism is no literary invention. There is nothing more real.

What happens next is curious, and not commonly appreciated. (How could it be? We are in deep denial about what we do. How might we then attempt to understand the dynamic of what we set in motion?) When punishments predominate in the environment, so too do the conditioned punishers: the same smoky pall touches everything. As they proliferate, so does our unhappiness, anxiety, even despair. "If we encounter punishment frequently, we learn that our safest course is to stand pat and do as little as possible." This is known as learned helplessness, and it is precisely the state of the dogs who have ostensibly achieved "calm acceptance" on that famous dog-training show.

Not only do many of the things we do and say before, during, and after delivering a punishment themselves become secondary punishers (the sound of the car in the driveway at 5:28 . . .), but whole environments become tainted. And, to contradict myself a bit, fear does teach something: to be afraid. Its colors become hard to remove; they are enameled to both the inner world (where its indelible inkstain is posttraumatic stress disorder) and to the outer—to the entire view available to the eye at the moment of distress. This can be the social environment, in which terrible words (signals predicting loss of a

safety we held so dear) are exchanged, or the physical environment
to which threat of unpleasant outcome is tightly bound (the school
building; even the thought of the school building). Then there is the
meanie himself, a conditioned punisher: a person hated, feared, or
avoided by others. "Anyone who uses a shock, becomes a shock."*

Negative reinforcement—that which provokes us to do something
not because it brings something nice but because it helps us avoid
something not nice—"generates escape." It's punishing to have good
stuff taken away, and so negative reinforcers and punishers "are the
same events functioning in different ways." Shock is, unfortunately, the
example at hand: in the lab we learn what to do to make a shock stop,
such as pressing a lever; negative reinforcement. Or we receive a shock;
positive punishment. ("Yes, I'm positive I received a punishment.")

Yet how often we are unaware that we are punishing others. It
happens reflexively: We coerce friends, spouses, employees. They
naturally seek to escape. When they do, it can appear a complete
surprise, and we feel like the offended party.

This desire to escape control by negative reinforcement manifests
the opposite effect of behavioral modification by positive reinforcement. The student who has been rewarded for offering something
clever begins to try all sorts of new ways to repeat the performance,
even if it was something you intended for him to do all along.† (In

---

* And a hand is transformed, in the emotional world of the dog, to an object to fear.
The movement of a hand comes mainly to signal an impending punishment—the
smack, scruff shake, alpha roll, removal of valuable possession—and it doesn't take
long before it is treated as an enemy about to attack. Confrontational approaches to dog
handling are known to increase aggression, which from the dog's point of view is really
self-protection. That's sad. What may be sadder is the breach of trust it represents in a
relationship where mutual trust is a source of the deepest pleasure. Punishment trans-
forms an appendage into a weapon.

† Here might be the appropriate place to note again the distinction between a reinforce-

Lads Before the Wind, Karen Pryor describes how she made one of these "nuisance" students out of a porpoise who was reinforced only for coming up with novel behaviors out of her own imagination—a display of creativity, or higher order "deutero-learning," that had hitherto been thought the sole province of humans. The experiment permanently changed the animal, from one who was "docile, inactive" into one who was "active, observant," and "full of initiative." Dogs can easily be turned into nuisances, too, as anyone who has ever lived to regret playing shaping games with their already too-smart border collie knows.)

In his mind, the reinforced student made the world all over again, from some sticks he found lying around. Now he wants to make another one, and another. He's glad to be at it all day. He gets good at world-making, too. It feels wonderful. And he gets paid for it. More win-win-win.

The reduced-to-a-robot creature who is afraid to do anything outside of whatever narrow repertoire of behaviors hitherto proved safe from nasty repercussions, on the other hand, is a dull boyfriend/child/student/dog. Dull and possibly depressed, a known outcome of frequent "corrections." (Interesting that the same term is used as a euphemism for both the prison system and for the leash jerks of traditional dog training.) It seems not to matter whether the punishments are physical or emotional: both are "felt" by the same areas of the brain,

---

ment and a bribe. They may be the same item—say, a ten-dollar bill—but they have dramatically different effects due to their temporal placement in regard to an action. Briefly, a bribe: "If you get an A on that paper, I'll give you ten bucks" (the reward is presented before the act). A reinforcement: Paper comes home with an A on it, ten dollars given (unexpected but pleasant consequence of freely doing A work). Bribery is coercive, while positive reinforcement is not; the very structure of a bribe is implicit threat ("*If* you . . ."). Moreover, bribes have unintended side effects, like all coercive methods of changing behavior: motivation and performance are both dampened.

the anterior insula and the anterior cingulate cortex. (An experiment revealed that taking acetaminophen for heartache—not the literal kind, though maybe we can't use that distinction anymore—is effective in lessening the dolor of loss.)

In the employment of both these behavioral controls—punishment and positive reinforcement—timing is critical. Punishment that is mistimed increases fallout from the fallout: "When punishment is delayed, as it often is, the action that is actually punished becomes not the intended one but instead, whatever was being done just as the punishment was being delivered."* That's just the way brains work. Sidman here, Donaldson a few pages ago, Pryor before that, all the way back to Skinner, in effect repeat the same fundamental message: *That's just the way brains work. So it only makes sense to work with the way brains work.* Steel can be bent, but only in accordance with its physical properties. Asking, wishing, or cajoling it to change

---

* The classic illustration of the delayed punisher is prison. As a punishment, it is delivered so long after the misdeed, the actor associates it with everything *but* the act. The people who are responsible for producing the sentence are the conditioned punishers, and the only response they are likely to generate is a desire to escape. And to never get caught again. Jail sentences are primarily motivators to get better at committing crimes.

The increase in the number of prisons is not explained by the commonly accepted rationale for their existence, as a deterrent to further disobedience. If that were the case, their numbers would be falling, along with the percentage of population incarcerated. The unabating growth of both, then, can only be understood as a response to successful reinforcement for those who imprison. Among imprisonment's powerful rewards for us is the removal of miscreants from society. But the most alluring is that it feels good as only revenge can, carrying the peculiar emotional release of retaliation.

On the other side of the equation is one of the prime deleterious side effects of all severely aversive behavioral controls: increased aggression. (Like dogs, like man.) In Pennsylvania in 2012, a convicted felon, a forger named Andrew Thomas, was stopped by Officer Brad Fox. He had already sworn he would not go back to prison and intended to "commit suicide by police"—but he took down the officer, too, a young father of two.

shape avail not. So, too, with behavior. While we have resolutely denied the evidence, a lot of time, and lives, have gone by.

Social reliance on punishment is a method ripe with irony, as Sidman notes. "Because delayed punishment suppresses whatever actions just happened, it may make us stop doing things that are perfectly permissible, while we continue to do whatever the punishment was supposed to stop." *Argh.*

On the other hand, the greatest hazard with a delayed reinforcement is the formation of so-called superstitious behavior. Whatever happened between the target behavior and the late reinforcer becomes incorporated into the behavior when it is repeated: I had hit RECEIVE/SEND when the message came in telling me my article was accepted, so the act of hitting RECEIVE/SEND now takes on an anticipatory happiness, as if it were the act that caused the welcome news. I start doing it a little more often. (I won't tell you how often.) Of course, it had nothing to do with the acceptance: the absurdly hard work of writing did, but given the glacial pace of editorial reply, the mind is hard-pressed to connect the two distant events. The feeling of reward attaches less to the slog of writing and more to sitting mindlessly in front of the email scroll. Guess which act I am more likely to repeat.

The phenomenon known as "punishment-induced aggression" (encountered previously in the example where Cesar Millan zapped the German shepherd fitted with a shock collar, who then turned on his "innocent" owner sitting nearby and bit her arm) is a fascinating, if supremely dismaying, one. Almost all animals are prone to it, including us.

If a sudden aversive is visited on a laboratory subject, he will immediately attack any other animal who has the misfortune to be present. If no other flesh-and-blood creature is there, a so-called bite bar receives the frenzy—and, unlike the fellow rat, is able to digitally record aspects of the aggression, including how many bites and how hard. More disturbing, a punished subject will go to any lengths to *find* another individual to attack, even an animal behind a closed door that requires the physical and intellectual expense of figuring out how to get through. Anything, so long as we can take out our fury on someone else.

And then, the blissful relief of having vented this urge to retaliate reinforces *further* expressions of violence. A cycle begins.

The coercion cycle of control-countercontrol-anticountercontrol can occur between individuals or within entire systems, such as repressive governments and schools. (Sidman betrays his academic background by reaching for schools more often than any other illustration of the modes and methods of coercion; indeed, they are the single most detailed and persuasive example he cites. He thus also follows his teacher and philosophical forebear B. F. Skinner, who was figuratively frustrated to tears by what he considered the dim-witted, counterproductive educational model that has so long predominated. There are too many ways in which school is an aversive experience, conducive to avoidance, escape, and retaliations both subtle and altogether dramatic. Does anyone else find themselves wondering why school shootings seem to have become practically quotidian? Rarely are there grocery store shootings, or arboretum shootings, or bowling alley shootings—though what really goes on in post offices needs immediate deep analysis. Of the sixty-two mass shootings in the U.S. between 1982 and 2012, more than half occurred in either a school or a workplace; the latter are, interestingly enough, Sidman's second or third most often blueprinted example of coercion's peculiar architecture.)

Now the coercive cycle's progress comes right up on our heels. It is time for the big question. "Coercion is responsible for so much misery: why does it persist?" The behavior analyst knows what to do: look for the reinforcer, as it must be there; we must look at what happens right after a punishment is received.

"Usually, punishing people makes them stop what they were doing. That is our reinforcement . . . the basis for our belief in punishment." Unfortunately, though, "All the side effects come later." And late is no good to be of any use, remember. The delayed punishment—the usual cascade of negative fallout—is not connected with the act of punishing. Ironically that comes out smelling clean and fresh; it is obviously not the problem.

Finally, we gloss the unconscious compulsion to punish with a veneer of intention: *discipline* (a favored euphemism for punishment or threat, along with "leadership" and "consequences") is necessary. Even good, morally superior. We justify what is personally pleasant because we wish to protect our supply line to our preferred high, no more and no less. Also because we are conditioned by the avoidance of what we find more than a little punishing itself: the idea that we are controlled by circumstances beyond "free will."

> *Punishment is seen as more acceptable than positive reinforcement because "people believe they are free to choose to behave in responsible ways to avoid punishment." (Maag, 2001)*[18] *Our societal values of independence, and a tendency to view the world in terms of being punished for bad or immoral behavior tend to predispose us to treat inappropriate behaviors with punishment, rather than focusing on the value of positive reinforcement for doing the right thing.*[19]

So this is what total remodeling of entrenched habit is up against: fluency, practice, legacy, a powerfully long history of reward. How to replace something like that with what amounts to a mindfulness practice? Stand back and calmly consider the science? Carefully engineer a plan and stay the hand, when it wants to strike?

As a society, much less as dog trainers, bosses, parents, we need a twelve-step program to dry us out from our long punishment drunk. It would be so much easier (notwithstanding the eventual outcome of all addictions, disaster) to remain in denial that we have a problem. To continue to permit ourselves the blessed release of pouring the day's first drink (temporarily forgetting that it is only the first of many, and that the last is far uglier when stripped of its fictive glow). Then proceed to sink slowly into the warm embrace of consciouslessness.

The price of relinquishing oneself to any such compulsion is always finally too high. As with drink, so too with human society, both ensnared in great webs of lies. The first is semantic. We call it freedom, but we are enslaved. Our master's name is coercion.

* * *

IT IS ironic, a suck on a lemon, that the behavioral methodology that instilled such fear in people who imagined it was going to strip free will from us is in fact the wellspring of initiative. (And that might well be just another word for free will.) A dog who has been pushed around will never know the joys of playing 101 Things to Do with a Cardboard Box—and his owner will never know the complementary bliss of seeing her beloved doing what we may well have been put here on earth to do: fall in love with learning. It's ecstasy in a minute of time, in a look, a body. Which is, after all, all we have been given. Ourselves, here, inside this skin. In the midst of experience.

A revelation: we can choose to be kind.

It is not easy. It doesn't come naturally. But it is worth it.

This is the experience of the so-called cross-over trainer, one who started as a traditional trainer but who, often in a single moment of epiphany, saw a naked truth no longer possible to turn away from. One of them described the veil torn off when she was getting ready for yet another training session for competition obedience and found her dog hiding from her under the porch.

Who can say what caused her in that moment to step back and suddenly see, instead of furiously grab the dog and pinch and jerk him just a little harder that day? Whatever changed her view, it is a story told and retold by hundreds. This may be the true power of the love of a dog: that sometimes it makes us see for the first time.

The only opposing force against the depressingly daunting challenges inherent in crossing over that dread divide is the fact that, just as punishment is reinforcing to the punisher, so positive reinforcement becomes reinforcing to the reinforcer. You just have to start. Soon they will come, a few hits of this particular happy drug: working, learning, quickly becomes addictive for both dog *and* trainer. A sparkle in the eye of the beloved, a new liveliness in the carriage, a strangely visible thought process—how sensuous is thinking!—and the confidence of growing safety in and control of one's environment.

Withholding every possible chance to learn all they are capable of, and so to feel that native joy, is mean, in the original sense of the word: miserly, stingy.*

I confess that I am still just a tiny, painfully regretted, bit mean to Nelly. But she gives back as good as she gets. She is my shadow.

---

* Jean Donaldson, once more, can't quite contain herself. On the subject of compulsion trainers who loudly justify their staunch commitment to withholding any pleasure to their dogs, she said in a webinar: "The sad objective of these trainers seems to be to reach the end of the dog's life having dispensed as few rewards as possible. It's difficult to explain why an animal trainer would strive to be as stingy as possible, given the evidence of how powerful and safe positive reinforcement is. Maybe it's psychological."

CHAPTER TEN

We need another and a wiser and perhaps a more
mystical concept of animals. Remote from universal
nature, and living by complicated artifice, man
in civilization surveys the creature through the
glass of his knowledge and sees thereby a feather
magnified and the whole image in distortion.
We patronize them for their incompleteness, for
their tragic fate of having taken form so far below
ourselves. And therein we err, and greatly err.
For the animal shall not be measured by man. In
a world older and more complete than ours they
move finished and complete, gifted with extensions
of the senses we have lost or never attained, living
by voices we shall never hear.

—HENRY BESTON, *THE OUTERMOST HOUSE*, 1928

The more deeply one goes into a specialized topic,
the more one realizes how intimately that topic
is related to everything else. Real specialization,
although frowned on by so-called generalists,
eventually brings one into contact with the rest of

the world. One cannot really know how general
anything is until one has gone into it deeply.

—MURRAY SIDMAN, "REFLECTIONS ON

STIMULUS CONTROL," 2008

In time, Nelly and I melded our lives on paths that psychically came together the more they physically diverged. Our daily walks were both silent communications and, to our systems, autonomic. Like the pumping of the heart, walking separately together was basic to survival. Perhaps it also became an addiction. But the substance I was abusing was air, sight, thought. I think those walks, in the cornfields, on the rail trail, bushwhacking on DEP lands and sometimes, *shhh*, private owners', kept me alive. They kept me moving, anyway, and what is more like life? We were born to move and, as we do so, to absorb the world through senses that conscious thought cannot access. Though sometimes the world accessed my mind in turn; once, at the top of a long uphill climb on a trail in the middle of the thousands of acres of the Mohonk Preserve, a fully formed sentence simply unrolled itself in my head. I have no idea where it came from, but maybe the mountains themselves. I had not been thinking of anything, except the perennial wonder about where Nelly had got to. (During a significant portion of our walks, maybe half, she was not visible to my eye, although she always knew where I was; one of the ways in which we grew together was the evolution of my trust that she would, eventually, return. This was sadly misplaced again and again, but each new day I forgot the anguish of the past and went out yet again in search of yet another opportunity to appreciate Nelly's spectacularly predatory nature. It is also not out of the realm of possibility that she was racking up frequent-flyer miles to Mexico.) A mile of one foot carefully placed in front of the other, advancing among the rocks and tree roots and muddy patches, with the peculiar joy of having small challenges continually met. Then, it was there. The final sentence of a review that had stumped me for days.

I knew I would lose it, too, on the way back down unless I got it on paper.

Sometimes things work out just right. Well, rarely they do. But that still qualifies as sometimes.

Given the size of the pockets in my jean jacket, there was no way there would be anything of help in them. But life continually overturns expectations, pessimistic same as hopeful, and so it turned out I had a stub of a pencil in one pocket and a matchbook in the other. I leaned against a boulder and scrawled the sentence around the front and back of two inches of cardboard. It was very hard to read later. But it exemplified the kind of comprehensive miracle that came again and again to me on the trails. For all their generosity to me, I would never have permitted myself their luxury now (much though I had depended on aimless wandering for my primary pleasure as a youth) had it not been for the excuse that I was really giving my dog a brief opportunity to be herself before I demanded that she suppress everything that she was for the rest of the day. She had to, and uncomplainingly did, conform to inexplicable demands. No human could do for more than a moment what we routinely, without consideration, make our dogs do for most of their lives.

Then I turned to look for Nelly.

She often came back filthy, burr-studded, carrion-enriched, and very late. She was living her life, which in at least half had nothing to do with mine. And why should this not be so?

Because she was my responsibility, and my insensible love, too, I would spend hours retracing my steps, certain she was in this corner of the state because that is where I last saw the flash of her trundle-tail. That is when I would find she had rounded the territory and was now back on the other side of the map, well ahead of me. It was my own damn fault, but that did not stop me from being angry. Most of the time, anger is really fear, chemically transformed, but on rare occasion it truly is just anger, when your kindness is being taken for granted (not even taken for kindness)—and the school bus is about to arrive at home. You are torn in two, but of course the half containing human progeny weighs more. That makes you angrier, and you get in your car and drive furiously away while loudly telling yourself you just don't care: *Do you hear me, I don't care!* Though of course you do care, heart-in-throat care, and once the bus is met, the child hustled into the backseat with a snack, you drive back as fast as you left with two versions of the future alternately superimposing themselves in your head: the sight you dread most, unspeakable, appearing and reappearing around every corner of the road you now hurtle along; and the little beast, standing innocent but unharmed in the parking lot as if she simply didn't understand, waiting alertly for your return.

So far, the eventuality has always been the latter. It just as easily might not be, the next time. And yet, you always repeat and return. To the trails where she can be her wolfish self. To the trails where you, too, recover a piece of the history that made you.

* * *

AT LEAST I knew enough, from my former life as a student of Polly, to not make a common error: that of punishing Nelly for coming back (or rather, for my own stupidity, garnished lightly with anger at being so stupid). One of the most elementary techniques in filmmaking is to arouse sympathy in the audience for any character, no matter how unsympathetic, simply by shooting from that individual's POV. Polly, as director of a movie on the true life of dogs, never before seen, made the camera the eyes of the other: the dog's. Always the dog's.

Furious as I might have been when Nelly e-v-e-n-t-u-a-l-l-y returned from her extended travels—her departure always presaged by a wild yet vacant look in her eyes that signaled the switching on of the primitive hind-brain; I imagined I could see it glowing toxic green right through her skull—I resisted the desire to detonate the atom bomb made of my colliding fear and frustration. I heard Polly whispering from the past: *Bad idea*.

She had said: What are you really punishing when you yell at your dog, or clip on the leash to end the fun, after he finally comes back? The act of coming back, of course.*

So restrain yourself. Set the dog up for success. (Here, heeding this leading mantra of the positive movement means managing the environment so the dog never has the chance to fail at coming back: you are supposed to arrange it so the only option he has is to come back and get paid for it, foreclosing the possibility of landing a bigger reward by his own doing somewhere in the wild blue yonder. He will simultaneously learn that it is always a great, happy thing to return and that "Come" is not an arbitrary sound endlessly repeated, but actually attaches to a meaning.) Let Nelly drag a twenty-foot long-line, in other words, and let me step on it quickly if she looks like she is about to bolt. Then just stand there, quietly; inevitably, she will look around, confused as to what has just impeded her progress.

---

* Last week I witnessed this—with the added bonus of a perfect example of "poisoning the cue," soon to be described—when a family member, who routinely crated her Bouvier at night and when the family went out, called "Come!" when she wanted him to go to the first floor and into his crate. His displeasure was obvious; sometimes he stuck so fast to where he was she had to go and drag him by the collar. The result was that when she called "Come!" for dinner or to go out for a walk, he hesitated in confusion: did that sound signify impending imprisonment away from his beloved people, or something good? When he stood at the end of the driveway, having relieved himself and ready to go back indoors, she called "Come!" again to by now predictable results. Oh, don't bother, she said to herself. He doesn't listen.

At some point, her gaze will fall on me. *Click*. I have just taken the first step in shaping a highly useful behavior: the habit of checking in with me. It took Nelly only a few trials to figure out what she had to do to claim the prize, and from then on it was a regular thing (Nelly likes her tasty morsels). Now I could start to raise the criteria: a click only for a close-by check-in. Soon she was running back to me, standing by my leg and looking expectantly up. Damn, this works almost too well.*

If at this point she still managed to get away and I felt like coming unglued when she finally came back, I had to put a cork in it. First, it could only be my fault. Second, by making it end badly for her, I would only ensure she would think twice about coming back in the future.

I loved these walks, in the way one loves the smooth skin on a man's chest. I needed these walks: they gave me what is impossible to get in any other way. The repetitive motion that is their essence is the theme of the world itself, expressed in one melodic line that goes away, followed by another that returns. I got good thinking done. I tired myself, and my dog as well. I meditated without trying.

I also cemented the type of friendships of lasting strength that only come with shared adversity: Janet's Willy disappeared with some regularity, too. It was as if he and Nelly conferred, deciding to give us a bit of a break, so that usually only one of them was gone at a

---

* Here, another of positive reinforcement's crazy wildflowers pushes its tender head up through the earth: it instills self-control. The individual learns when to reward herself, as it were, on her own say-so. Here, behavioral control is a motivation originating in the organism. It is not imposed from without. You can't learn self-control if someone's always one step ahead, arranging the means to control you.

Score another one for the Chomskyites, for turning this around so completely: they accuse Skinner of imposing control, but it is *precisely* the opposite. In the world according to operant conditioning, you are given nothing but opportunities to control yourself. And this is how an individual reaps social benefit.

time. We cursed, at the same time we acknowledged that, knowing full well the mischievous proclivities of our dogs, we willfully chose to walk into the same ambush day after day. We needed each other as well as the walks. Janet, Bonnie, and I for years walked together: Malcolm and Nora, Willy and Dixie, and Nelly had their own conclaves with nature, while the three humans solved every problem of a personal nature as well as the travails of the world. They became my sisters, and together we should have been crowned triumvirate of all known nations, because we would have fixed them and made everyone happy.

Then, too, even as Nelly ran away, she and I drew together. The connective filament between us, stretched thin though it might have been, was spun of understanding. I learned what was likely to cause her to sprint, and I learned under what conditions she would come back. I could not will this knowledge into being, study it or look it up online or ask an authority. I had to bloody walk through it. It was going to take as long as it was going to take: the three-mile trail was three miles. Every step had to be taken. When it is all over and not a moment before is when you realize the best knowledge is so hard-won it comes this close to killing you before it enlightens you immeasurably.

When living with another species—that backhanded, irreplaceable privilege—understanding is the root of trust. Sometimes I trusted her to be untrustworthy. That felt most solid of all. I knew she was more likely to disappear, farther and for longer, when we walked with anyone else, either people or dogs, than if we were alone. I learned, ridiculously late in the game, that she would never, ever come back when she was in her walkabout mode if I stood waiting by the car. No, I had to be in it—with the door closed and windows up, only. It often felt like an eternity, but I rarely had to watch the sideview mirror more than ten intense minutes before a bedraggled dog would appear from the weeds, moving left to right. Objects in mirror are closer than they appear.

If I didn't happen to be near a car, I could try to find a building to go into for the sole purpose of shutting the door. She might have been gone forever until I disappeared inside: within seconds she would materialize. A shriek would erupt from the universal center of sound. Matter tore.

I do not compliment myself that Nelly had fallen for the inimitable me, the little girl entrapped in this aging cage who still believed she was worthy of love for her own sake, for the very particularity of her irreducible self. I was something useful to Nelly, as she was something useful to me. Love is—as we do not wish to see it—relative.

A dog surveys the scene and it begins pixelating. The tiny visual building blocks quickly rearrange themselves until a new picture emerges. It is composed of objects of value. Everything that doesn't matter is reabsorbed into the background. What the dog sees out of the window is very different from what you see, because your history—evolutionary, cultural, and personal—is wholly different. What you desire most is different. You both note the garbage can, but for opposing reasons.

The verbal scene is the same: I will bet my admittedly small investment portfolio that your dog has no clue what "Good dog, Bella!" means, nor does she care, except as far as the sound of "good" or "dog" or "Bella" may once have occurred in proximate relation to something she truly valued. The concept of "good" in a moral sense is probably ungraspable by Bella, and as a rewardable state is a peculiarly human construct that presupposes, impossibly, that a dog enjoys "approval" the way human children do. Some dogs do appear to enjoy attention, it is true, but not half as much as our vanity would like. In fact, not only do most dogs not enjoy it—consisting as it does in body language their species especially deplores as threatening, such as pats on the head, direct stares, and hugs—to many of them it is punishing. The attention is desirable only inasmuch as it has been conditioned as a signal of an incipient primary reinforcer, something necessary to survival. For children and dogs both, your attention—which represents something of essential value to you as an organism, your time—stands in for affection, which in turn is a sign that you are the one most likely to offer the care and feeding a dependent requires.

Three small terriers were enjoying the rocky shallows of the stream with their owner. One of them persistently ran up to Nelly and exhibited what to me (though undoubtedly not to the dog) seemed oddly contradictory behavior. She got in front of Nelly and immediately submitted by rolling onto her back, while Nelly did what she increasingly does in her late middle age: look away and refuse to engage. She has lost the intense desire of her younger years to play ferociously until exhausted and wet with the saliva of her playmates. (This is the gift of the dog park to the owner of a young dog: a tired puppy, which is a good puppy.) Nowadays, Nelly wants only to be left alone to walk and sniff, intent on the work of covering ancient pee marks of previous generations with her own. But, from submissive to pesky in the space of an instant, the little sand-colored dog leapt up when she stood still in apparent plea to be left alone and started biting her ear. Now, Nelly is not one to stand down. She can be patient, but only until that patience has been tried enough. For her, "enough" is about thirty seconds. Before that could elapse, happily, the owner called. The small terrier rushed away. And, as soon as she got to her person, she was punished for it.

Now, that is not how the nice young woman saw it. "Good girl, good girl!" she cried, immediately bending down to lavish her touch on the dog's head and shoulders. The dog visibly flinched. To her, there was a loud sound (remember dogs' hearing, far more acute than ours) and then something of monstrous size reaching over her: nothing in the dog's repertoire of affection resembles a pat on the head. It is to them nothing good; in fact, in their language it is a threat. (Most dogs submit, while a few will fight back; but to none is a pat on the head a reward unless it has been previously conditioned as one by being paired with the receipt of something desirable. People are only convinced their dogs like to be patted when they have not yet learned how subtle are dogs' expressions and how different their communications from ours; in the presence of a blank screen, we project onto it our understandings. Self-interest works both ways.) The woman, by reacting as a primate, using a primate's body language, had discouraged her dog from repeating a desired behavior.

Sometimes you say "Good girl" but your actions say "Bad girl," and you know what they say about which speaks louder than which.

*   *   *

TO NELLY, I am very nearly everything. Not because I am as startlingly complete as an object of affection as I so clearly am, but because there is a wall between her and what she wants—the joys of running and chasing and sniffing; almost all food; other dogs; the prey that she truly lived for—and I am a door. I am a resource to her, as the conduit to other resources. I am even regarded by her as a tool, and if dogs are not counted among tool-using species, I know better. Or maybe Nelly is alone among her kind: one night I sit on the floor by the woodstove, as I do on winter nights, as close as I can get without setting my sweater on fire. She had gotten a particularly large knucklebone for dinner and had been propelling it around the floor, trying to get a purchase on it so she could tear the last remaining shreds of tendon off. Suddenly she picked the bone up in her mouth, trotted over, and nudged the newspaper out of my hands she crawled into my lap. She deposited the bone in my hand and I reflexively held on. Now that it was stabilized, she proceeded to tear into it. She had reduced me, Ivy League education and all, to a bone holder.

I am useful to her. I provide and I care for her. In the spring and fall, I pull ticks from her, some days by the dozens. My primate fingers are reflexively busy whenever we are at rest; I have tapped into an ancient instinct, the origin of all that Homo sapiens would become. We groomed each other, long ago, in the trees. And we became cooperative beings above all else. Our brains grew and grew as our fingers found vermin. I find I have a natural talent for it.

It hurts, though, when I pull them off. Nelly won't let anyone else do it without whining, crying, or even placing her teeth, a gentle warning, on their skin. With me, though, she knows: She has asked somehow for this. She sits patiently for it. She turns to look me in the eye, and silently says, *I know: you didn't mean to hurt me; it is in service of my request, after all.* And how do I know what she is asking for next, proof? I just do. I open my hand and show her the repulsive creature, legs waving, before I rejoice in crushing it. (Sorry. I would make a bad Jain.) She observes it for a moment, is satisfied, then turns away again: *Carry on.*

One day on a walk, I saw Mercy up ahead suddenly lurch, then refuse to put her right front paw down again. She wheeled around and hobbled on three legs back to me. She sat down and held up her paw until I took it. I felt around her foot as she looked off into the middle distance; it was her intention that I do exactly this. I found it, as was her plan: a gigantic thorn embedded deep in a pad. She winced as I pulled it out, but the pain had already been accounted for by Mercy. She knew it was coming and that its momentary prick would be subsumed by permanent relief. She had manifested intentionality, as well as foreknowledge of my usefulness. My Androcles, to her lion. (In George Bernard Shaw's telling, the slave informs the

Roman emperor: "Never be afraid of animals, your Worship: that's the great secret. He'll be as gentle as a lamb when he knows that you are his friend." I am my dogs' friend. But are they mine? I will not venture farther with this line of thought. It is bound to be unpopular. As all stone pragmatism ends.)

This is the basis of my dogs' storied love for me, their one and only. Only I know the real truth. It is not this Melissa they love. If they bark menacingly at someone who approaches, they are not doing it to ensure my safety. There is but one thought in their minds: do not harm this person, for she is my most valuable possession. My large Swiss army knife, the one with all the extra attachments.

•   •   •

YET, YET . . . love. Is this another of our compulsive narratives, created only to elevate the lowly, inescapable physicality of existence, that which begins, then ends? Who among us will be remembered a hundred years hence, or more than a generation or two even among our own progeny? At best, we will be some yellowing papers and time-shredded handkerchiefs in an attic trunk: "Look—great-grandma's stuff." "Huh."

Of what is my child's love for me composed? (I know what mine is of him: everything I am, or ever will be.) As he nursed at the breast, or cried as if his heart would break upon parting from it, I had an unsentimental thought even as I was washed in the waters of the greatest sentiment I had ever experienced: our children love us because we feed them.

Yet, yet . . .

The rescue dog tells another story of love. The one who was found, terrified and alone (terrified *because* alone), in the park and then taken home. The one who has been through one owner or more already, and who knows deep under his fur unto his bones what sudden loss feels like. This is the one who clings, who with piteous eyes closely watches every movement of his new owner as if to say *Not you, too?*

Janet's Dixie is such a dog: how much loss in her previous life she was made to experience we will never know, though we can guess. But now she examines Janet for signs. Dixie is the one who never disappears on walks, while Willy and Nelly take turns exploring the wide countryside and their owners' tolerance of intense fear and frustration. She is also deathly afraid of thunder. She takes to trembling with every cell.

The day the weather report indicated a line of severe storms and possible hail, Janet dashed from the house in the pressing rain to move the car under the carport. Dixie weighed her options in a quick second. She attached herself to Janet's leg and burst through the door, too. It was better to face the monstrous with her beloved than safety without her. Is this love?

Yes. Call it that.

*   *   *

WE CALL them by name. "What are you going to call him?" Our own act of genesis, for in the beginning was the word. Naming begins everything. The baby, still bearing gills and a tail, is named before she breathes. It makes her real, and it makes her her.

So we call our dogs. "Olive, come!" As if the dog (1) knows of a thing called "my name," referring to this entity, "me," and (2) knows what "come" means.

That darn dog doesn't listen to me!

She listens, but what does she know of what she hears?

Dr. Jesús Rosales-Ruiz, in a ClickerExpo seminar on "the poisoned cue"—the conditioned reinforcer that has been recklessly deployed—used an example that hit close to home for everyone in the room. One's name may be the most poisoned cue of all. Sometimes hearing your name called meant your favorite dinner was in the offing; sometimes it meant you were about to get a hug or your allowance. Other times it meant "Who tracked this mud through the kitchen?" or "We need to have a talk about your report card." You never knew if you should run to the source of the sound or go hide in the closet. So you froze instead. A dog who has heard "Buster, bad dog!" followed by a swat, as well as "Buster, time for nyum-nyums!" knows his name is another word for trouble. Unless he was trained by the greatest, most consistent positive reinforcement trainer on the planet, upon hearing his name your average dog is likely to evince anxiety, expressed by a quick lip lick or a sniff of the grass (a subtle sign, true, often misread as, well, sniffing the grass).

As someone who not only poisoned cues like a real champion but who was able to poison the whole experience of living with my dog—sometimes I guided her pretty well, sometimes I made head-slapping errors large and small—I never mastered the high art of the recall. This, despite taking a whole class in one specific protocol, developed by trainer Leslie Nelson, called Really Reliable Recall; it depended heavily on keeping a tight grip on all resources. I thought of it as constructing a metaphorical chute: nothing of interest available to the dog by his own wiles, so the only option was to come through the tunnel to you, the light at the end. It was said to work without exception *so long* as it was followed to the letter: impossible for me, since I kept insisting on giving Nelly access on our off-leash hikes to the most delectable buffet of reinforcers there was, to which she could go and fill and refill her plate with clouds of aromatic delights. What need could she possibly have for lamb roll or even Vienna sausage? Nothing man could make could compete with the

excitements of the world in which one evolved. If I insisted on permitting her access to these glories even occasionally, I was devaluing
anything I could offer. I got what I asked for.

Not that I let my dog roam completely free, with no constraints
whatsoever. I did try many things, some of which met with partial
success. And partial, in my worldview, is often complete.

Over the years, I essayed—and one by one abandoned—many
fine techniques. I bought stuffed toys and anointed them with eau
de bunny from the hunters' supply, on the theory that an owner who
makes herself more interesting than anything else in the environment will have a dog who will always come to her. Uh-uh. No obviously fake dead animal wearing fake perfume could interest Nelly
for long, when there were genuine potential dead animals doused in
their own alluring scent out there hiding. (I should have done a better job of being secretive with the prize, since that was an essential
aspect of the rabbit's appeal. Or, come to think of it, any object of
one's affection.) I trained, but then neglected to proof or to maintain,
a "down-stay at distance"—the skill of hitting the ground and staying there until released on cue, crucial in case, say, your dog ended up
on the other side of a road then decided to come back at the instant
a car was coming. I tried to get her fixated on tennis balls, getting
all excited about the fact that if she came I may or may not release
one for her to chase, just wait and see! She, too, got all excited, especially about the surprise aspect of the release, ran after the ball like
a shot, then dropped it and trotted off to better things. She was no
retriever and no herder, the two types of dogs most likely to become
ball-obsessed, although I did succeed in installing a "bring it back"
cue. (Hint: easy to do with two balls. Make the reinforcer for the
retrieve the instantaneous release of the second ball. You can keep
a dog going this way for longer than your arm will hold out.) For a

while, I remembered to attach a couple of jingle bells to her collar every time we set out so I would at least be able to tell inside which impenetrable thicket of briars she had made herself unreachable. All of these items eventually found their way to the bottom of the dried mud that coated the pockets of all my truthfully named dog coats. And stayed there.

Only one lucky thing I taught Nelly ever succeeded more than once in truly saving my ass. It seemed innocuous enough when it was suggested to me while she was still a puppy. In the kitchen or in the yard (strike when the iron was cold: teach when the pressure was off), clip her leash to her collar, give a treat, release. Repeat. When she's already coming, under her own volition for some other reason, give the act a name—"let me put on your leash" was my ingenious cue—and repeat, repeat, repeat. The fact that it never cost her anything, for she was always released immediately to beloved freedom, and with a slightly fuller stomach, made it to her a behavioral freebie. Soon I had it under "stimulus control," meaning it was a sure thing.* Where "Come!" failed as a supremely poisoned cue (it sometimes ended her fun), "Let me put on your leash" never did. Functionally, it was the same: Nelly ended up safely attached, often in the last opportunity before danger. She has never made the connection about the connection, one of the few end runs around my feeble mental defense she has not effortlessly enacted.

---

* From the glossary on Karen Pryor's Clickertraining.com (what gorgeous literature is science!): "A conditioned stimulus becomes a discriminative stimulus (or cue) when it is followed by a specific learned behavior or reaction. The response is said to be 'under stimulus control' when presentation of the particular stimulus fulfills these four conditions: the behavior is always offered when that cue is presented; the behavior is not offered in the absence of that cue; the behavior is not offered in response to some other cue; and no other behavior occurs in response to that cue."

· · ·

I CAN never fully understand the mind of another—another human's, much less one of another species—but I can certainly misunderstand them.

Nelly's world is enclosed and unknowable. It is also penetrable to the extent of my willingness to venture into gaps below which there may be no ground. I must turn myself around and feel my way to the edge of the cliff. At some point, my foot will find the place where it finally drops, and then I trust to the rope and space. I lower myself down backward by feel. When I attempt to know what she experiences, I rappel into her mind.

In the late seventies, a two-headed black rat snake came to live in a lab at Rockefeller University. It happened to belong to Donald R. Griffin, the man who as a biology student made the radical discovery that bats navigate using echolocation. Griffin later broke a major sound barrier in science by suggesting that what went on in the interior world of animals, not just their observable behavior, was a legitimate object of study; he is thus the father of cognitive ethology. Decades later, it is still a young field. "Argued Animals Can Think," runs the surprised headline on his 2003 obituary in the *New York Times*. It would have contained an exclamation point if the *Times* countenanced such frivolity.

The snake was studied at feeding time for five years, during which it killed and ate some 400 mice. But *who* killed and ate them? It was a two-headed snake.

If it was aware that both its brains served the same body, then one would have crowned itself king and ordered the other to do all the work of feeding. But the real king, or tyrant, is instinct, and these brains could not rise above it. The two heads on the one body often fought over prey. As if only one stood a chance of winning. The snake was named IM, for "instinct" and "mind," the two heads each of us, too, possess.

Of the many motivational urges that rule us but of which we seem equally unaware, acting as though speech has substantive powers is one of the more amusing. If we were truly the rational beings we so desperately wish we were, one would never hear things repeated in increasingly loud tones to an uncomprehending foreigner, as if the word (in one's native tongue) were universal, of course, and the problem could lie only in volume. The same is true of people yelling over and over again "Come!" or "Sit!" or "Drop it!" to that foreigner with four legs with whom they share a home but not an essential world.

Speech is a set of arbitrary sound symbols. Like all symbols, words themselves lack meaning beyond the substantive thing they have been paired with. Structurally, they are conditioned reinforcers. This does not explain the generation of language, or a whole lot else about it, but it is an inarguable basis of a word's function.

If you want to teach a Frenchman the meaning of the word *bread*, you would do well to show him a baguette; he'll get it pretty quickly. If you stare at him and repeat, louder and louder, this strange complex of sounds (especially that godawful hard *R*) you'll only end up hoarse.

And smacking him in the face at the end of the recitation because he "refused" to understand is likely to win a very unpleasant reprisal, as ought all such absurd acts.

Yet such is the essence of what goes on, and on, with a million dogs at this very moment: a smack for the insolence of not instinctively knowing English. And it's not just "English," i.e., one language of nearly 7,000 known to exist. It's a thing that emanates from somewhere so deep inside us—say, the historicoexperiential center of being—that we cannot differentiate it from Skinner's "homunculus," the chimera of the internal self. (And in fact I now wonder, from the vantage point of advanced age, if what appears to be the intense hold the notion of free will has on our minds wasn't really just hormones all along.) The person actually believes *Come!* has some internal power to *make the dog come.* Four letters. Conveying messages to will and bone.

We have fallen so far down the well of speech's imagined powers that we are often unable to pull ourselves up to the rim to peer out at a world wider than 6 feet in diameter. We so naturally expect to receive a response to our words, since we are surrounded by listeners who speak the same tongue, that talking is like the engine that continues to run even though the vehicle is in park.

(This reliance, against all logic, on speech as if it magically made things—as if it were a factory made of soundwaves—may be the proof of Skinner's contention that consciousness is a social construct. He maintains it never would have taken conceptual shape if people hadn't talked about it with one another. It did not cause us to reflect on it. Rather, our reflection on it caused it to appear to exist. Moreover, this absorbing search for the "self" is really a search for a Creator, he said. Which makes cognitive psychology the Creationism of science. Words bound to anger many, even if true.)

We seem constitutionally unable to understand that speaking does not get things done, that there is no invisible yet powerful motor that once started up by speech will originate actions left and right. The word for this is "deluded." What we say is so often at odds with what happens. As for me, 90 percent of everything that comes out of my mouth is utter horseshit.

And then I go and repeat it. As if it wasn't stupidly ineffectual the first time, I say it again as if this were somehow going to imbue it with undeniable power. Repetition: the top habit of highly ineffectual people. It also marks the difference between requesting and nagging. With a dog, as with a teenager, the wall of white noise that emanates so often from our mouths—wishful thinking at its most bizarre, imagining that the eighty-seventh repetition is finally going to pull off the trick—teaches only one thing: it's all meaningless. So tune it out.

Give your cue, or your request, one time only. Then be quiet. Each repetition saps meaning until there's nothing left. Except the sound of your frustrated voice revolving into outer space.

I am never as good a dog trainer (or parent, for that matter) as when I keep my mouth shut.

Dog training can be done, and possibly done best, in the near-complete absence of spoken language. Stripped of the crutch talk represents, the magical thinking that enwraps the act, suddenly you are able to *see*. Disengage the mouth and vision suddenly clears: timing improves; witnessing occurs. You can't call things what they aren't anymore, by way of projection or dissimulation or false hope. Suppress speech, and you are left before only what is there.

It makes no sense to believe either that we already understand their language or that they have none. We need a Rosetta Stone course in dog, just as we would in Mandarin if we hoped to move to China. We are like foreigners to one another, and one of us needs to stop chattering as if we were the only one with something important to say.*

---

* Someone who calls himself "BfSkinnerPunk" wrote on the Click-L listserv about his realization that verbal behavior is the preeminent distinction between us and the other animals—yakking and "the slew of fancy behavior it creates." At the same time, he says, it is also the behavioral attribute that gave rise to the idea that we possess "some extra-special soul-like inner self." One that eclipses notice of other species and their communicative parity: what a bird says to another bird is every bit as important (to the birds) as what I say to you. Our ignorance of the birds' communication does nothing to diminish its primacy to them.

We were sitting in fat armchairs in the lobby at a ClickerExpo, I and a dear friend who was once also Polly's acolyte (having had the same revelatory experience I'd had, she had gone full speed ahead into the new technology: eight years later and she is a trainer of some note, with a book and a podcast to her credit). While I poured out yet another tale of Nelly woe to the friend who patiently fielded years' worth of emails, calls, screams of pure frustration, and visits back to Brooklyn, returning reams of information and advice on training protocol, she was doing something. So distraught was I that I barely noticed her tossing minuscule bits of lamb roll to Nelly, who was intently—and, holy shit, *quietly*—watching my friend as if she were about to reveal the numbers to tomorrow's Mega Millions. She was talking to me, but not to Nelly. She was just waiting for something, and when she saw it, she tossed a bit of food. To the right, to the left, and after each time she scrambled away to get the morsel, Nelly hurried back to throw herself down again and direct at my friend a gaze that might have cut iron pipe. She was being shaped.

For a while, she had been "throwing" behaviors—tossing out things that had worked once upon a time, to see if they might work again. But in my friend's mind an idea had taken form, and with it the changing criteria that Nelly would have to meet in order to arrive at a finished product. Only one of them knew what this was to be, until the final clapping of hands and huzzahs: shaping is a little like playing charades. The next thing I knew, Nelly had her chin glued to the floor, and she was being reinforced heartily every time she returned to her place at my friend's feet and immediately lowered her head. She would have kept at this all night. No words were spoken during the entire episode: the treats along with their well-timed delivery said everything.

Years and years later. Every time we sit at the dinner table, Nelly's hope springs eternal. On occasion, Nelly has been tossed a bit off a plate, but only if she is absolutely quiet. If she's in another room, it's even better; I can throw her a tidbit anywhere I like, and because she comprehends that lying in the next room is the payable job, she runs back there. Fun game, for the dictatorial spirit in all of us.

But when I'm in a mood, or Nelly is (the mood to whine), the reward refuses to appear. Now she's frustrated. And my lack of timing is what has frustrated her. But Nelly is nothing if not persistent, the cause of my deeply held belief that she must have terrier in her: she has the terrier's never-say-die attitude, along with its profound attraction to rodents. She is so persistent that what happened to her nearly a decade ago, over the course of maybe twenty minutes in a hotel lobby, is so entrenched it is now her go-to behavior. Whenever she can't make food dance off a plate just by willing it, she puts her chin on the floor and looks up through brown eyes that could melt stone: Isn't this what you wanted? I am giving you all I've got.

And indeed she is.

* * *

THE CLICKER is not magic, but it is a symbol of the sudden change from nothing into something—the rabbit appears—that communication brings into being. The clicker is magic.

I watched doors swing open one by one down an endless hall when Mercy first understood what she could make happen: the opportunities to make me click were to her endless, exciting. She watched my every movement so minutely, as dogs are made to do, that I'm sure she saw my hair grow. Years later, in agility class, Nelly would consistently and maddeningly miss the entry to some piece of equipment. Until the instructor pointed out that my dog was watching my eyes, where my foot was pointed. At the same time, she was racing flat out in and out of tunnels and over jumps. A barely noticeable (to me) correction in the direction of my look, a quarter-inch shift in my path, and now she would go where I wanted. It was all a fine game.

Tell these dogs the clicker is not magic, though.

For anyone who is wondering about using a clicker for training, I thought I'd share the following from some sessions I did with my foster dogs yesterday: Leroy, hound mix, aka TOTAL MESS . . . I taught Leroy in two, less-than-ten-minute sessions to go lie down on a mat. No words. No physical *manipulation. And I'd never taught him to lie down before. He went from grabbing the mat up and thrashing it around like a toy when I laid it down, to running over and laying down on it. I was* stunned.

Doogan, handsome boxer mix: Taught him to high-five in less than five minutes. Seriously.

—Susan Mitchell

Susan, this post brings tears to my eyes as I remember the day I stopped luring. I was training my second dog (both adopted from rescues) and I was used to a dog who just loved training and handled stress by getting more bold and in-your-face vs. shutting down. Penny taught me right away she wasn't Lola . . .

Four months into the training process for lying down, I still didn't have a reliable behavior without a lure. It was so frustrating, I was a good training intern, . . . why couldn't I get Penny to lie down? For heaven's sake, she's part hound, all she ever does around the house is lie down! I came back from my first ClickerExpo shocked that what I had been learning was not clicker training at all and decided to give pure capturing [waiting till the behavior is offered and clicking for it] a try.

In five minutes (and I am not kidding), Penny, who was usually somewhat cowering into a down when we worked on it even though

I never even touched her, was throwing herself at the floor as hard and as fast as she could with her tail wagging a million miles an hour. She finally got it. My heart just sang as the realization came over her face: "You mean I, little old Me, I can MAKE you click?"

—*Crystal Saling*

Animals [problem-solve] all the time, of course, but most people are not used to setting up a training scenario and having an active, conscious (but hands-free) role in helping the animal "figure out what works." People want "sit," so they push down the butt. They get the result (dog's butt on the ground), they think the dog learned the behavior, but the dog learned to have his butt pushed down, not to put his butt down himself. Capturing and shaping are very hard for most people. They want to make the behavior happen, rather than allowing the animal to do the behavior. It's a control issue, mostly because they can't imagine training could happen any other way. Can't blame them.

I have no illusions; I'm a walking, babbling, arm-waving slot machine, to our four horses and two dogs. But they sure are glad to see me every day! They certainly appear to "love" me more than they did when I tried to train them with the best of intentions but a sad lack of skill or learning theory. Still, it's humbling for most people to reach that understanding.

—*Cindy Martin*

These stories were posted to online clicker-training forums by trainers whose lives had been transformed by learning about how dogs learn—because doing so transformed their dogs for the better. There are other stories where these came from, figuratively speaking, not about dogs but about people being washed in the same white light of understanding. They are all about one fundamental act: speaking.

In the most profound sense, to find a common language means having the power to communicate information, that upon which success in all aspects of life is based.

One woman, director of community outreach for a humane society, describes providing the demo dogs for a pilot clicker-training class run for the benefit of at-risk families. She brought her three dogs, all of whom had their Canine Good Citizen badges; one of these was a Labrador retriever who had "flunked" out of Guide Dogs for the Blind due to a certain lazy demeanor and an inordinate affection for food. A five-year-old boy, who had witnessed his mother's extreme abuse at the hands of his father, who was now in prison, was reluctant to engage in anything, much less interacting with intimidatingly large dogs. But the Lab, though wide, was gentle, and when the boy was persuaded to ask him to sit and he did, the child seemed to bloom. There was the emotional give-back of immediate success; there was a sense of mastery; there was a free exchange of meaning. Immediately, the boy began to participate in the class, every clicking game (most of them played among people) adding to new stores of confidence. In school, too, things began changing, especially after his mother asked his teacher to compliment good behavior and ignore bad. He was soon able to join a sports team previously off-limits on account of behavioral issues; he made an unprecedented run of earning good behavior points at home; and he finally went to his first birthday party without his mother, and without being asked to leave. The humane society worker followed his progress after the class to discover that he no longer needed counseling. He had been clicked back to society.

One of the prime benefits of clicking, either dogs or kids, is the product of paradox. When we stop using words, we can begin to truly communicate. No more nasty if unintentional inflections, rising tones, temptation to repeat commands (aka nagging); all the emotional baggage that comes along for the ride when we open our mouths. The click is clean. It sounds the same way every time, and only needs to be made once. The click is unable to sneer or criticize. Theresa McKeon, the co-creator of TAGteach and the teacher whose lessons enabled nine-year-old Hrafnkell to tie his shoes for the first time, describes the stickiness of our addiction to words: "Because of our reliance on verbal language, people need a bit of practice when transferring clicker training skill to other people. People teachers can quickly progress from using language to abusing it. Important points get buried in long lists of criteria and even longer explanations. Social responses divert concentration. We resort to nagging and escalate from there. Nagging doesn't work on cougars and it doesn't work on people."

On the other hand, punishment *does* work: "Put a gun to someone's head and you can get them to do anything." Or so says a man who knows whereof he speaks, trainer Kevin England. "I was a compulsion trainer for twenty years before changing to positive reinforcement training. I got the obedience dogs and awards to prove it works." But it's the way it works that is a problem for England. He didn't particularly like doing it, and his Dobermans liked it even less; the people in the classes rarely cracked a smile, and the instructors "yelled at their clients so their clients could yell at their dogs." He crossed over, never to cross back. Now he asks his clients, when they inevitably ask how to stop their dogs from jumping on people, to first examine *why* their dogs jump: it's because they're excited, happy, and want to kiss your face. The traditional method of stopping the behavior is a knee to the chest. It's usually effective. No more joyful greeting. "But think about trying that on your significant other when they get home and want to kiss you. Knee them in the groin! I bet they will not do that again. But what did you just do to the relationship?" For England, the problem with punishment—

beyond its destructive effect on trust and the relationship—is that "it leaves a void. We say what not to do but not what to do. Which leaves the door open for a 'new' behavior which can be even worse than the first." Then the only option is an escalation of aggression.

It seems so obvious when you look at it this way. Of course! Turn around and walk in the other direction. That is all you need to do.

Yet why is it so difficult to see? I've just spent a couple hundred pages trying to enumerate some of the many factors that militate against seeing a simple truth—one of which is that it's so simple. Toward his own explanation, England quotes Dr. Phil ("You can only change what you acknowledge") and offers his experience with traditional trainers, most of whom "have no use for research or seminars" because of the magnetic qualities of the status quo: "There is one method to train and everyone uses it so why switch. It just becomes an endless debate." Endless, yes, given the evidence of online forums. I have spent years collecting unrelenting discussions of pros and cons—and have the empty inkjet cartridges to prove it—and know I have not skimmed the surface. But maybe it all boils down to something simple anyway. "We can only lead through example."

Example, colored on occasion with a tinge of spite. I walk into the open field at the local park to find a circle of people standing with their dogs, most of them starting to spin on the ends of leashes fitted with choke chains as soon as Nelly and I appear. They strain to bound forward while their owners yank and yell. To the dogs, it seems as though the acceptable price of their natural curiosity is a pinched windpipe and aching eardrums; there's only one prize for their attention on offer, and it's a small black-and-white sheltie mix. She in turn looks at me in question, since doing so in circumstances of some confusion—giving attention, receiving direction—has been shaped over several hundred trials with the receipt of something she finds valuable. Not that attention to such as I is not reward in itself.

But it's actually a half-cent worth of cheese she finds abundantly more appealing.

The class is taught by the instructor I privately, to myself only, let it be clear, refer to as the Nazi. A dozen dogs are now going wild, no matter how many times a dog's name is yelled, no matter how many times the instructor seeks to polish his students' sharp pulls on the leash. That's when I say to Nelly, "Heel." Off-leash, she positions herself at my left calf and walks with her head craned at a nearly impossible angle (sorry, Nelly) so her eyes stay glued to mine. Barks from the field avail not. She mirrors my every step; I have—cheating awfully in the clutch—put my left hand in my pocket, a clue of great hope to my dog, who is aware that often enough my jeans come out of the wash with a disgusting soggy clot of brown in their pockets. I just can't remember details.

Thankfully, the trail soon disappeared into the woods because Nelly's heel was not so solid it could have held out much longer. I gave her her treat and she bounded off. But she had held her position, with nothing more than anticipation binding her to me, all the way past the class of uncontrollable dogs.

I did this, infantile as I know it is, as a protest. What I really wanted to do was run up and set every one of those dogs free. If only to prevent the cervical injuries they surely (veterinary study right here, next to me now) face. But really to say: That's unnecessary. And unfair.

The crossover trainers know more than I do about unfairness. Their stories, to a one, are heartbreaking, because they will openly admit breaking something in a dog. Al's moment came when he showed two dogs in the same competition: one was a German shepherd he had trained in the traditional manner, "with choke chains, and a bit of shouting and a slap now and again"; the other had only known reward-based training, as Al was transitioning. Both his dogs took a first. He was well pleased, until someone later asked him why his two dogs looked so different in competition. At first he didn't understand the question. It was explained that one worked "with his ears back, tail down and a generally worried body attitude" while the other "was very happy, bouncy, ears erect, tail wagging and full of positive expectations from me. In my stupidity I had never noticed the difference. The dogs were telling me what was best; one worked out of fear, one worked out of willingness. Both did everything well, both got the ribbon, but only one enjoyed and was really willing to work and had the potential to continue learning so much more." The German shepherd had passed on, but, Al said with rueful humor, he would probably deliver one well-earned bite when the time came for him to cross the Rainbow Bridge too.

• • •

OUR BODIES bear the impress of memories, bad or good. This is what Pavlov taught us, and this is finally what positive reinforcement is about. (It is finally what we are about, too, the bodies.) Nelly knows in her bones, after four years (when I write this) of knowing that when she runs to me, (mainly) good things happen to her. So she never needs to think twice about it. It's part of the more important part, on which the brain sits like an afterthought.

Before I ever learned anything about how we learn, I was given a startling lesson in the body, by a body. It is nothing if not absorptive.

It's group therapy night, a long lifetime ago. One of our members had come in complaining of a darkness that had descended suddenly on him; he couldn't explain the oppressive cloud that stayed inches over his head, wetting him with its gray tears. He kept looking for the cause: Work? Something a friend did? The weather? And finally the therapist said quietly, "Isn't this the week, eight years ago, that your partner died?" He was silent. Then he said, "Yes. Yes, it is."

• • •

WE ARE officially in the Age of Information. Also of "content," but that's another matter.

When were we ever *not* in an age of information, I'd like to know? Our cells communicate with one another; our neurons hum like the telephone wires of a century ago. Parasites communicate with their host. We live to exchange information, and we live because of it. (Excuse me. I have to go open the door for my dog; she's barking to be let in.)

Science has now formally addressed the universality and position of communication in all natural systems. The name of its study is biosemiotics. It's not exactly on fire, in the way neurology is today. But it has given a stamp of approval to the notion that all manner of creatures encode meaning to be interpreted by those to whom it should matter.

It should matter to us that when we reach down to pat a dog and he rolls onto his back he is not "asking for a tummy scratch" any more than the person who puts his hands up when a gun is pointed at him is asking for company in doing the hokey pokey.

Relationships are rooted, as a word and as a fact, in relating. One can relate to no one without understanding the language in which expression is made. If you don't speak dog, you don't have a relationship with one.

It's important, in the context of dogs, to reiterate the difference between *speech* and *language*. It is true that dogs do not have speech, for while they make an unappreciatedly wide range of vocalizations that each "mean" something, they cannot form words. And frankly probably don't want to: they already have another, even richer and more subtle visual language of more parts than we have yet discerned, even though we have compiled several quite extensive encyclopedias. Also, their language is obviously sufficient: its evolution helped their wolfish progenitors survive over the small matter of a couple of million years.

They are in truth Keatses, maybe Wordsworths, with four legs, commanders of their language with the lyrical precision of poets. But it is a poetry whispered when compared to our rude shout. To each other, it is loud enough. But we have a problem in that we are not accustomed to hearing with our eyes. We are bound so deeply to the effects of our speech, we insist it is the only communication there is. But we risk not hearing, both a loss on our part—dog is a balletic language, and one adept at negotiating peace, which should be of interest to the likes of us—and a grave loss to them. We end up punishing or even disposing of dogs because we can't hear what they're telling us.*

Karen Pryor agonizes, in her quietly measured way, about the consequences of our visual deafness: "Considering how long dogs and people have been living together, it's amazing how thick most people are when it comes to reading the domestic dog's emotional signals. Even some dog experts may misinterpret dog threats or be

---

* In addition to Turid Rugaas's *On Talking Terms with Dogs,* there are many detailed resources, or foreign-language dictionaries, if you will, on canine body language. A good overview is on the ASPCA website (http://www.aspca.org/pet-care/virtual-pet-behaviorist/dog-behavior/canine-body-language). Books include the excellent *Canine Body Language: A Photographic Guide Interpreting the Native Language of the Domestic Dog* by Brenda Aloff; *Canine Behavior: A Photo Illustrated Handbook* by Barbara Handelman; and *Dog Language: An Encyclopedia of Canine Behavior* by Roger Abrantes, Sarah Whitehead and Alice Rasmussen. Thorough as these are—most people will be astonished, and possibly abashed, by the extensive communications previously dismissed as dogs' random movement—I don't know that they even convey the half of it. Dogs are such masterful watchers of our body language, it should surprise no one if their own language were more subtle than the apparently comprehensive language we have been able to decipher.

totally oblivious of blatant signs of stress and fear." I see it all the time—not because I am an expert, but because I have availed myself (easy enough to do) of the work of experts. There are enough. With one of the most popular of those encyclopedias of canine body language running to 370 pages, there's a lot not to know.

Pryor goes on to relate what happened when her nonprofit research foundation set out to scientifically assess what experience had already proved to her: "clicker is quicker." Some of these so-called crossover trainers, fluent in both positive-reinforcement and force-based training, were to teach some shelter dogs "down," first using the traditional method of placing the dog in the position, by either gently pulling out the front legs or pushing down on the neck. Fairly tame stuff compared to some traditional techniques. By the sixth dog, however, the experiment is halted: the trainer who is operating the video camera is in tears. Dogs have an automatic opposition reflex, so if you push them one way, they can't help but push back the other way; they are confused by all this pushing. They are being forced to do what they have not been given any option to do on their own, yet would. Confusion is stressful. In Pryor's words, it is clear to all that the dogs are "suffering" and "miserable." And so are these trainers, for when their "methods [changed], so [did their] eyes."

The language problem is huge, but its solution, education, marks a passage that hearteningly goes in one direction only: forward. Once you understand a language, you can't unlearn it. It's like losing your virginity. An unknown foreign language is simply noise, but knowledge makes the noise resolve itself into meaning. Meaning, you can't turn away from.

•   •   •

I AM not sure which of the transformational revelations Polly gave me shows itself as greatest, but it might be this one, in the form of a question: why *wouldn't* we think animals have every bit as rich and complicated an inner life as the one we know is within us? The allowance that another's needs and desires and thoughts, no matter how inaccessible, are every bit as important to them as ours are to us is the beginning of compassion. When we seek to tutor the dog for whom we realize the full extent of this compassion, we look for a method that takes into account their integrity as separate but equal.

Operant conditioning is the only method that respects this fact. It begins with the assumption that every individual's interests are self-determined. No matter how much I would like my human values to matter to Nelly, if she doesn't agree, well then, she doesn't. (And she doesn't.)

She has already informed me how important lamb roll is in her cosmology—very near the top. It thus takes the same place in hers that the evening glass of wine—or, in times of yore, the coffee-break cigarette—does in mine: a powerful motivator for which I'd do almost any trick. So I decide to try what I'd witnessed at Clicker-Expo done with such ease: let's just sit out here in the garden and "free shape" some behaviors! It's often so cute to see what comes of an open-ended plan to let the dog decide where to go; sort of like hitchhiking in the hippie era. Where you going? Seattle? OK, that's cool.

I diced some roll into tiny cubes; the wisdom from higher-ups was that training treats, if nutritive, could take the place of a meal so as not to end up with an obese, if well-schooled, dog. In fact, if there was work to do outside the home—habituating a dog to a public place, outside the entrance to the mall, say (where we spent many not altogether happy hours, on the idea that I would keep Nelly literally under threshold so she could eventually tolerate going inside a store without screaming)—it was advised to feed an entire meal by hand there, piece by piece. Giving a dog a meal "for free," or driving right by its potential to either reinforce behavior or to countercondition an unpleasant situation, was to squander an opportunity. (Free feeding, or leaving a bowl of kibble available at all times, not only wastes a chance to build a meal's worth of new behavior, it does nothing to strengthen the bond between the provider and the recipient. Otherwise, the house becomes as important to the dog as you do, for it is the house that appears to provide the food.)

It was not as easy as they made it look. Nelly watched me closely; I waited for her to do "something." Waiting was my first mistake: high rate of reinforcement at the beginning, please. *What* the heck was she supposed to do? I wasn't giving her any instruction, and I wasn't giving her any reward. Once the screaming commenced, which it did almost immediately, the game was up: any movement that followed could be construed (especially by quick little dogs) as a part of a sequence, or chain: *Oh, I see. You want me to scream,* then *turn around.*

Nonetheless, I succeeded, against all odds, in quickly teaching Nelly a handful of cute tricks: the best was one I'd also taught Mercy, to "spell." It played directly into the credulity of those who didn't understand that dogs don't speak English as a first language: the cue for down was "d-o-w-n" (actually, to the dog, the cue was more like "duh," or the sound of the word's first letter, with the rest given solely for the benefit of the amazed onlooker). We rarely performed it without causing a moment of confused silence: *Your dog knows how to spell . . . ?*

Otherwise, I had in Nelly a half-trained dog who was capable of so much more than a short list of easily learned tricks: on your side; wave; high five; shake (also "your other hand"); ask nicely (up on your haunches); drop it; leave it (necessary to pass the Canine Good Citizen test, in which a dog—Nelly!—had to walk by a biscuit on the floor without lunging for it); kiss! (she jumps up and bumps her muzzle against my lips); in your car! These were the simple things. How many more I could have taught her, and still can, for old dogs can learn new tricks.

One day on a walk, when Nelly had disappeared for the thousandth time to who knew where—that was the problem—I stood and fretted, because it was all that was left to me. My son looked on, too: he was used to his mother's self-made travails. We had been having a good time, until then. My delusions of togetherness, where my dog read my thoughts and was mindful of the aesthetics of the pretty family picture. All of a sudden, he said, "If I were to draw a picture of the way Nelly really is, I'd show two cars that had crashed into each other. One would say 'Sweet' and the other would say 'Pain.'" They would have become one. Sweet pain. My dog, and the life she led me on.

· · ·

IT WAS on our walks that I had the worldly amplitude to consider the organizing principle not only of dog training, but of human society itself. When I wasn't composing grocery lists or obsessing over a wide variety of meaningless trivia, that is. There had to be something behind it all. One piece, like dopamine, that spanned both the beautifully functional and the howlingly inexplicable. The piece into which dopamine itself fit, as the grease on the skids to make sure we got the stuff our physical systems most critically needed and that had to be the explanation for all that we did, the extravagantly strange at the same time as the obviously necessary.

Resources.

One of the most common behavioral problems a dog can manifest, the one that gets them surrendered to shelters, that causes them to bite and suffer the consquences, is resource guarding. Food, toys, dirty dishes, their bed (or yours, which they understandably mistake for their own), and the person who provides what in the Maslow

Hierarchy of Needs are called D-needs, the essentials. The stuff of survival: worth a raised lip to show the gleaming incisor.

We hate it when our dogs do that. And we take action. Yet we growl, too. Threaten our stuff, or what we consider our stuff, and we make war. We may be aware only that the aggressors speak and look different than we do, or pray to a different god for their victory, but that is not the real motivation of conflict, just a convenient gloss. Dig, dig underneath, and there is always a threatened resource at stake in all acts of aggression. Religion as a motivator for anything beyond the most superficial aspects of human behavior is a straw man.* (I have just spared myself the pain and expense of reading the many recent screeds against empty religion and all the damage it's caused over the centuries; I am in complete agreement already—I think—with *The God Delusion* and *The End of Faith* and their ilk.) Instead, it's the shell that hides the little pea of truth. We would rather not think ourselves as low as chimpanzees, biting each other in a screaming battle over bananas. It's somehow more worthy of our self-conception to believe we are biting each other in a screaming battle over precepts concerning invisible entities. But resources—more specifically the reinforcement of the dopamine rush they naturally provide, as we were conditioned by evolution to have our behavior conditioned by it—can be the only logical motivation for something so calamitous as intraspecies violence.

---

* And maybe not even in the case of superficialities like religiously prescribed costuming and food taboos. (It is just my personal opinion, but I figure that any god who cares that much about underwear or what can go in one cooking pot but not the other is not a god I can respect, especially when at the same time that he's getting upset about the length of your beard he's letting breathtaking numbers of people and animals suffer horrifically.) The cultural-materialist explanation of these "riddles of culture" feels so logically rock-solid it would take an amazing act of willful ignorance to deny them. See *Cows, Pigs, Wars, and Witches* by Marvin Harris, for one.

The moment I heard about stringent but sound dog-training protocols like Nothing In Life Is Free and Learn to Earn—prescribed for the most difficult cases, and based on strict, complete control of resources, so the dog can only get what he needs and wants by behaving in an acceptable manner—I heard the kerthunk of two distant pieces of idea coming together with the force of supermagnets in my head.* From long-ago freshman anthropology and encountering the cultural materialism of Marvin Harris to learning about the most powerful method of altering behavior in our canine pets, one commonality emerged: it's all about the resources. "The answers to our riddles [everything from why we go to war to what is behind our social and religious laws] do not lie within the participants' consciousness," Harris wrote, echoing Skinner's rejection of "mentalism" as an explanatory fiction for behavior's causes.

This means, though, that we didn't really know, nor could we, what Vietnam was really about (resources). Or the Seven Years' War (resources). Or why adultery is banned by the Bible (resources). Explanations usually centering on concepts such as "right" and "wrong" are portrayed as causes.† But we are *wired not to know*

---

* Only later did I come upon this post in an online forum by a trainer named David Smelser, a further aperçu birthed by the subject and yet more proof of the breadth of thought alive and well in the outwardly dismissible field of animal training:

> One reason I think that social groups tend toward threats of punishment (-R) instead of positive punishment is when resources are limited, it is more economical to threaten punishment than to give a reinforcer. A trainer's supply of treats is limited: it costs time and energy to give a treat or play with a dog, but threats of corrections are essentially free—it only costs time and energy when you have to deliver the correction.
>
> One of the benefits of a NILIF program is that it educates the trainer to the abundance of things a dog is willing to work for. It turns all of them into potential reinforcers.

† "Ethics is mainly a matter of the conflict between immediate and remote causes," Skinner explains in "Why We Are Not Acting to Save the World." He attempts to understand why we haven't *done* anything: because all we do is *talk* about doing some-

ourselves. Robert Wright, author of *The Evolution of God,* says we underestimate "the cleverness and ruthlessness with which our inner animals pursue natural selection's agenda. We seem designed to twist moral discourse—whatever language it's framed in—to selfish or tribal ends, and to remain conveniently unaware of the twisting." In other words, if it's all about resources, we're the last to know about it—and Skinner might very well be right, that our behavior is always acted upon by forces outside of ourselves, up to and including the creation of a *sense* that we are not being acted upon by forces outside of ourselves. Or, in a gorgeous understatement, "The absence of facts has not deterred [people] from developing stories about why they behave the way they do."*

Another long-standing piece of the behavior puzzle drifts into place. The burning question of my own adulthood, wondered at because it was not only before my eyes but behind them, was why in almost all cultures—with only differences of degree—are women consistently subjugated, controlled through means insidious or violent or both? Before now I never could come up with an answer that had the polished feel of truth, hard as I would think. Then, there it was. We are the greatest resource of all, worth keeping a boot heel on. We are the agents of humanity's ultimate survival, because we produce and keep alive—our unique and critical ability, by way of the bond of our care and the milk of our breasts, for which there are no substitutes—more humans. A secondary cause may well be all the props men get for behaving this way: Marvin Harris believes, for

---

thing, and talk alone has never motivated change. Humans' patterns of behavior were "selected for" in a different environment than exists today (the past of both great plenty and great deprivation), so many of our behaviors are now maladaptive.

* Quoth Carl D. Cheney, professor emeritus of psychology, Utah State University (from "The Source and Control of Behavior" in Waris Ishaq, ed., *Human Behavior in Today's World.*)

instance, that fierce male-warrior societies (of which modern America is a subset) arise because fierce male-warrior behavior is heavily rewarded with primary reinforcers that especially encourage such behavior. The fiercest warriors get the best girls and the most goods.

Similarly, the phenomenon of self-flagellation, which is an expression of a multitude of faiths, is possibly the closest human analogue to the hyena in the zoo who has been trained to offer his jugular for blood draws. Rest assured people don't do it for the feeling of blood trickling down their scored skin. (Although the release of endorphins reportedly helps enormously.) Rather, there are big human-style rewards at stake: "When Shiite adults and male children . . . beat their naked chests with iron chains" in religious ritual, "they are lavished with abundant reinforcers by family-members, friends and neighbors. People surround the men and boys, praise them, bathe their wounds, bring them fresh milk, fruits, nuts and cheese, press them to eat the special dishes cooked for them by their mothers, aunts, sisters, female cousins," writes behavior analyst Waris Ishaq.

"And ye shall know the truth, and the truth shall make you free" (John 8:32). But how will I know the truth? Does not new truth come along all the time and supplant the old? Or did it only appear to be the truth because there was an absence that needed to be filled? Now that it was, we can stop searching. We have arrived.

Um, maybe. Well, then, how will I *know*?

When I was younger, I projected on the screen in my mind elaborate films in which I watched myself dramatically leave the family that I thought could never understand me; after packing just a few things, I would run off to live in the woods with the *only creature* with whom I could truly commune: a dog. I lived in a world of fiction, which seemed the only container expansive enough for all the lonely mysteries, the earnest longings, that poured out of the factory that was producing them night and day in my imagination.

Like a seesaw slowly reaching homeostasis for a moment, some decades later my desire hung evenly between fable and fact. And then, it started to fall to one side. Only that which was real—in all its byzantine, tendriled, conflated glory—seemed rich enough to interest me now. The tales we made up, our fictive metaphors, appeared pointlessly thin and drained, when even the most elementary thoughts about how all this—the physical world—had been put together were so wildly imaginative you might as well have dropped acid. (But it was still safe to drive a car.) Wouldn't it be cool to understand *everything*? To venture upriver to the mouth of the final explanation in provable science's impeccably built craft, instead of on speculation's nostalgically disintegrating wooden raft?

How will I know?

Work backward. If that is the way the dog learns the long freestyle dance that will ultimately make the viewer weep although she has no understanding why, then start with the last piece first. The first step is the final one. Backchain. From the observable to the invisible. From the border collie's bow, head on paws, accepting the riotous applause that is due, to Fly's first entry on the stage, as the music comes up from the silence that was once all there was.

My dog, here now on the bed next to me, watching out the window while I type, watching out for number one, is an old beast. I don't mean herself—although she is that, at ten more than halfway through her life, as I, too, am more than halfway through mine, closer now to the end by a significant margin than I am to the beginning; in this ten years she has kept her own counsel while accompanying me through the hardest and, if it weren't for her, loneliest years of my life. I mean that she is ancient in the truths she holds. She is a cross, I would swear, between the Ethiopian wolf and (except for the startling blue eyes) the Siberian foxes that for generations have been experimentally bred for tameness and are now piebald and doglike. Nelly-like, to be exact.

She is her own ancestor. She is truth itself. She is the answer to the question. How will I know? I will know I have found some part of the world's truth when she tells me so.

When she learns with alacrity both what I want her to and what I don't—her self-interest always one step ahead of my dumb slowness to realize that our interests diverge, indeed sometimes oppose— and I see her unalloyed joy at learning more, always more, she is telling me: This is the truth. This is how it is. In my brain, therefore in yours. In the mysteries of the world unfolding.

You get the dog you need.

AFTERWORD

꧁

WHEN *A Clockwork Orange* was rereleased in an R-rated edit in the United States in 1973 (originally, a year earlier, it bore an X), I was just about to turn sixteen and was terribly in love with movies. To miss seeing a Kubrick film as soon as it was legally possible seemed almost to transgress a law of physics.

The problem was, there in the dark, I found it impossible to look at. It was a philosophical argument, the sort of thing that acted as food or water to my system in those days, but here was the discussion in incontrovertibly physical terms, not at the safe remove of verbal dialectic. The postulation of a vicious subjugation of society's weakest members—of which I was one, being female and just coming to realize that by virtue of natural accident I had been born into a class of prey—was made flesh before my eyes. Flesh either stolen or bloodied, or both, three rows ahead on a large screen in brilliant, irrefutable color (a theme made manifest in the opening credits, each one set on a background of aggressively hypersaturated hue, with the unmediated red of life, not to mention death, standing behind the title). The movie smashed home its full point, logically muddy though it was, even in the sporadic snatches I watched from between the fingers that covered my eyes. I didn't really need to be subjected to the full treatment; I got it. At the end, I watched as Kubrick added another layer to that of his source material, Anthony Burgess's 1962 novel. When Malcolm McDowell's Alex is receiving "aversion therapy," his inability to look away from the films that would prove powerful enough to change his very essence is meant to mirror the act we ourselves were engaged in at the same moment.

The whole experience felt deeply, complicatedly, wrong. At that time, in the way of the girl who had long been told she thought too much (an observation that maddened me since thinking was the protective reflex I had come to rely on), I figured it had something to do with me—I was too sensitive, too afraid, too female. Decades later, I would again sit before the movie, still just as unsettled by something in its get-go, but strangely untouched this time by the repugnance of the imagery. It all looked now like just some ostentatious clothing on a straw man. What had me squirming in my seat now was the creepiness of falsehood. Experience—and I had naturally had some, in the intervening years—had changed the movie itself. I had not seen it before, the two bad guys as concoctions shadow boxing with each other, projections of the author's mind and nothing existing in any real world I knew. What was repulsive about the movie was no longer its wanton violence, but its wanton untruth.

Two years after the film's release, a disgruntled Burgess sought to take back what he believed was stolen from him: the unimpeachable tangibility Kubrick gave to the writer's fictionalized exploration of morality and free will had invited the charge that it glorified violence. It also, like the book's American edition, neglected to include the twenty-first chapter, in which Alex *decides* to reform. That represents a hokiness one can hardly imagine Kubrick ever embracing, but Burgess felt it necessary to his final intention: to issue a warning about governmental mind control, which he feared would rob us of what makes us human. He believed our possession of free will—to do either good or evil, and it was no one's business but the individual's to decide which—differentiated us from all other animals. And he believed there was a devious politician, a psychologist, out there promoting a platform of revoking our freedom. It was necessary to do anything to stop him.

In 1973 the novelist wrote an essay (unpublished until *The New Yorker* did so in 2012) redressing the injuries done by Kubrick and his American publisher to the novel. He explained it now as a manifesto of the individual's right to freedom from control, even "scientifically imposed contentment," which renders "the slaves happy in their slavery." He comes out with the name of the author of these perfidious means of depriving man of his central humanity: B. F. Skinner.

At length he describes Skinner's brand of behaviorism, and Skinner himself. He is the kind of man, Burgess offers, who is deaf to deepest truth, that conveyed by "imaginative writing" (by which, obviously, he means his own). Skinner so little appreciates the wonder of the human being that in attempting to cure society's ills he would turn us into mere trick animals, thrown sops in return for better behavior. Burgess gives full cry to his derision of such travesty: Skinner derived his notions of social betterment from experimenting with lab animals; indeed, "some of his achievements in animal conditioning approach a high professional circus level." The effrontery! The absurd, terrifying perils of extrapolating from what *animals in a box* would do!

And this would be an awful leap, too, should it be true as Burgess believed that humans are fundamentally different from other animals. Philosophers have done their due diligence on the question from ancient times to the 1960s of *A Clockwork Orange*, but only recently has science begun to go full throttle into research on the question, and the results contradict over a thousand years of philosophy, religion, and popular opinion alike: with each study new evidence emerges for collective similarity of species. Our differences are every day revealed to be more superficial than fundamental. And the gene does not lie.

(Only one of many such examples is the 2002 study published in the journal *Nature* that revealed how closely the mouse's genome resembles ours: we both carry somewhere around 30,000 genes, which were the legacy of a common ancestor 75 million years before. One has to wonder exactly when, where, and by what means in subsequent years man was given something—what?—that separated him so utterly from his forebear. Of what material? Lodged where? Why doesn't an MRI pick it up? This stuff keeps me up at night.)

The study given to the investigation since then in the fields of ethology, neurobiology, comparative psychology, and genetics has amounted to so much new knowledge, however, that the sixties might as well be the Middle Ages. To continue framing the "Are we different from other animals in any essential way?" question as a philosophical rather than a scientific one seems as sensible now as asking a shaman to perform hip replacement.

The historical record is repetitive, and one of the most common themes there is concerns adhering to religious or superstitious beliefs in the face of discovery to the contrary. In retrospect, we discover exactly how it has slowed the intellectual, and frequently material, advance of humankind. Ironically, in this case, that ability— to advance ourselves as a species by way of scientific inquiry—may well be the one and only difference that will remain to mark us as apart from our cousins the other animals, if research continues in the same direction it has been going. As record keepers (another difference, though perhaps not one that qualifies as essential), we are in possession of an expanding list of scientists whose ideas were originally met with hostility, or worse, but were eventually vindicated.

If we were prone to learning from history instead of repeating it, the list would have been cut short at 1543, with the publication of Copernicus's *De revolutionibus orbium coelestium,* and Galileo would have been spared that nasty business with the Inquisition. Much less the withering ridicule turned on poor Darwin, the Wright brothers, Edison ("the Sorcerer of Menlo Park"), and Nikola Tesla, among others. (Evolutionary psychology has interesting things to say about the mechanism that resists acceptance of the radically new; it's an animal thing, it turns out.)* Considering this aspect of scientific history is a bit like reading famous literary rejection letters: *Lord of the Flies* is "absurd and uninteresting"; *Animal Farm* can't be published because it "is impossible to sell animal stories in the USA." One of many scientists who revolutionized our understanding of the physical world, that same William Harvey who in 1628 published his theory on the circulatory system that should have retired the prevailing notion that there were two types of blood, had to take what was coming to him: "I tremble lest I have mankind at large for my

---

* It stands to reason that animals distrust novel situations; danger lurks there. But what about the "reasonable" animal, man? Now, since at least 1988, when the concept of "status quo bias" was first presented, it is a staple of marketing knowledge. In "Status Quo Bias in Decision Making," researchers William Samuelson and Richard Zeckhauser (*Journal of Risk and Uncertainty* 1 [1988]: 7–59) open by citing three cases in which people unreasoningly chose the known over an unknown option with decided benefits: one of these concerned a colleague who for twenty-six years ate the same lunch every day. For the record, ham and cheese on rye. "The lunchtime diner's relationship with his chosen sandwich outlasted several marriages," the authors reported. They also suggested that "the greatest marketing error in recent decades"— the substitution of New for "old" Coca-Cola—resulted from the "reasonable" assumption that since consumers preferred the taste of the new formulation in blind tests that they would therefore prefer to buy it. They did not.

enemies . . . respect for antiquity influences all men." We hold fast to what we believe, even if it hurts.

In 1912 an Australian inventor named Lancelot Eldin de Mole sent sketches of an armored tank to the British War Office; his idea was rejected. He tried again several years later, but through a combination of bad luck, bad communications, and uninterest, his design (now seen as having held far more promise than the machines of limited use that were built) languished. "Caterpillar landships are idiotic and useless. Nobody asked for them and nobody wants them," said the voice of knowledgeable authority in the form of the 4th Lord of the Admiralty. What has never previously existed cannot be desired. But in this case one's imagination teems with ghostly swarms of young men in Brodie helmets, and the aching thought of what might have come of their lives if they had not been blasted to bits to gain a few inches of No Man's Land, should such a vehicle have been used.

Half a century later, in 1977, the president of the Digital Equipment Corporation stated confidently, "There is no reason anyone would want a computer in their house."

Thus remains B. F. Skinner's legacy to a certain extent: not fully appreciated in his time, because his discovery challenged received wisdom about what made us tick. Like everything radically new, it felt threatening. Only when it was applied to lesser beings could it fly under the radar undetected; only when it was transferred to the hands of dog owners in the form of toy clickers could its powers be exercised without censure, although not without controversy: there are two opposing methodologies in dog training, and the vehemence of their proponents has led to fairly intense squabbling. All things are not equal in terms of ethics or effectiveness, or even truth. The fight parallels every major argument in politics or philosophy throughout history.

. . .

SKINNER CALLED *A Clockwork Orange* a brilliant film. He also pointed out that it travestied the use of conditioning—and "not my kind of conditioning." Noam Chomsky had perpetrated the error that Skinner was a "stimulus-response" psychologist, as Pavlov had been, when in actuality he was a "stimulus-behavior-reinforcement-stimulus-behavior-reinforcement" psychologist. Numerous papers were written and conferences convened to set the record straight, but the distinction could no longer be appreciated after *Walden Two* and *Beyond Freedom and Dignity* ventured into the sacred territory of philosophy beyond the reach of data. Except, perhaps, in the dog park. There, I attended it very well. Or rather, I did so because Mercy . . . made . . . me.

NOTES

Ⅴ

1. J. Matson and J. Boisjoli (2009). "The Token Economy for Children with Intellectual Disability and/or Autism: A Review," *Research in Developmental Disabilities 30* (2009): 240–248.

2. Available on FORA.tv.

3. http://theoryfundamentals.com/

4. As reported in the understatedly titled "Skinner's Utopia: Panacea, or Path to Hell?" *Time*, September 20, 1971.

5. M. Sundberg and J. Michael, "The Benefits of Skinner's Analysis of Verbal Behavior for Children with Autism," *Behavior Modification* 25, no. 5 (October 2001): 698–724.

6. "Mental Health: A Report from the Surgeon General," http://www.surgeonge neral.gov/library/mentalhealth/chapter3/sec6.html#autism

7. G. Green, "Evaluating Claims About Treatment for Autism," In Maurice et al., eds., *Behavioral Intervention for Young Children with Autism* (Austin, Tex.: Pro-Ed, Inc., 1996).

8. John R. Platt, "The Skinnerian Revolution," in *Beyond the Punitive Society,* ed. Harvey Wheeler (San Francisco: W. H. Freeman, 1973). Platt was also a physicist, scholar, and author; his obituary in the *New York Times* in 1992 read in part, "From 1965 until his retirement in 1977, he was professor of physics and associate director of the Mental Health Research Institute at the University of Michigan. From 1945 to 1965, he taught at the University of Chicago. His areas of research included molecular biophysics, the biophysics of vision and perception, and social trends. Pondering the future, he once argued that 'the world has become too dangerous for anything less than utopias.' "

9. The book in which these statements appear is a collection of papers presented at a symposium on *Beyond Freedom and Dignity* held by the Center for the Study of Democratic Institutions in Santa Barbara, California, and represents

a wide-ranging appraisal of Skinner's most audacious work, including some trenchant critiques of Skinner's overreaching.

10. "Harvard-Trained Dog," May 20, 1952, p. 17.

11. Primary sources for the material in this chapter include: IQ-Zoo, http://www3 .uca.edu/iqzoo/; Robert E. Bailey, J. Arthur Gillaspy, Jr., "Operant Psychology Goes to the Fair: Marian and Keller Breland in the Popular Press, 1947–1966," *Behavior Analyst* 28, no. 2 (2005):143–159; Gail B. Peterson, "A Day of Great Illumination: B. F. Skinner's Discovery of Shaping," *Journal of the Experimental Analysis of Behavior* 82, no. 3 (2004): 317–328.

12. https://www.patriciamcconnell.com/theotherendoftheleash/are-clicks-better -markers-than-words-comments.

13. Polar Bear Thesis: "Enrichment Program Implementation to Modify Stereotypic Behavior of Captive Polar Bears at the Central Park Zoo" (Laura Venner, Columbia University, Department of Ecology, Evolution and Environmental Biology; Yula Kapetanakos, Central Park Zoo/WCS; Prof. Stephanie Pfirman, Barnard College, May 1, 2006: http://www.lauravenner.com/curriculum-vitae/ research/polar-bear-thesis/ [retrieved April 7, 2013]).

14. M. H. Herron, "Survey of the Use and Outcome of Confrontational and Non-confrontational Training Methods in Client-Owned Dogs Showing Undesired Behaviors," *Applied Animal Behaviour Science* 117, nos. 1–2 (2009): 47–54.

15. M. Schilder and J. Van der Borg. "Training dogs with the help of the shock collar: short and long term behavioural effects." *Applied Animal Behaviour Science* 85 (2004): 319–344.

16. *UC Davis Journal of Juvenile Law and Policy* 12, no. 1 (Winter 2008):1–50.

17. "Prehistoric Dog," *The Atlantic*, July 1999.

18. John W. Maag, "Rewarded by Punishment: Reflections on the Disuse of Positive Reinforcement in Schools," *Exceptional Children* 62, no. 2 (2001):173–186.

19. https://wikispaces.psu.edu/display/PSYCH484/3.+Reinforcement+Theory: "3. Reinforcement Theory" (Created by Brian Francis Redmond, last modified by Karin L. Housell on September 29, 2013).

ACKNOWLEDGMENTS

IT SEEMED as though this project might have no end; certainly, my gratitude to numerous individuals does not. For contributions large and small, I thank:

Polly Hanson, who started it all: I don't know where I'd be without you. Not here, at any rate.

Stacey Tabellario and Mindy Babitz of the National Zoo, for sharing their expertise and time.

Jean Donaldson, for answering a hundred follow-up questions after a galvanizing seminar.

Dot Hayhurst, for saving Nelly (and so many others).

Kim Wilson of K9Crazy Playskool, who taught us so much.

Devorah Sperber, an honor to know and from whom to receive profound insights on art and training dogs, which are often the same thing.

Michele Murteza and Jennifer Andersen, for sharing their experiences at chicken camp.

Julie Vargas of the B. F. Skinner Foundation, for agreeing to read a portion of the manuscript and correct its errors.

Susan Mitchell, Crystal Saling, and Cindy Bennett Martin, my appreciation for permission to quote from their astute observations on the power of the clicker.

Barbara Mansfield, Bonnie Cooper, Suzanne Finnamore, Sue Sanders, Lynn McCarty, Melissa Cohen, Lee Harrington, Mindy Pickard, Gary Jacobson and Sissy, Beatrice Weinberger, Valerie Torrens, Janet Steen, Jim Gardner, Martha Frankel, Kim Hunter: for your friendship, support, ideas, and conversation.

Marge Carlson, for making Nelly a part of your family in my absence.

Jolanta Benal (along with Sarah Egan), who early on extended to me their friendship, hospitality, and, in Jolanta's case, expertise and patient explanation of wide-ranging technical matters in training.

Joe Sokohl, the best friend a writer (or anyone) could have.

Erica Lansner, for the provision of two sequential pieces of electronic equipment on which I have written four books.

Lloyd Westerman and Carol Meyer, for shelter from the storm—literally.

John Chicoine, for generosity, friendship, and kindness of a hundred different sorts.

Julia Szabo, whose help to me and especially to innumerable dogs and other creatures is deeply appreciated.

My agent, Betsy Lerner, to whom I owe abundant thanks.

My editor, Amy Cherry: I have no words to express my appreciation for the dogged work she performed here. If there is anything of worth, she coaxed it out of me; if there is not, it is by my insistence alone.

Editorial assistant Remy Cawley, always at the ready with help of many kinds.

More than to just about anyone, I bear enormous gratitude to Janet Harrington (and her husband, John) for countless expressions of generosity to Nelly, to me, to Raphael. I can't imagine life (and wouldn't want to) without her kind understanding and friendship.

Tarara Bheumdier, Mercy, Roscoe, and Nelly: my dogs have truly taught me everything. I miss some of you every day of my life.

The two men in my life, who make me wish every moment could last a lifetime, Bob Krause and Raphael: I had no right to expect such luck, but now that I have it, I never want to let it go.